# PLANNING IN TEN WORDS OR LESS

*For Adriana*

# Planning in Ten Words or Less
## A Lacanian Entanglement with Spatial Planning

MICHAEL GUNDER
*University of Auckland, New Zealand*

JEAN HILLIER
*Newcastle University, UK*

ASHGATE

Published by
Ashgate Publishing Limited
Wey Court East
Union Road
Farnham
Surrey, GU9 7PT
England

Ashgate Publishing Company
Suite 420
101 Cherry Street
Burlington
VT 05401-4405
USA

www.ashgate.com

**British Library Cataloguing in Publication Data**
Gunder, M. (Michael)
Planning in ten words or less : a Lacanian entanglement
with spatial planning.
1. City planning--Philosophy.
I. Title II. Hillier, Jean.
307.1'2'01-dc22

**Library of Congress Cataloging-in-Publication Data**
Gunder, M. (Michael)
   Planning in ten words or less : a Lacanian entanglement with spatial planning
/ by Michael Gunder and Jean Hillier.
      p. cm.
   Includes bibliographical references and index.
   ISBN 978-0-7546-7457-3
   1. City planning. 2. Regional planning. 3. Geographical perception. 4. Space perception. 5. Lacan, Jacques, 1901-1981. 6. Psychoanalysis. I. Hillier, Jean. II. Title.

HT166.G859 2009
307.1'216--dc22

2009005300

ISBN 978 0 7546 7457 3

**Mixed Sources**
Product group from well-managed
forests and other controlled sources
www.fsc.org Cert no. SGS-COC-2482
FSC © 1996 Forest Stewardship Council

Printed and bound in Great Britain by
TJ International Ltd, Padstow, Cornwall

# Contents

# List of Figures

# Acknowledgements

Previously published works have been drawn on to partially produce this text. In all cases prior publications have significantly been revised and undated, in several cases whole papers largely form the basis of a discrete chapter in this work. Other articles have been pulled apart, deconstructed and re-territorialised in a manner constituting a jigsaw throughout these and the other various chapters. Published works drawn upon and reprinted with permission of the publisher include: Gunder, M. (2003) 'Passionate Planning for the Others' Desire: An Agonistic Response to the Dark Side of Planning', *Progress in Planning* 60:3, 236-319; Gunder, M. (2003) 'Planning Policy Formulation from a Lacanian Perspective', *International Planning Studies* 8:4, 279-294; Gunder, M. (2004) 'Shaping the Planner's Ego-Ideal: A Lacanian Interpretation of Planning Education', *Journal of Planning Education and Research* 23:3, 299-311; Gunder, M. (2005) 'Lacan, Planning and Urban Policy Formation', *Urban Policy and Research* 23:1, 91-111; Gunder, M. (2005) 'The Production of Desirous Space: Mere Fantasies of the Utopian City?' *Planning Theory* 4:2, 173-199; Gunder, M. (2005) 'Obscuring Difference Through Shaping Debate: A Lacanian View of Planning for Diversity', *International Planning Studies* 10:2, 83-103 (Chapter 7); Gunder, M. (2006) 'Sustainability: Planning's Saving Grace or Road to Perdition?', *Journal of Planning Education and Research* 26:2, 208-221 (Chapter 8); Gunder, M. (2008) 'Ideologies of Certainty in a Risky Reality: Beyond the Hauntology of Planning', *Planning Theory* 7:2, 186-206 (Chapter 4); Gunder, M. (2009) 'Imperatives of Enjoyment: Economic Development under Globalisation', in Rowe J. (ed.) *Theories of Local Economic Development: Linking Theory to Practice*, 285-300 (Aldershot, Ashgate) Copyright © 2009 (Chapter 6); Gunder, M., Hillier, J. (2004) 'Conforming to the Expectations of the Profession: A Lacanian Perspective on Planning Practice, Norms and Values', *Planning Theory and Practice* 5:2, 217-235; Gunder, M., Hillier, J. (2007) 'Planning as Urban Therapeutic', *Environment and Planning: A* 39:2, 467-486 (Chapter 3); Gunder, M., Hillier, J. (2007) 'Problematising Responsibility in Planning Theory and Practice: On Seeing the Middle of the String', *Progress in Planning* 68:2, 57-96 (Chapter 9); Hillier, J., Gunder, M. (2003) 'Planning Fantasies? An Exploration of a Potential Lacanian Framework for Understanding Development Assessment Planning', *Planning Theory* 2:3, 225-248; Hillier, J., Gunder, M. (2005) 'Not Over Your Dead Bodies! A Lacanian Interpretation of Planning Discourse and Practice', *Environment and Planning: A* 37:6, 1049-1066.

# Chapter 1
# Planning as an Empty Signifier

## Introduction

*Political language* ... is designed to make lies sound truthful and murder respectable, and to give an appearance of solidity to pure wind.

George Orwell, *Politics and the English Language*, cited in Watson 2004, 1

Cities are places of contested desire. Some of these strands of aspiration and hope are shaped and channelled into collective action for a better tomorrow through the deployment of techno-political narratives which strive to signify potentially better futures. These spatial planning narratives and the words that summarise and label them are largely predicated on the implication that something in the present is lacking or incomplete. The city would be better, if only ...

Spatial planning practice performs a dialogue between planning and urban governance that is full of signifying terms and labelling buzzwords, or 'weasel words' as Watson (2004) terms them, many of which imply innovative means to achieve desired states of urban well-being, such as deploying 'Smart Growth', 'new urbanism' or 'bohemian indexes' to plan for 'sustainable', 'globally competitive', and 'liveable' cities. We argue that these terms, and many others, are mere 'empty signifiers', meaning everything and nothing – comfort terms – all things to all people. These desirous states of living and being, which most of us would aspire towards and, accordingly, attempt to shape our cities to achieve, are often illusions, attained, at best, with limited success.

In this book we demythologise ten of the most heavily utilised terms in the spatial planning literature and practice: certainty, the good, risk, growth, globalisation, multiculturalism, sustainability, responsibility, rationality and 'planning' itself. Our analytical 'debunking' frame for this 'game of buzzword bingo' is predominantly Lacanian in origin and especially the contemporary Lacanian-inspired thought of Slavoj Žižek, although we also refer to other poststructuralist authors including Michel Foucault, Gilles Deleuze, and Jacques Derrida and touch on the sociology of Ulrich Beck, Pierre Bourdieu, Anthony Giddens, Jürgen Habermas and Henri Lefebvre. Our specific objectives in this book are:

- To engage with the ideological underpinnings of orthodox spatial planning theory and practice – city-making – from a post-structuralist cultural studies perspective.

- To understand the dimensions of desire, aspiration and fantasy embedded in our construction of human settlements and how our dreams are integral in the shaping of social reality and the actualisation or materialisation of our built environments.
- To illustrate how these desires are channelled by mechanisms of power in situations of contemporary governance.
- To consider alternative perspectives from which to engage with, and challenge, contemporary spatial planning practice.

We explore each of the ten heavily used, but often contested, planning words drawing on examples of planning practice and process from the UK, North America and Australasia. We conclude that 'city-making' in the 21st century should shed its tradition of seeking impossibly idealised end-states through means-end orientated planning. In place of this still largely instrumental form of planning, we suggest that spatial planning might be more effective as a process of contingent emergence and trajectory without closure. We trust that the readers of this book will gain a new insightful understanding of city–shaping and the role that contemporary spatial planning plays in this process. We also wish to illustrate the important role of ideology in this approach. Indeed, we will contend that social reality is largely constructed by the materialisation of our fantasies through our actions. We hope that this book contributes to the exposure of such constructs and empty signifiers, including that of 'planning' itself.

This introductory chapter will begin by questioning the ontological nature of spatial planning. Is planning an art, is it a science, or is it merely an ideology? We will suggest that planning has dimensions of both art and science largely tied together via constructs of ideological illusion. The chapter will then suggest why the psychoanalytical insights of Jacques Lacan, and his adherents, are useful to engaging with the ideological constructs of planning and that of wider social reality. It will also outline why the application of Lacanian thought is often criticised. We then introduce the reader to the Lacanian concept of 'master signifiers' and the implications that these have for both the construction of knowledge and our identifications with others through our social, political and cultural networks, which in aggregate constitute society. We apply the concept of master signifiers to our ten contestable words of spatial planning to illustrate how we will deploy this concept, as well as other aspects of Lacanian theory, to demystify the symbolic[1] equipment of planning. The chapter concludes with an overview of the book's structure.

---

1   That which can be put into language, either spoken or written text.

**An Introduction to Spatial Planning: Art, Science or merely Ideology?**

[P]lanners are strange characters. They traffic in fiction, and at the same time ask us to take it all seriously. Even more surprising, those of us who are not planners do take them at their word and grant them the authority they crave. This open-eyed reliance on fiction as a basis for public policy is remarkable, to put it mildly, and requires explanation. (Van Eaten and Roe 2000, 58)

According to the 19th-century founder of linguistics, Ferdinand de Saussure (2006, 67), all words in any language have two dimensions. The first is the word's identity, what it looks or sounds like, the shape of letters or utterance comprising it. This is called its *signifier*. The word 'cup' is composed of the letters 'c', 'u', 'p', in that order and pronounced 'kʌp' in the International Phonetic Alphabet. The second dimension is what it means, its *signification*. A cup is 'a small bowl-shaped container' (Concise Oxford Dictionary 1992, 283). A cup is an unambiguous word. Other words are more complex, with multiple significations, take for example the word 'sound'. It can be a adjective, noun or verb and mean to be 'healthy', or a 'noise', or a 'narrow passage of water', as well as mean, to 'test the depth of water'. Saussure (2006) observed that any connection between the signifier and what it signifies is largely arbitrary. Some words, such as 'democracy' or 'freedom', have many significations, often with conflicting meanings, which may be both of slight and of a more profound differential nature. Laclau (1996, 2000, 2005) argues that politics arise in the gap between signifier and its signification: where conflicting meanings are employed and we try to fill this gap. Here the signifier gives coherence to a grouping of conflicting meanings by signifying it or giving a general label of explicit connotation and agreement for this contested ground. Laclau (2003, 2005) calls this an empty signifier.[2]

---

2    Sometimes Laclau calls it a floating signifier. An empty signifier is 'strictly speaking, a signifier without signified' (Laclau 1996, 36). However, it is not possible for a signifier to have no signification. What the term implies is that the signifier has been 'emptied' of any one particular meaning and takes on a universal function of representing an entirety of ambiguous, fuzzy, related meanings such as a social order, an ideal or aspiration, or a difficult to define concept, such as 'planning'. It no longer signifies a particular phenomenon but can articulate different elements, to which it stands in relation and becomes the privileged nodal point that binds these particular points into a discursive formation (Laclau 1996, 44).

Where a signifier can indicate different significations in different contexts – i.e., its meaning is indeterminate or 'suspended', Laclau (1996, 2005) terms this a floating signifier. For example, the term 'sustainable development' has signified different meanings over time. For the Club of Rome's *Limits to Growth* this understanding, or signification relates to an ecological balance (Meadows *et al.* 1972) is in contrast to the WCED/Brundtland definitions of sustainable development which integrated environmental rhetoric to developmentalist ideology (WCES 1987) – as will be discussed in Chapter 8.

For simplification in this book, we will use the term empty signifier to stand for both empty and floating signifiers.

We contend that planning is an empty signifier. The label or signifier, constituting the word of 'planning' acts as a holder of meaning: what it signifies, its signification. Another way of thinking about an empty signifier is that it refers to a word that acts just like a cup, which can contain almost anything as long as it can be poured or placed into it, for example, milk, wine, oil, blood, water or sand. Planning is a signifier, similar to a cup, which can contain many diverse meanings and nuances. This can be narrowed down to some degree by putting another adjectival label before it, such as regional planning, urban planning, strategic planning, development assessment planning, communicative planning or spatial planning. For the purpose of this book we consider planning to be about the 'co-ordination, making and mediation of space' so we have chosen the term 'spatial planning' as delineated by the UK Royal Town Planning Institution (2001) and articulated in 21st-century British government policy (Doak and Parker 2005). This will at least allow the planners, the planned, and the topic of planning that we wish to address, to not be confused with, for instance, financial planners or wedding planners who have little to do directly with shaping the built environment. Yet, this focus on a partially defined 'spatial planning' still allows much room for contested meaning. We suggest that planning is inherently a contested and contestable term and will remain an empty signifier in this regard.

Perhaps one reason for planning's diverse and contestable meanings is its complex historical evolution. Planning largely evolved out of the art of architectural design and the science of civil engineering in the built environment. It was initially deployed largely to address issues of public health and housing to offset the adverse impacts of industrialisation in the late 19th and early 20th centuries, with a general aim to produce a rational and progressive city (Ashworth 1954; Boyer 1983; Sandercock 1990). Its early adherents, if professionally qualified at all, were generally master design practitioners (Brooks 1988). However, the positivistic[3] social science model tended to dominate planning after the Second World War, especially in the United States (Banerjee 1993; Dagenhart and Sawicki 1992; Perloff 1957). For many planning practitioners, academics, or commentators, in the mid-20th century, planning was a scientific engagement with place making, often predicated on instrumental rationality and positivistic physical and/or social science (Faludi 1973; Friedmann 1987; Hopkins 2001). This scientific rationality still tends to dominate spatial planning education and practice in many parts of the world, although this worldview has come under challenge increasingly since the 1980s (Healey 1997; Hillier 2002, 2007; Sandercock 1998, 2004).

We agree with this challenge to purely predictive scientific planning for we argue that spatial planning can never be just about the facts which constitute empirical science – what we know to be true – because facts in science must be inherently observable and measurable. Facts must always inherently reside in the present and

---

3  A philosophical system recognising only material facts and observable phenomena, deployed in science to develop predictable models based on cause and effect (Giddens 1974).

the past, not in the future. Yet, we contend that planning is ultimately about what will, or might be, the future. Planning thus incorporates components of human values, desires and aspirations at its core. Analytical science's conceptualisations of causal relationships cannot fully engage with such intangibles. Intangibles, by their very nature, are unable to guarantee predictability to 'allow planners to propagate principles and laws across an undulating and often resistant social landscape' (Beauregard 2001, 437). Science has limited predictive power when it comes to human hope, ambition and values (Flyvbjerg 2001). We argue, therefore, that science and the application of facts have a definite, but limited application in planning practice, no matter how much we might wish to rely on universally applicable scientific techniques. Spatial planning practitioners, we suggest, also need to engage with other means of understanding when attempting to shape the world.

Eugenie Birch (2001) refers to planning as an art-form of design, craft[4] and presentation, while Heather Campbell (2006) describes spatial planning as 'the art of situated ethical judgement', since value judgement is an inescapable dimension of the planning process. In this light, Campbell and Marshall (2006, 240) suggest that planning is 'an activity which is concerned with making choices about good and bad, right and wrong, with and for others, in relation to particular places.' We suggest that most planning theorists would agree (see, for example: Flyvbjerg 1998, 2001; Forester 1989, 1999; Healey 1997), although we indicate in later chapters that others would argue for 'better' or 'worse' choices, rather than 'good' or 'bad' ones in the quotation above.

With planning's loss of its architectural dimension in the latter half of the 20th century, Talen and Ellis (2004, 22) suggested that the literal 'art' in planning diminished, or at least its aesthetic dimension of 'the artistic side of urbanism'. The authors suggest that a 'review of city planning journals from 1960 to 2002 reveals that the artistic component of city planning is rarely discussed' (22). They call for a re-establishment of the aesthetic in planning as a merger of art, life and nature to create 'beautiful cities [which] inhabit the edge between order and disorder', that is between novelty and certainty of order (27).

We suggest that spatial planning practice has indeed an artful dimension. This is an art partially predicated on aesthetic values, but also one drawing on the wider emotions and affects of its constituents. Beyond aesthetics, Nigel Thrift (2008, 240) refers to this 'artful' manipulation of built environments, or cityscapes, as technologies and engineering of affect: 'a series of highways of imitation-suggestion' often producing behaviours of anxiety, obsession and compulsion. We suggest that this 'art of affect' may impose ideological effects on the populace,

---

4  Perhaps the descriptor 'craft' is a particularly useful dimension for planning for 'craft blurs the boundaries between universal principles and particularistic applications' of planning practice (Beauregard 2001, 438).

what Foucault refers to as governmentality[5] (Gunder and Mouat 2002; Hillier 2002), and we suggest that this is a central mechanism of many contemporary spatial planning processes (Gunder and Hillier 2007a). Further, in this work we argue that planning both induces ideological belief and behaviours in the populace it plans for; and is, in itself, at least partially constituted as a discipline for its practitioners and supporters by a set of ideological beliefs.

Back in 1960, Donald Foley identified a strong ideological dimension to British planning; an ideological factor that 'tends to build around seemingly self-evident truths and values and, in turn, to bestow a self-justifying tone to its main propositions and chains of reasoning' (Foley 1960, 212). Eric Reade (1987, 98) also argued that planning offers an emotively satisfying ideology for its supporters; one that justifies their social position in 'what they do and are'. Reade attributed six dimensions to planning's ideological construction:

- It is 'a body of thought devised to serve an interest', in this case the planning profession (or possibly, more recently, cynics might argue, that of the development industry);
- It is one that 'relies heavily on unstated and often unconscious basic assumptions' about the 'big questions' based on 'presuppositions' that are often 'unclear';
- 'It is prescriptive' about 'states of affairs we "ought" to prefer', but 'frequently omits to mention that the states of affairs which it regards as self-evidently desirable can only be justified in terms of values, and instead seems to suggest that they have been shown objectively or scientifically to be inevitable or desirable';
- It 'tells us *how* to bring about the states of affairs which it urges', but subsequently, often fails to achieve this state when subject to dispassionate scrutiny;
- It 'appeals both to our emotions and to our intellect, but confuses us to which is which'; and
- It 'succeeds at one and the same time in being both very confused, and yet apparently forming a psychologically satisfying, coherent, interlocking system of explanations, providing a clear and understandable view of the world' that blurs distinctions of 'fact', 'value', 'theory' and 'untruth' ... 'into an impenetrable web of mutual supportive arguments' (1987, 98 – emphasis in original).

The following chapters will test and show support for Reade's assertions as to planning's ideological nature. Planning, we also assert, tends to be both an

---

5  Governmentality is a mentality of governance and management on the part of the state to set standards of normality for populations co-variant with a mentality of self-governance of individuals in society to conform appropriately to what is expected of them as responsible citizens: i.e., to act normally (see Dean 1999).

ideology of belief and one of identification for its practitioners as to what is 'good' planning practice behaviour. These practitioners, in turn – often while thinking that they are acting in the public's best interest – ideologically impose these beliefs (scientifically grounded, or otherwise constructed) as their professional normative values, on the public via their plans and other strategic planning processes. Consistent with Flyvbjerg's (1998, 2001) earlier findings, rationality in spatial planning will be shown throughout this work to not be always as evident as it is made to appear.

The French sociologist, Pierre Bourdieu's, concepts of *habitus*[6] and *doxa*[7] well illustrate this ideological process. Planning's key terms, especially the ten words primarily addressed in this book, provide the 'mental structures' – the holding 'cups' – necessary to produce a 'social space', or field of spatial planning for popular socio-political engagement. These place markers, as 'empty signifiers' are essential in order to construct and structure a dynamic *habitus* that produces, reproduces and evolves social practices, be they those of spatial planning and city-shaping, or society's wider issues constituting the 'common sense of the day' (see Bourdieu 2000, 164-172). The latter constitute Bourdieu's concept of *doxa*, the unquestionable orthodoxy of any one time and spatial location – including what we may lack but must strive to have (Chopra 2003, 426). A spatial planning example would be the potentially contradictory rhetorical planning assertion that: we must be 'sustainable' to be a 'globally competitive' city (Jonas and While 2007)! In this regard, the 'habitus serves to transmit and "embed" attitudes, values, norms and beliefs of the social group or "social world" within an individual as to what constitutes desirous and appropriate sustainable behaviours as the individual practises those activities normally associated with such attitudes, values, norms and beliefs' (Searle and Bryne 2002, 8). 'Though thoroughly individualized, the habitus in fact reflects a shared cultural context', it is 'an unconscious formation' that 'develops as an *unconscious* competence' as 'a result of an experiential schooling stretching back to childhood' (Adams 2006, 514 – emphasis in original). Of course, the dominant *doxa* or 'ideology of any historical moment or spatial location – Bourdieu's "orthodoxy" – will of course reflect the orientations of the dominant social group(s)', e.g., the desire that *we all must share* in support of global economic competitiveness (Rankin 2003, 716).

So, in this light, is spatial planning practice merely an ideology, or can it still have dimensions of science or art? Or, can it have all three? Beauregard (2001, 438) attributes to planning both a scientific and craft (or art) dimension, but also states that planning is 'an ideology and thus infused with prescriptive judgements

---

6  *Habitus* is a set of acquired guidelines for thought, behaviour, and taste. These acquired criteria, or dispositions, are the consequence of the internalisation of objective social or cultural structures through the life experience of an individual or group (Bourdieu 1998).

7  *Doxa* denotes what is taken for granted in any particular society, the unquestioned ways and values that constitute the dominant common sense of a culture (Bourdieu 1977).

and normative visions'. We tend to agree and suggest that ideological belief acts as the binding core of the discipline to tie all three dimensions to planning practice.

Wildavsky (1973) went so far as to claim that planning, at least for its adherents, is a faith, i.e., a set of unquestioned beliefs without factual foundations. Because human actors 'can only create the future' they desire 'on paper', they transfer their 'loyalties to the plan' so that 'the process of planning becomes holy' (Wildavsky 1973, 152). While planning might not have been reified as a secular faith for all its practitioners, let alone its vociferous opponents, such as property developers, protesting residents, or environmentalists, we suggest that there might be some dimension of validity in Wildasky's assertion. Wildavsky (1973, 127) observes that we 'think through language'. He therefore draws a link between how we 'think about planning' and 'how [we] act'. We turn to consider language and planning in the next section.

## The Language of and in Planning

Whilst spatial planning practice may couple knowledge – scientific or otherwise – to public action (Friedmann 1987, 1998), it is through language[8] that planning debate is framed and focussed. What sells the 'vision' in the plan? How do we bundle complicated and often obtuse planning issues together in a manner where actors with contesting positions can grapple jointly with the problem? How do planners foster public debate and participation? We suggest that language is core to this process of belief, aspiration and especially, psychological identification, with desire and the concept of empty signifiers often playing a uniting role in this process.

John Forester (1989, 1999) documented how planners effectively focus attention, shape debate and generally try to minimise mystification, or other distortions in communications, as well as provide hope and understanding through their language games of planning practice. Other planning theorists, such as Bent Flyvbjerg (1998, 2001), take a less optimistic perspective and indicate how planners often distort language and rationality in seeking their strategic

---

8   Here, we differentiate the word 'language' from that of 'narrative' or 'discourse'. When we refer to 'language', we are referring to the general text and speech acts that we use to communicate. Narratives or discourses are sets of sentences constituting speeches, arguments and conversations that have become institutionalised into a particular way of thinking. However, in this book we will also differentiate between discourses and narratives with the former used to denote particular technical psycho-linguistic structures seeking to evoke an effect on the listener within speech and writing (after Lacan 2007) and narratives used in the wider context of sets of sentences comprising meanings, practices and arguments. Accordingly, narratives, such as planning narratives, contain explanations and claims justifying 'truths', values and beliefs, i.e., they claim legitimacy as knowledge and set the boundaries of acceptability.

ends. James Throgmorton (1996, 38) documents the important role of rhetoric and storytelling in planning practice, particularly when appropriately shaped and tailored to the perceived desires of their specific audiences. As Brent (2004, 216) observes 'illusion and rhetoric are indeed an important part of social reality, which is not based only on a rational instrumentality, but has strong aesthetic and narrative components – human cultural activity, with all its creative energy, and is a major part of social construction'.

We suggest that, just as images and catchy phrases sell commodities in our consumer-oriented world, they also encourage both debate and public acceptance of planning initiatives and ideas. 'What is seen and imagined, practiced and understood, as [planning] today operates through and as the materialization of publicity' (adapted from Dean 2001, 626). Iconic labels capture our hearts and minds. Images of desirous futures capture our aspirations. We identify with these sublime potentialities and wish to make them ours. In such a context the role of spatial planners is to create, mediate and facilitate common goals and visions of a desired future for our communities (Ferraro 1995). As Throgmorton (1996, 5) demonstrates: through the deployment of narratives and *tropes* – rhetorical devices such as metaphor[9], metonymy[10] and synecdoche[11] – 'good planning is persuasive and constitutive storytelling about the future.' As Sandercock (2003a, 26) further asserts: 'stories and storytelling are central to planning practice, that in fact we think about planning as performed story'. We suggest that planning is more than mere 'science fiction' of what should be. Yet, until realised (if ever) these stories remain but virtual fictions and fantasies of what actors desire. It is these virtual hopes and aspirations that shape actors' subsequent actions.

Planning, then, has dimensions of science and art in its practice. It also has ideological dimensions, which appeal to our emotions and our intellects. Central to all three dimensions is the fundamental role of language and communication in planning, and the effects and affects these have on 'subjects', both planner and those for and with whom planning plans. The importance of language and communication has given rise to one of the most significant and influential fields of recent planning theory and practice: communicative planning (Innes 1995).

Probably the most important influence on what has become known as the 'communicative turn' in planning theory has been the work of the German sociologist Jürgen Habermas. Habermas examined issues of intersubjective

---

9   A metaphor is a descriptive signifier that may be used to give signification to an object or action where 'it is imaginatively but not literally applicable', e.g., the world is a stage (Concise Oxford Dictionary 1992, 745).

10   A metonymy is 'the substitution of the name of an attribute or adjunct for that of a thing meant' or signified, e.g., 'Crown for king, the turf for horse-racing' (Concise Oxford Dictionary 1992, 747 – emphasis removed).

11   A synecdoche is 'a figure of speech in which a part is made to represent the whole or vice versa' e.g., 'new faces at the meeting', Italy won by two goals (Concise Oxford Dictionary 1992, 1237).

communication and social action from a perspective of communicative rationality. His early critical theory of communicative action drew heavily on the work of the Frankfurt School[12] and its basis in the work of Karl Marx and, importantly for our purpose here, Sigmund Freud.

Habermas wrote that his 'point of departure is the assumption that the development of interactive competence regulates the construction of internal behavioural controls' (2001, 131). He regarded language as a means of organising wants and needs that are communicatively structured and subject to interpretation. As such, the concept of reciprocity – or mutual recognition – in which actors define themselves in relation to one another, is important.

Habermas' general theory of communicative action was partly developed from Freud's psychoanalytical theory of distorted communication,[13] which Habermas believed necessarily presupposed non-distorted communication and 'the intention of universal and unconstrained consensus' (1972, 314). His wider concern was that the state is forced to deal with dysfunctional side effects of the economic process under fairly restrictive conditions. Habermas' desire was that communicative action might bring about 'social relations in which mutuality dominates and satisfaction does not mean the triumph of one over the repressed needs of the other' (1979, xxiv).

Habermas' 'desire' clearly resonated with the values of planning theorists. His work was developed initially by John Forester (1989, 1993, 1999) who was conscious of the importance of power in decision-making, a dynamic which Habermas has tended to understate. Judith Innes (1995, 1996, 2002) applied communicative theory in practical consensus-building strategies in the United States, extending her work to incorporate consideration of complexity theory (Innes and Booher 1999, 2002), which itself has undergone a new iteration to include a psychoanalytical understanding (Medd 2002; Stacey 1996).

Patsy Healey (1997) has developed collaborative communicative theory in a context of processes of governance. She is particularly interested in 'the qualities of the social relations through which collective activity in relation to urban management is accomplished' (Healey *et al.* 2002, 12), which has led her to explore interrelationships between theories of organisational management and communicative theories in a 'new institutionalist' framework (Healey 1999, 2002, 2003, 2007).

---

12   The Frankfurt School was an informal name for a group of famous German thinkers drawing on neo-Marxist critical theory, sociology and philosophy including Max Horkheimer, Theador Adorno, Herbert Marcuse and more recently Jürgen Habermas. The School held that basic socio-economic concepts had to be integrated with psychological concepts due to a belief that an emancipated society and an autonomous self were interdependent (Wollin 2006). Habermas (1979) similarly believed in the interdependence of forms of social integration and forms of identity.

13   See Habermas (1972), Chapters 10-12.

Organisational management theories regularly incorporate psychological and behavioural aspects (Haslam 2001). With regard to planning and management theory, Howell Baum (1989, 1991a, 1991b, 1994, 2000) has referred to the work of psychoanalysts (such as Sigmund Freud, Melanie Klein and Wilfred Bion) with regard to examination of group culture, participatory consensus in planning decision-making and delusion in development partnerships and bureaucratic practice. Tore Sager (1994) has also drawn on Freud's concept of parapraxis to explain planning dysfunction and misunderstanding as a consequence of failed communications.

Leonie Sandercock (2004, 139) has observed that, until recently, the contemporary planning and urban policy literature has lacked recognition that there is a need to understand both *'language and a process of emotional involvement,* of embodiment', in planning processes. Sandercock continues that this is especially so, because 'many planning disputes are about relationships, and therefore emotions, rather than [just] conflicts over resources' (139). She asserts that effective spatial planning needs to understand and work with the emotions that drive ethnic and other forms of urban conflict (Sandercock 2003b, 322).

One of the authors of this present volume, Jean Hillier (2002, 2003a), attempted to build theory that explains planning decision-making practice more fully than does Habermasian communicative action. She not only investigated the potential contribution of Michel Foucault[14] in terms of including power relations between actors, but also traced Chantal Mouffe's objections to Habermasian theory back to their Lacanian roots. Hillier made reference to Lacan to explain the impossibility of a complete and comprehensive 'truth' and hence agreement or consensus about an issue. She argued that agonistic dissensus may be understated, but that it is a key constituent of the arenas and forums of planning practice. The other author, Michael Gunder (2000a, 2003b, 2005a), has also utilised Lacanian theory to expose pernicious elements of planning practices, hegemonic rhetorics and action, as well as to prescribe an agonistic alternative to consensual communicative planning.

Parallel to these developments in planning theory, the references to psychogeography in the work of authors such as Steve Pile (1996, 1998, 2000, 2005), Ed Soja (1996, 2000), David Gregory (1997), Jane Jacobs and Ken Gelder (1998) and Nigel Thrift (2000a, 2000b, 2008), have opened up spaces for psychoanalytically informed analyses of practices of everyday life; microanalyses of what people do, how and why they do it. Pile (2000, 84), for instance, suggests that 'cities are like dreams, for both conceal secret desires and fears, for both are produced according to hidden rules which are only vaguely discernable.' These 'rules' and practices may not be consciously articulated or readily observable (Lefebvre 1991). They reflect

---

14   Foucault also initially engaged in psychoanalytical discussions of Freud's and Lacan's theories of the subject in *The Archaeology of Knowledge* (1972) and *The History of Sexuality, Volume 1* (1979).

practical, experiential, phronetic[15] knowledges generated through 'the remorseless buildup of small and fleeting detail in speech and objects which "points" towards certain concerns'; 'the oblique, the transparent, and the haunted: the latent' (Thrift 2000a, 404-405). As Thrift (2000a, 405) continues, 'these are knowledges of what is permitted and prohibited, present and absent'. They also comprise the uncanny[16] and the repressed, all of which are dimensions engaged by psychoanalysts in analytical practice with their patients, often referred to as the 'talking cure'. However, like the psychogeographers, we wish to extent this type of analysis from the individual to wider society so as to encompass an understanding of spatial planning: its art, its science and above all its ideology. We argue below that the work of Jacques Lacan, and that of his followers, offers us psychoanalytic perspectives from which to do so.

## Why Lacan?

Arguably, one of the most significant French intellectuals of the latter half of the 20th century, Jacques Lacan was a neo-structuralist philosopher and practising psychoanalyst (Marini 1992; Foucault 1998, 279). Central to Lacan's theory of the individual as subject is a focus on belief, knowledge and desire. Lacan drew on Freud's metapsychology[17] and 'other theoretical traditions, prominent among them phenomenology and existential philosophy' derived from Heidegger, Kant, Kierkegaard and Hegel, 'structural linguistics' from Saussure 'and anthropology' from Sartre (Boothby 2001, 9). As a consequence, 'Lacan's account of symbolic subjectivity contributes more to social theory than to psychological theories of the individual' (Dean 2000, 2).

Jacques Lacan's body of work (1988a, 1988b, 1992, 1994, 1998, 2006, 2007) has become widely influential outside the field of psychoanalysis as it provides a comprehensive critique of social interaction and ideology. As Bowie (1987, 133) writes, Lacan 'provides workers in other fields with a cautionary portrait of thinking-as-it-happens'. This creates the opportunity for self-reflexiveness, a way to think through complex issues of choice and responsibility (Sarup 1993), which we argue are extremely pertinent to spatial planning practitioners; responsibility being one of our 'ten words'.

Lacan was not a prolific writer, nor formally an academic. Rather he was a practitioner and teacher. His major written work was the *Écrits* (2006), originally published in French in 1966. The majority of Lacan's publications are transcriptions of his teaching seminar series that ran for 27 years in Paris from 1953-1954 until 1978-1979, two years before his death in 1981.

---

15    From Aristotle's intellectual virtue of *phronesis* – a virtue of excellent judgement in human affairs developed through learning from experience (Flyvbjerg 2001).

16    Freud's (2003) unheimlich or 'unhomely'.

17    Psychology concerning the fundamental assumptions of the Freudian theory of mind (Boothby 2001).

Lacan and his followers allow a new insight into how ideology shapes social reality. As Jameson (2003, 37-8) observes, we may attribute to Lacan 'the first new and as yet insufficiently developed concept of the nature of ideology since Marx'. Drawing on Lacanian-inspired work by Louis Althusser, Jameson states that ideology is 'the "representation" of the Imaginary[18] relationships of individuals to their [r]eal conditions of existence', so that 'the individual subject invents a "lived" relationship with collective systems', such as the fantasy that we are wanted by society and that it will look after us, if we only give 'it', this 'big Other' with a capital 'O', what it wants. This, in turn, induces symbolic and materialised relationships of common practices and rituals (Krips 2003, 149), which we suggest are largely synonymous with Bourdieu's (1998) concept of *habitus* (Steinmetz 2006). It is the abstract aggregate of this 'big Other' – which constitutes society, and the illusions and fantasies that we generate about it and ourselves – that we respond to and materialise in our actions. This in turn, ideologically shapes the social reality that is observable in our behaviours and is articulated in language. That is, it constitutes our lived space.

For Lacan (2006, 300) 'the function of language in speech is not to inform but to evoke' an effect upon the other actors. Lacan engaged with language throughout his work, but it was in his teachings of 1969-1970 – *Seminar XVII*, that he engaged most directly with the power of speech when he proposed his *Four Discourses* (Lacan 2007). Lacan's 'theory of the four discourses is without doubt the most important part of the Lacanian formalisation' (Verhaeghe 2001, 19). The discourses represent, respectively, the language games, or linguistic structures, which underpin and produce four fundamental social effects that resonate strongly with the roles and practices of planning (Bracher 1993, 53):

1. governing/commanding (the master's discourse);
2. educating/indoctrinating/administrating (the university/bureaucracy's discourse);
3. desiring/protesting/complaining (the hysteric's discourse); and
4. analyzing/transforming/revolutionizing (the analyst's discourse).

Each of the discourses affects how knowledge and desire is created and used as well as the conscious and unconscious ordering of the individual's relationship both with some 'truth' and society's capacity to (re)interpret and define the individual's conformity with normative behaviours (Stacy 1997).

Moreover, central to Lacan's theorising is the insight that while the human subject, or society, cannot exist without language; neither the subject nor the material world can be diminished to the symbolic – words and text – alone. Some type of symbolic structure, or system, is critical to enable us to constitute and integrate our perceptions of social reality. However, th relationships between

---

18   That which can be put into images, either in the symbolic realm of media, art, or in human consciousness, or human dreams.

structure (such as the class system) and agency (our individual performativity) within our social reality are often symbolically obscure, because these relationships extend to a dimension external to language or even that of our imaginations (Hillier and Gunder 2005). Lacan (1988a, 1994, 2006) called this indeterminate registry, or dimension, the 'Real'. The Real resides completely externally to that of the symbolic or the image(ary). The Real is impossible to grasp, to visualise, or to describe. We therefore (albeit often unconsciously) deploy fantasy and illusion to obscure this 'impossible thing', a noumenon[19] that exists but cannot be symbolised or even envisaged (Žižek 1997a, 1999c, 78). The Real is a lack in the symbolic that provokes the subject to produce an imaginary element to obscure what is lacking and to give some type of consistency to what cannot be signified within language (Stavrakakis 1999, 27). Hence, what ensures the possibility of a coherently-appearing social reality is 'the intrusion of fantasy, especially the manner in which fantasy screens over the void, lack, or absence' of the Real that we fail to articulate or even conceptualise (Elliot 2001, 76). This insight on the Real, and the fantasies that it induces, are a core dimension of Lacanian-derived theory.

However, the application of Lacanian theory to the understanding of society is not without concern for some authors. For instance, numerous clinical practitioners of Lacanian psychoanalysis are 'suspicious of the wider "application" of the theory to those not actually in analysis' (Parker 2004, 69). Alternatively, Lacan's teachings have been criticised by social theorists as being far too theoretical and void of empirical material (Sarup 1993, 26). Further, for others, the inability to reconcile the nuance of each particular psychoanalytical case to a meaningful universal and testable theory of the unconscious is a fundamental constraint for considering psychoanalysis a science, or by extension, a valid scientific body of thought applicable to the understanding of aggregate human behaviours (Fink 2004). In this regard, Lacan was unable to legitimise and advance Freud's psychoanalytical theory successfully as a *science* of the unconscious even with his application of mathematics (mathemes) and linguistics to Freud's metapsychology (Althusser 1996; Fink 2004; Morel 2000). Consequently, we view Lacan's work as best understood as a 'philosophy of psychoanalysis' from which subsequent understandings of society and culture may be derived (Althusser 1996, 93).

Within feminist theory the value of Lacan's metapsychology is hotly debated. While some regard it as a useful set of concepts from which to challenge phallocentric knowledges and patriarchal power relationships (for example, Judith Butler (1990), Joan Copjec (1989), Elizabeth Grosz (1990), Julia Kristeva (1970) and Juliet Mitchell (1974)). Others perceive Lacan as privileging masculinity, where women are signified as a lack that is a substratum of the androcentric subject (for example, Luce Irigaray (1985), Germaine Greer (1999) and Dale Spender (1980)).

---

19   An object that is independent of human perception, appearance or observation. Kant (1934) called it a 'Thing-in-itself' in contrast to a phenomenon that can be observed.

We agree with those feminists who defend Lacanian theory and contend that rather than interpreting his work substantively, Lacan's work should be used as an explanatory analytic tool for understanding power relations (Grosz 1989; Mitchell 1974; Ragland-Sullivan 1986), or bodily life and desire as significant explanations of causative relationships (Copjec 1994, 2002). While Lacan constructed his undeniably male-gendered theories without apparent acknowledgement of patriarchal domination, we agree with Elizabeth Grosz (1990) that Lacanian theorising provides scope to change our perspectives on power relationships and how they are replicated in society. Through transcending Freud's focus on biology, Lacanian thought permits us to understand gender domination in the context of the ideological constructs that constitute the social realities of society.

Our critical understanding of Lacan's teachings and their application to the sphere of social analysis owes much to the interpretation of Slavoj Žižek. Whilst Žižek's particular Hegelian and Marxist readings of Lacan are controversial (see Butler 2005; Dean 2006; Dews 1995; Gigante 1998; Johnston 2008; Kay 2003; Myers 2003; Parker 2004), Žižek does build up a rich and dense texture of associations, which, we believe, afford useful explanatory insight. This includes, for instance, Žižek's (1993, 1997a) argument that the truth of the subject is always outside itself in the object. That is: we can never know ourselves because this truth resides in the unknowable Real, hence we look to the Other, i.e., society, to tell us who we are. Yet, this response is always inherently incomplete. If our symbolic identity is situated in the Other, this position radically challenges the traditional conceptualisation of the subject and object as mutually opposed. Žižek brings Lacan out of the clinic and into popular culture and everyday life, he deploys jokes and uses popular culture[20] to explain his philosophical positions and arguments.

## A Dash of Lacanian Insight: Master Signifiers, Identity and Knowledge

In this section we introduce the Lacanian concept of master signifiers and how these function in language to allow us to create a symbolic set of identifications for ourselves and in our relationships with others in society. We, as humans, use words to describe to others who we are and what we believe are our truths. For example, someone might describe themselves as *US-American, white, single, female, able-bodied, thirty-something, post-graduate* educated *planner*, who is religiously *agnostic*, but who believes in *sustainability* and *social justice*, who likes to *throw pots, cycle,* play *tennis, travel* and *cook Thai* cuisine, etc. The aggregate of these words would constitute a person's identifications such that they can convey to

---

20    For example, his analyse of the Director's Cut of the Ridley Scott's film *Bladerunner* is deployed to explain and illustrate the above position about the truth of the subject. Žižek (1993, 40-41) illustrates how for the film's main character, Deckard, this truth is inherently ambiguous – is he human or robot? Is what appears as his subjective truth only an artificial construct of his manufacturer to give him a sense of human identification?

others. Yet each word is much more than itself. Being *US-American*, or a being a *planner*, each comprises a multiple range of subtexts constituting what it means to be and act as an American or as a planner. Moreover, being a *US-American* or a *planner* conveys a wide ranging set of contestable rules and values grounded solely in themselves: 'it is so because it is so, because it is our custom' (Žižek 2008a, 22). In Lacanian thought these identifying labels are called 'master signifiers'.

Identifications with a range of master signifiers constitute the subject as an individual in culture and wider society (Verhaeghe 2001). Master signifiers include descriptive signifiers, e.g., of bodily appearance, ethnicity and gender, through to more abstract signifiers of intellectual and spiritual beliefs (Bracher 1999, 45). The totality of a subject's master signifiers constitutes their ego-ideal, which comprises the core beliefs, values and a sense of self producing who, at least they believe, they are. Master signifiers thus describe and articulate who individuals are to others. Although Lacan (1988b, 2006) would argue that there is always a lack in the subject's identifications that prohibits a complete identity, as a consequence, it is this search for completeness, which actually constitutes the human subject.

Each abstract master signifier of identification is in turn comprised of a complex aggregate of ordered words constituting diverse narratives of contestable sets of knowledges and beliefs. These contestable narratives give a master signifier its meaning, i.e., its signification. For example, the narratives explain what it is to be an *US-American*, or a *planner*. Master signifiers are thus empty words, or signifiers, without explicit meaning in themselves (Laclau 2003, 2005). They tie together multifaceted and often muddled and conflicting, arrays of narratives under one universal and iconic signifier. These narratives may be academic or cultural in context and may, or may not, also incorporate other master signifiers within their own particular description. While harbouring these diverse narratives, master signifiers permit us to amicably arrange, clearly outline and communicate our descriptive, as well as abstract, identifications.

Master signifiers are crucial for sorting out our sense of self in society's complex sea of conflicting and contradictory knowledges, beliefs and values. Without sufficient master signifiers to anchor our identifications we could be driven to psychotic madness. With too many, and/or if too rigid in their structure, we could be driven to neurotic despair and obsessive self-sacrifice (Bowie 1991, 74). Master signifiers allow us to identify with others in our lifeworlds; they allow us to form our diverse groups and communities of interest. Master signifiers allow us to have shared and harmonious social identifications. Yet at the same time, in their competing sub-texts of what it means to be a *US-American* or a *planner*, they also allow us to accommodate difference and disagreement within, and across, each identification. They constitute and embrace the structuralisation of our socio-political life (Stavrakakis 1999, 30).

Lacan calls these master signifiers '*points de capiton*', 'button ties' that pin narratives, or networks of signifiers, to both the individual subject and wider society (Stavrakakis 1999), so as to order the world (Žižek 2008a, 30). Each master signifier is a 'nodal point ... which "quilts"' sets of knowledges, beliefs and practices, 'stops them sliding and fixes their meanings' (Žižek 2002a, 87). Each provides an anchoring point or concise signifying label for a 'whole field and, by embodying it, effectuates its identity' (Žižek 1989, 88). What constitutes a signifier as a suturing and ordering master signifier, is that it is isolated from the rest of the narrative, the sets of knowledges, codes and beliefs that comprise it (Fink 1995, 77). While the master signifiers remain unchanged, 'their descriptive features will be fundamentally unstable and open to all kinds of hegemonic rearticulations' (Laclau 1989, xiv). For example, sustainability has many contested interpretations, but the master signifier 'sustainability', itself, does not change (Gunder 2004, 302).

**Ten Contestable Words: Demystifying the Symbolic Equipment of Planning Practice**

Master signifiers related to spatial planning and engendering contemporary policy discussion include: *certainty*, *the good*, *risk*, *growth*, *globalisation*, *multiculturalism*, *sustainability*, *responsibility*, *rationality*, and *planning* itself. This inventory, of course, is not comprehensive as terms such as 'new urbanism', 'liveable cities', or 'environmental justice', could be readily added to the list (Gunder 2004, 303). These 'empty' signifiers have given up explicit, concise, significance to secure multifarious points of view, chains of significations constituting conflicting narrative, or unique interpretations pertaining to particular situations, all under one common label (Stavrakakis 1999, 80). In this book, we will examine these ten master signifiers and the contestable knowledge sets that vie to articulate what each master signifier means.

Diverse sub-texts or narratives – sets of knowledge, stories, and symbolic practices – describe and support their master signifiers prior to any hegemonic rearticulation or fine-tuning as to what these master signifiers should actually embody. For example: the dissimilar narratives of regional science and communicative rationality, both fundamentally support the master signifier *planning*. These diverse sets of knowledge also constitute our normative behaviours, the subcodes that fix the master signifiers, describing their ambiguous characteristics, acceptable behaviours and values (Bracher 1999, 45). The acquisition of these knowledges, stories and practices constitutes learning, which also includes the disciplinary and professional codes that constitute spatial planning and related urban policy disciplines.

This introductory chapter has introduced arguments that spatial planning, while drawing on art, craft and science, largely acts as a set of ideological beliefs for its practitioners. We contend that this is not a derogatory claim. Rather it is an interpretation that can lead to an improved understanding of planning practice and hopefully make us better practitioners and recipients of spatial planning. We introduced Lacan and his strengths and weaknesses, the concepts of master signifiers, Lacanian identification and the narratives that contest for meaning within each abstract master signifier. Finally, we have begun to suggest what this might imply for our ten words of planning deconstructed over the following chapters. In doing so the wider aims of *Planning in Ten Words or Less* are:

- To develop stronger and deeper theoretical perspectives for understanding spatial practice and governance. We contend that spatial managers and planning practitioners need strong theoretical foundations in order to understand and to be able to transform current practice effectively.
- To demonstrate how spatial planning policy responses often attempt to achieve impossible end-states without possibility of clear definition, let alone material achievement, constituting a supposedly 'better' social reality and spatial order. These are often ambiguous end-states that constrain and structure our urban policy responses by excluding other potential alternative responses to address problems and make appropriate improvements.
- To broaden the potential of spatial planning's ability to engage with issues of repressed desire/aspiration and deflate the pernicious illusions we sometimes sustain in our current spatial planning processes about city-making and our wider hopes for the future.
- To fundamentally challenge spatial planning's solution-led orthodoxy and demythologise several of the frequently unquestioned notions current in spatial planning processes. This is in order to delineate the potential of alternative planning processes that may be more open to continued social movements of dynamic change, progressive community self-determination, spatial planning innovation and ethical responsibility.

## Book Structure

In Chapter 1 we have hopefully persuaded readers why our approach to spatial planning is useful for understanding contemporary city-making. We considered how the art or science of *planning* is largely ideological in its techno-political policy intent and tentatively explored the mechanism of hegemonic articulation deployed in its shaping of the built form. Personal and group identification is central to this process. We then introduced the ten words selected for investigation as systematic of contemporary near-universal planning practice orthodoxy.

In Chapter 2 we commence with a detailed discussion of the place of 'lack' in Lacanian thought, commencing with the primordial maternal lack of young humans yet to be integrated into language and culture; and how it is then deployed in contemporary political and technocratic processes to inspire desire for a particular solution or policy process. Examples will be used to illustrate how this is nurtured as a popular desire underlain by a promise, or illusion, of harmony and fulfilment, which, of course, never materialises. The metaphorical framing of spatial planning fantasy will be discussed and its ideological power in shaping and guiding desire for specific community aspirations as the only 'correct' consensual belief will be explored. The chapter will argue how it is the desire for veracity of prediction – truth – which we claim is synonymous with the desire for *certainty* towards the unknowable future, which underwrites the very ontological purpose of spatial planning and gives it its popular support.

In Chapter 3 we will examine the concept of the *good* from a Lacanian perspective. We first consider the impossibility of the idealised, utopian city where 'good' for all can be achieved. We will suggest that fantasy and misrecognition are central to this process. The metaphor of the city as healthy body will be explored in this context. The chapter will then provide an appreciation of how our personal striving, to be perceived by the Other as 'good', shapes our very concept of self and our wider outwardly-materialising behaviours which, in turn, shape our empirically measurable social world. The chapter will also consider what constitutes 'good' urban behaviour, at least for our agents of governance, and how this is shaped through our media and other arenas of socio-political life. The chapter will then have regard to the fantasy constructs deployed in this manner to shape 'our' desired cities: what they ought to be, but without questioning for whom!

Chapter 4 takes the discussion of the desire for certainty as a core human 'good' further, drawing on Ulrich Beck's concept of *risk* society. We start with a discussion of realism and constructivism as alternative ways of constituting knowledge in the social sciences, including spatial planning. We then expand the constructivist position into a discussion on representation and non-representation, which introduces and draws on the Lacanian Real. Derrida's concepts of undecidability and hauntology are in turn engaged to argue planning's very ontological being as papering over of the fear of risk and uncertainty of the unknown risky future. We will suggest, however, that the ontological nature of planning, to provide an illusion of certainty towards the future, impairs its ability to engage with emerging problems. Planning is largely solution-driven, and without a solution to frame an emerging issue, spatial planning, as currently practised, has great difficulty tackling the new.

In Chapter 5 we explore the American signifier *Smart Growth* to consider the concept of economic growth in the contemporary world of finite carrying capacity. We use this metaphor of American city and regional planning to explore both the dominance of liberal global capitalism and how much of the orthodox international response to city shaping and making is derived from its hegemonic values. The Lacanian concept of *jouissance* – pleasure – will be defined in this chapter and then further explored in the subsequent two chapters. However, as we will explain, with Lacanian *jouissance* 'we are not dealing with simple pleasures, but with a violent intrusion that brings more pain than pleasure'. We will argue that to enjoy in such a context 'is rather something we do as a kind of weird and twisted ethical duty' (Žižek 2008a, 343).

Chapter 6 builds on Chapter 5 to argue that city policy management in areas of spatial planning and economic development are largely predicated on the imperatives of competitive *globalisation*. Our primary focus is on the way the

Lacanian concepts of *jouissance* and desire are deployed by both markets and governance to create desiring citizens who respond appropriately. We introduce Lacan's (2007) Theory of the Four Discourses, with particular focus on the discourses of the 'master' and 'university/bureaucracy'. We conclude the chapter by asking the question: in whose interest is enjoyment actually articulated and achieved?

In Chapter 7 we expand further on Lacanian *jouissance* in the context of *multiculturalism*, largely drawing on Žižek's (1993) conceptualisation that the Other always steals my enjoyment. We also engage further with Lacan's discourse theory (2007) and introduce the discourses of the 'hysteric' and 'analyst'. We illustrate how difference constitutes the contemporary metropolitan city. Yet we argue that this is, by necessity, a difference of exclusion and agonism that should be engaged with, not papered over by fantasy constructs of tolerance that, again drawing on Žižek (1997a, 1999c, 2008c), are shown to be mere arguments of, at best, subtle racism.

Chapter 8 explores *sustainability*. We argue that sustainable development is the now dominant spatial planning narrative, although perhaps implicitly trumped in achievement at the city-region level by the desire to be a 'globally competitive city'. Sustainable development is explored to illustrate how the term acts as a foil to give the appearance of doing something about global warming and the environment, when in effect it is largely deployed to maintain the priority of economic growth for achievement of global competitiveness. We suggest that sustainable development is considered so wonderful for all of us, for as we drive our hybrid car we can think we are saving the environment and making our cities better, when in reality we are simply perpetuating the idea of economic growth or 'business as usual'.

The penultimate Chapter 9 engages with the signifier: *responsibility*. We consider the traditional placed-based concepts of responsibility and city-shaping largely deployed in contemporary orthodox planning practice. We then broaden this concept of responsibility, drawing on Lévinas, Derrida, Iris Marion Young and, primarily, from Lacanian-derived literature, what is often titled an 'Ethics of the Real' (Zupančič 2000) to argue for an ethics for planning and city-making that is globally conscious. We suggest that such an ethics might involve practising an understanding of responsibility that is predicated on a premise of 'avoidance of avoidance', especially when we are aware of the global implications of our actions. The chapter concludes with a reflection on these implications for contemporary placed-based planning.

In Chapter 10 we summarise the prior chapters in the context of the signifier *rationality*, its relationship to *jouissance* and the materialisation of ideology. We consider the rationality which has traditionally underlain spatial planning and argue that it is often not a rationality of balancing facts, but rather a rationality of balancing desires. We then consider the spatial planner as a Lacanian subject. We suggest the need for alternative ways forward beyond continued imposition of transcendental ideas and the ideological deployment of language to structure our cities within wider social reality. From this perspective we indicate how spatial planning might engage with new potentials, inclusive choice and openness, rather than its traditional focus on exclusion and enclosure of a prescribed orthodoxy seeking only one, or at most a few idealised, but limited, end states.

# Chapter 2
# The Lack of *Certainty*

## Introduction

> ... underlying the production of cities are the hidden workings of desire and fear.
>
> Pile 2000, 76

To some degree most, or perhaps all, people desire to be safe, secure and to have control over their environment in order to sustain their regular and habituated ways of life: what the British sociologist Anthony Giddens[1] (1991) calls a desire for 'ontological security'. These concerns apply to all dimensions of the built and natural environment, from issues of our personal physical security, well-being and sense of belonging; through material considerations, such as housing and employment needs; to the protection of our wider heritage and ecology (Brand 1999; Dupuis and Thorns 1998, 2008; Grenville 2007).

Spatial planning as a discursive set of practices and processes plays a central role in all of these dimensions (Pløger 2001a). Further, we suggest that one of planning's fundamental purposes and key justifications is to produce an illusion of certainty in order to provide a sense of ontological security in an unpredictable world. This is particularly so in relation to the future, or what Friedmann (1987, 168-169) refers to as 'the veil of time':

> The desire to know what does not yet exist but may happen at some future time is a very powerful human desire ... [yet] Despite the invention of various ingenious methods for spying through the veil of time, the outlook for social and economic forecasting is fairly bleak.

Core to spatial planning practice is the provision – or at least the appearance of provision – of future 'certainty' in a complex, unstable, dynamic and inherently uncertain world. As Christensen (1985, 63, 1999) wrote, 'planners hate uncertainty as much as other people do, and spend their working lives trying to reduce it'. Other authors also indicate the need for planning practice to offer certainty: 'Planning means, essentially, controlling uncertainty – either by taking action now to secure

---

1   While Giddens (1979, 1987) does not put forward a Lacanian position he has engaged with Lacan's work, although Thrift (1993, 114) observes that it is 'quite difficult to work out whether Giddens has a theory of the unconscious or whether it is simply a supplement which enables him to privilege practical consciousness and knowledge.'

the future, or by preparing actions to be taken in case an event occurs' (Marris in Abbott 2005, 237). Moreover, as Silva (2002, 336-338) observes:

> Dealing with uncertainty is a duty of planning. Basically, all planning approaches in one way or another manage uncertainty about the future … [Regardless] 'of reality, planners, managers, and politicians persist in their efforts to impose certainty (administratively, bureaucratically, legally, and politically) in an uncertain world.'

What purpose does a blueprint, a master, or a strategic plan serve, but to provide a template of future certainty of land use or spatial design? Even if the planners drafting the plan realise that it will never completely achieve its projected end state, planners, and the public, must 'continue in their faith that their [original] plans will be successful, and [completed], so planners and those "planned" have the belief necessary to carry on planning' (Gunder 2004, 301). Or, to paraphrase Wildavsky (1973, 152), if we cannot put our faith in achieving our desired future, we should be able to put our faith certainly in our existing plans and planning for the future, which reside in the here and now.

Wildavsky indicates the perceived value of regulatory planning in the seeking of certainty as compared with the unpredictability of a discretionary planning system in which the play of politics could lead to uncertainty of outcomes (Tewdr-Jones 1999). In this regard, planning practice and its related regulation act 'as a process in which knowledge, risk and public concerns are [first] constructed' to produce unambiguous rules that ensure predictable and consistently reproducible outcomes (Lidskog *et al.* 2006, 89). Or, at least they provide the illusion that this will be so in a traditional modernist view of a project's progression to a materially better world.

In maintaining a belief of control and future certainty, deficiencies or lacks must be quickly addressed and solutions prescribed. We suggest that the political or technical deployment of a 'lack' or 'deficiency' is a powerful planning and political trope for response and action. For who would wish to live in a 'deficient' city lacking in *safety, competitiveness, sustainability* or some other shortfall? As Laclau (1996, 2000, 2005) has illustrated, the identification of lack represented by an empty signifier: such as a lack of *order* or, perhaps, *security* and the subsequent hegemonic articulation of its resolution, provides a powerful and emotive political tool; one that underlies much political discussion at local and national scales (Stavrakakis 2007, 76).

Spatial planning practice is often centrally involved in processes of identification of 'lack' and its subsequent resolution (Yiftachel 1995). Indeed, planning may play a key role in giving the *appearance* of de-politicising much of this hegemonic function, at least for city-making and region-building, by introducing what appears to be a technical rationality to the identification and resolution of an urban (or rural) problem. This is particularly evident if policies are legitimised by being worded as scientific narratives, consistent with wider dominant cultural imperatives (e.g., public choice theory) and similar consumer-oriented contemporary values. In this role, spatial planners quantify the politically qualitative lack as a measurable symptom. A lack of economic competitiveness thereby becomes a lack of transport-efficient urban form, a lack of adequate infrastructure, or a lack of available commercial land for development (Filion and McSpurren 2007; Scott 2007, 2008). A perceived lack of safety and security becomes symptomised as high crime rates and anti-social behaviour to be 'cured' through effective urban design, including perhaps, gated communities (Dupuis and Thorns 2008). A lack of sustainability is resolved with urban containment and intensification and the 'better' management of energy consumption and waste-streams to reduce the city's ecological footprint (Gleeson *et al.* 2004, 351).

Laclau (1996, 122) argues that the construction of a solution to fill an identified public or community lack is a social operation. The constructed 'universally' desired answer which then dominates and provides the only acceptable solution is thus a 'pragmatic social construction': a vision or a desired state. It is inherently utopian. Moreover, this 'vision' is inevitably contaminated by particularity. Each vision is a 'unique, one off,' universal, which tends to serve a hegemonic function for a specific powerful group with vested interests: 'precisely because the universal place is empty [as in empty signifier], it can be occupied by any force, not necessarily democratic' (Laclau 1996, 65). The visions of dominant groups (such as professional experts, vocal residents or other pressure groups, or political or business elites) attempt to fill and resolve the identified deficiency. Consequently, the identification of a lack and its hegemonic resolution are both highly contestable and ideological (as is any deconstruction of them) representing the 'incommensurability between the ethical and the normative' (Laclau 2000, 81).

We develop this concept further in the following sections, where we engage a detailed discussion of the role of 'lack' – a fundamental Lacanian concept – commencing with the primordial maternal lack of young humans yet to be integrated into language and culture (Ruti 2008). We then further explore how the concept of lack and its metaphorical slippage and framing are deployed in contemporary political and technocratic processes to inspire desire for a particular planning solution or policy process. We draw on case studies to illustrate how such 'solutions' are nurtured as a popular desire underlain by the promise, or illusion, of harmony and fulfilment – which, of course, never quite materialises. We conclude the chapter by demonstrating how it is the desire for security and fulfilment – that we argue is synonymous with the desire for certainty towards the unknowable future – underwrites the very ontological purpose of spatial planning and gives it much of its popular support.

### The Concept of Lack: Thanks Mum!

The desire to overcome 'lack' and to become 'whole' is central to Lacanian theorising and defines the Lacanian subject. The infant 'in the first months of its life is unaware of any distinct identity of its own separate from that of its principle care giver' (Harding 2007, 1768). To be whole is being nurtured and secure with Mum, to be separated is to be incomplete and lacking. The infant then begins to realise that it must vie for the mother's attention in competition with another adult, or another child, or with her work. As Blum and Nast (2000, 198) suggest, the infant's desire and subjectivity are constituted in its recognition that it is not the only object of the (m)other's desire. This sense of lack drives the child to attempt to regain the central position as its (m)other's (or primary care givers) desired object. At a certain point of 'development the child comes to associate the absence of his [*sic*] mother with the presence' of the mother's partner or other sibling; initially, as a rival object, 'then as the one who is presumed to possess the' object of the mother's desire (Dor 1998, 115). In this manner, the infant works out a signifying relation to name the cause of its mother's absences by summoning up this symbolic other that has displaced the infant; the metaphor for the mother's desired object.[2] The human subject arises from the infant's original relationship with its (m)other: that is, 'by its desire for her desire – [it] identifies with the imaginary object of her desire insofar as the mother herself symbolizes it' (Lacan 2006, 463).

The Lacanian object of desire is a lacking but desired abstract 'Thing'. It is an imaginary object. Lacan's object of maternal desire functions as the injunction 'no' in the symbolic system 'as causative of a lack-in-being' (Ragland 2004, 2). Language and the cultures built by, and in, language separate us from our primordial state of original completeness with Mother. We fundamentally desire to return to this state, but, of course, cannot. This symbolic separation from the primary care giver is inherently fearful and the subject's fundamental repressed desire is to return to an idyllic state of maternal bliss. This impossible desire will drive the subject through life via metonymical displacement and metaphorical substitution where this initial 'desire is taken captive by language and its original nature is lost' (Dor 1998, 118).

---

2  Lacan was a practising Freudian psychoanalyst constrained to some degree by the orthodoxy of a profession derived from Freud's original conceptualisations, which reflected 19th century middle class middle-European norms of sexuality, authoritarianism and family structure (Breger 2000; Gay 2006). Lacan's significant contribution to his profession was to continue to deploy Freud's overarching concepts, such as the unconscious, transference, condensation and displacement, but often via a radical re-interpretation of them to align them with mid-20th century innovative theories of linguistics, structuralism, philosophy and anthropology, much of which also provided a precursor for contemporary post-structuralist thought (Stavrakakis 2007, 89).

This subject may materialise his/her desire sexually, or more often, through sublimation into alternative cultural activities that supplement the subject's existing identifications. This might be to become part of a 'prestigious' (or even infamous) club, profession, or 'gang', to acquire particular identity defining beliefs, knowledges and attributes, or the acquisition of material symbols of consumer success and distinctiveness (Apollon 1994; Stavrakakis 2007). This forgotten and hence unconscious infantile compulsion drives and shapes all human subjects. While needs may be met and specific fears overcome, desire is seldom, if ever, achieved and, if so, never sated. This is because we always desire more as we seek to repeat what we can never duplicate; our initial experience of maternal enjoyment beyond that of mere satisfaction (Lacan 2006, 431).

For Lacan, desire and subjectivity are inseparable. Subjectivity is characterised by uncertainty, anxiety, alienation, a desire for ontological security, originally that of the infant in relation to the mother. As such, desire to gain a sense of being, or a capacity to know, is inevitable. Actors desire some sort of control over the self, others and their environment, which Giddens' (1991) termed life politics. Lacan (2006, 689) would suggest that it is repressed desire which surfaces in actors (such as vocal interest group members) and is manifest in a particular demand, often expressed as a 'need'; such as 'we need better parks, schools, public transit, or road safety'.

There are important differences between desire, need and demand. As Fuery (1995, 97) explains, 'desire is not bolstered by needs, but rather the contrary; needs are derived from desire.' Whereas, 'need' and 'demand' can be tied to specific objects, 'desire' always exceeds those objects. Regardless of how well the demands of better social or transportation infrastructure are met, in the example above, or in other instances, desire can never be satisfied: subjects eventually demand more. Core to the Lacanian subject is that it is always split and divided, never whole. This 'is echoed on the level of the social' by '"antagonism", which persists in all social formations and renders any idea of social unification', contentment, 'or harmony illusory' (Jameson 2005, 192). Such search, or desire, for wholeness drives us, but it is never achieved. Fulfilment of a desire is never enough. It never recreates the sense of security provided by our original maternal completeness.

## Desire for the Harmony of Wholeness

As developed in Chapter 1, identification with a range of identity shaping labels called 'master signifiers' constitutes the person or 'subject' as an individual in society (Verhaeghe 2001). The totality of master signifiers constitutes a subject's ego-ideal. This comprises the core beliefs, values and a sense of self, creating the identification of who we believe we are, which we can articulate to others, as we seek the impossible task of becoming a complete and whole self. For in 'psychoanalytical theory the subject is never entirely at one with the social persona she has acquired and that she assumes in the everyday practices in which this unfolds and develops over time' (Lovell 2003, 13). The subject is constantly trying to define the self. We are always seeking 'further identification with something to fill' our 'existential lack' and become a whole subject (Van Houtum 2002, 42). But, our master signifiers can never succeed in completely filling this lack, leaving a void, or incompleteness in ourselves. This leads to an often perceived sense of unease, doubt and vulnerability that constitutes the human subject and its desire for ontological security. Indeed, for Žižek (1994a, 26-27) this void and the seeking to fill it is what fundamentally constitutes the individual as both a human and political subject. As Stavrakakis (2007, 25) observes:

> If lack is clearly central to the Lacanian conception of the subject, it is because subjectivity constitutes the space where a whole 'politics' of identification takes place. The idea of the subject as lack cannot be separated from the recognition of the fact that the subject is always attempting to compensate for this constituting lack at the level of representation, through continuous identification acts. This lack necessitates the constitution of every identity through processes of identification with socially available objects such as political ideologies, patterns of consumption and social roles.

In turn, each of our abstract master signifiers of identification, whether of nationality, political ideology, consumer habits, social roles, or intellectual belief act as empty signifiers that are themselves comprised and filled by contestable complex aggregates of ordered signifiers that tell us how to act and what to believe. These filling signifiers constitute diverse narratives of contestable sets of knowledges, beliefs and practices that vie to supply the one 'true' hegemonic meaning of the subject's defining words of identification. For example, this might be that all 'good' *US-Americans* must love and defend their country's actions, no matter what actions their President and government undertake. Importantly, these filling narratives also supply the expected behaviours of the individual identifying with that label, such as all 'good' *US-Americans* must stand and put their hands on their hearts when their national anthem is played, or that 'smart' *shoppers* must check and compare products to ensure best value for money. These master signifiers tie together diverse and often conflicting sets of narratives – intellectual or popular – under one universal representational label. The sharing of belief in these master signifiers constitutes social reality and consequently, they are central to the construction of the ideology deployed in spatial planning.

Empty signifiers are essential attributes of any orthodox planning narrative or strategy. They constitute the key components of concern and ownership of which all parties to the policies or plan must engage. They do so effectively by not precluding any one specific meaning. They act and substitute literally as 'motherhood' statements, a 'good thing' that promotes wholeness for all concerned (Gunder and Hillier 2007a). The corporate shareholder and the environmentalist can both, in their own ways, claim ownership of and identification with, for example, sustainability. For the former, the ideal of sustainability represents sustained profits for future generations of family and heirs, for the latter, a sustained world living within its carrying capacity and leaving a robust ecology for future generations.

Narratives – sets of knowledges, stories, and symbolic practices – describe and uphold their master signifiers before they attempt hegemonically to rearticulate or fine-tune what these master signifiers should actually embody for a particular group or individual. Of equal importance to any particular narrative are both what it asserts and what it does not. A fact or issue's absence is often more powerful to a particular narrative than its inclusion. For example, a problem only comes to public attention when stated. The gaining of these knowledges, stories, practices, and, importantly, what to exclude, constitute learning. These narratives also include the disciplinary and professional codes that constitute spatial planning and related disciplines of urban governance. Further, the narratives are drawn on to produce new stories and documents constituting our urban policies and plans, where they provide direction for a local authority or community to act (Gunder 2004; Hillier and Gunder 2005).

Narratives and the master signifiers that identify and engage them are inherently ideological (Žižek 1989, 2002). This goes far beyond just spatial planning practice. These ideological fictions construct social reality itself. Lacan asserts that the 'whole of human reality is nothing more than a *montage* of the symbolic and the imaginary … an articulation of the signifiers which are invested with imaginary – fantasmatic – coherence and unity' (Stavrakakis 2007, 42). Kant called these signifiers 'transcendental ideas'. If we refuse these illusions and fantasies, 'we lose reality itself; *the moment we subtract fictions from reality, reality itself loses its discursive-logical consistency*' (Žižek 1993, p. 88).

Since as humans we are always seeking new identifications by which to define ourselves and to fill in what we think is missing or lacking in our sense of self, we tend to welcome anything that gives us new positive identity and belief. We especially welcome new concepts and ideas that can somehow give us a sense of control or 'certainty' over the contingent complexities of life, including our environment and our futures. A belief and identification with spatial planning narratives, concepts and ideas – such as those provided in metropolitan or regional growth management plans and their key promises for future certainty that they appear to map out – can play such a role in reducing doubt and perceived vulnerability.

However, the symbolic creation and imaginary representation of plans always fail. Plans and their prescribed solutions lack. They are incomplete for they inherently fail to recapture the security and certainty of our lost primordial maternal fullness that we seek impossibly to replace. This completeness and certainty is inherently deferred, made impossible, by the subject's dependence on imperfect language, speech and image, for the symbolic must always be an abstraction of the whole. But 'it is this deferral, however, that keeps desire alive and socio-political creation open' (Stavrakakis 2007, 49). This is partly why we continue to plan for certainty, even if we know – in our heart – that it is merely illusion and rationalisation.

The desire to have control over one's uncertainty and exposure to perceived risk is a pure act of survival, both in a bodily as well as socio-psychological sense (Gunder 2008a). It provides the self with 'a sense of control in one's daily battles for our assertion of identification and self-respect' (Van Houtum 2002, 42). Strategic spatial plans, by providing a sense of certainty towards the future, can provide us with this sense of security and ease (Gunder 2004, 303). Spatial plans allow us the illusion of belief 'in the truthfulness of a self-devised pure and orderly scheme of reality, a fantasy' that is the direct 'consequence of the unconscious desire to be able to reduce' our feeling 'of uneasiness, vulnerability and doubts', both about ourselves and in our relationships to the future (Van Houtum 2002, 42).

Our master signifiers, including those we identify with in public policies of city-making, give us a perceived certainty of identification of who we are, and who we may become in society, even if on further analysis this identity proves inherently ambiguous. They also provide the fixed pivotal or anchoring points that fundamentally underpin the inherent ambiguous nature of social reality itself. Accordingly, effective strategic plans and related policy documents draw on and reflect these hegemonic labels. Desirable, popular or specialist master signifiers, and their metaphoric or metonymic symbolic substitutes, can carry highly emotive political power, especially when overtly identified as lacking in our communities. Urban examples include statements such as the city lacks: adequate transport mobility, security, harmony and liveability, sustainability, or global competitiveness; all of which were identified as applicable to Sydney, Australia in its three metropolitan plans presented to the public between 1995 and 2005 and subsequently played off against one another, in Sydney's case, primarily for the attainment of success in the global economy (Gunder and Searle 2007; McGuirk 2004, 2005, 2007).

In the San Francisco Bay region of the United States a lack of urban intensification, transport mobility, loss of agricultural land and generally perceived lack of open space, as well as a lack of affordable housing have justified a multi-tiered growth management strategic response originating in the 1970s and still ongoing (Pallagst 2007). One dimension of these issues, as expressed by San Francisco's Neighborhood Park Council (2007), as an example of lack and its proposed resolution, follows:

> San Francisco lacks the framework to effectively meet the needs for open space in the 21st century. It is crucially important to develop a strong network of stakeholders who can envision a greener future, secure the funding to realize the vision, and jointly devise creative maintenance strategies for existing and new parks and open spaces. Open Space *2100* will also address the existing gaps in San Francisco's current open space network and will work to ensure that all San Franciscans have access to open space …

The notion of spatial planning 'lack' was recently deployed in Toronto, Canada. An identified problem of regional sprawl and resultant lack of 'needed' urban intensification served 'as a public rationale for the primary municipal goal of increasing Toronto's economic and land-use development through private-sector investment and the attraction of skilled, professional labour to the [inner] city' (Bunce 2004, 180). Bunce (2004, 183) went on to illustrate how a 'lack of sustainability' was rhetorically deployed to imply that, regardless of perceived local adverse effects, 'if residents do not endorse intensification, then they can be considered insensitive to regional environmental concerns'. At the same time, the same planning vision promoted a 'green', but, more importantly, a 'globally recognised' Toronto. A perceived primary lack of the city's economic global competitiveness was overcome by a planning vision to attract and facilitate the accommodation of foot-loose high value-added knowledge workers in the city centre. This resulted in an 'urban renewal that dramatically changed the fabric of class and space in the parts of the inner cities that had yet been spared previous waves of gentrification' (Keil and Boudreau 2005, 12). The initiatives for public transit, environmental restoration, and affordable housing were thus 'subordinated to this imperative of competitiveness' within the global market place if economic certainty was to be assured and Toronto's 'lack' overcome (Kipfer and Keil 2002, 246).

Residents, understandably, respond to any 'identity lack' for their local communities and environments by asking, or even demanding, that these deficiencies be resolved. Politicians, policy planners, as well as others (e.g., 'key' stakeholders and the information media), play a central role in the filling of this lack by providing and/or supporting specific urban policy prescriptions: dreams and fantasies of what our future cities can be. For Stavrakakis (2007, 75), to 'stimulate the desire for identification, for social and political life, to imaginarise lack, is the function of *fantasy*'. These fantasies actually serve to stimulate or cause our desire in that they promise to metaphorically 'cover for the lack created by the loss' of initial security and enjoyment of maternal wholeness 'with a substitute, a miraculous' filling of the subjects' incompleteness (Stavrakakis 2007, 239). This occurs even if we are initially unaware of any urban deficiency and the need for its resolution, until framed on the public stage as an urban issue needing a desirable solution (Cochrane 2000, 540).

## The Fantasies of Certainty which Spatial Planning Provides

Fundamentally, we contend, spatial planning is predicated on a fantasy that the discipline successfully provides the solutions necessary in order to provide certainty and harmony for the future of our built and natural environments. Planners know intuitively that such solutions are but unachievable fantasies – why else do they constantly have to revise their plans? But they continue in the belief that the plans will succeed in achieving their objectives over the five, twenty or fifty year timeframe of the plan period. And so they have the faith to carry on planning. Further, the global spatial planning community (as well as the communities of other professions, disciplines and interests) constantly discovers or invents new iconic hooks (or master signifiers) of identification and desire on which to hang problems and deficiencies (lacks) which subtract from the security and certainty of well-being and which also provide their solution, often in terms of scientific narratives or ideas. We contend that these are largely fantasy constructs of, at best, ideological belief, which planning practitioners then deploy locally in their practices (Gunder 2005b).

Take Auckland, New Zealand, as an example. Over the last decade, the key anchor points for identifying the region's perceived major planning issues, or deficiencies, are problems of urban sprawl, car dependency and a lack of global economic competitiveness. The resolution of these problems is seen as being 'sustainable development,' 'urban containment' and 'nodal intensification' to facilitate 'transit orientated design' (Auckland Regional Growth Forum 1999), as well as in the now-familiar orthodox economic development response to make Auckland another 'world class city' (Rowe 2005, 5-6). All of these issues and resolutions are directly attributable to international spatial planning master signifiers and their dominant supportive narratives of *sustainability, global competitiveness* and *Smart Growth* (Gow 2000; Gunder 2008b). These master signifiers are deployed locally in Auckland (just as they are in many, if not perhaps most, other cities: including Sydney, Toronto, San Francisco) to provide the illusion of providing a surety of solution that guarantees resolution of the deficient lack by replacing it with a harmonious totality or wholeness.

Lacan 'proves our fantasmatic conception of the socio-political institution of society as a harmonious totality to be no more than a *mirage*' (Stavrakakis 1999, 73). 'This social reality is ... nothing but a fragile, symbolic cobweb that can at any moment be torn aside' (Žižek 1991, 17). 'Precisely because' subjects 'can never attain a state of wholeness', they are driven to look for substitutes that might compensate for their sense of lack. They are motivated to accept promises and dreams of security and harmony 'that can, momentarily at least, ease and contain the discomfort' of their incompleteness and uncertainty (Ruti 2008, 490). Fantasy negates the void, what is missing or lacking, by appearing to 'realise' it, by promising to close the gap between what is missing and what exists, 'by repressing the discursive nature of reality's production' (Stavrakakis 1999, 107). Both planners and those planned 'act as if the totalizing and reductive forms of ideology are true and serious, although we know they are not' (Torfing 1999, 117). We seek to satisfy our ontological lack through fantasy, but this satisfaction and 'guarantee' of certainty is only implied in fantasy; what is experienced is 'its promise, embodied in the object-cause of desire' (Stavrakakis 2007, 78).

For example, we gain much of our consumer information from advertising, or our political information from the media sound-bites of politicians on the news. We know both are highly manipulative – at best promises are merely implied – but we nevertheless use the information gained in channelling our wants and desires, as well as in making our actual choices. For example, we may often believe the political promises to upgrade the rail and/or bus links, or to improve residential consumer choice in our communities, but we may even more readily rationalise why these improvements so seldom seem to actually materialise (see Flyvbjerg 1998). These fantasies of implied truth and satisfaction, as well as the rationalisation of their lack of delivery or non-fulfilment, construct 'the safety net of ideology and thus provide the ultimate support of reality' (Torfing 1999, 117).

Similarly, spatial planning practitioners deploy fantasy onto those they 'plan' at two levels. First, plans and policies are used as persuasive storytelling in a manner similar to advertising or politics by utilising icons, images and rhetoric of a desirable future (Throgmorton 1996, Sandercock 2003a). Second, just like an advertisement presents the actor in the white lab-coat who demonstrates with upmost certainty that the whites are whiter-than-white, i.e., scientific and therefore true, planning is still socially predicated on its constituting fantasy of 'truth' that its practitioners are unbiased, rational, scientific technical experts serving the public interest (Gunder 2003a). Unfortunately, this is perhaps the greatest planning fantasy and is seldom, if ever, the case (Flyvbjerg 1998, 2001). Yet even with decades of critical planning research demonstrating inherent biases in planning practices and the multiplicities of public interests, the fantasy of unbiased experts seeking an idealised one and only 'public good' – originally instrumentally, now perhaps communicatively theorised and practised – continues (Flyvbjerg 1998; Gunder 2006; Hillier 2002, 2003a).

**The Framing of Planning Fantasy**

The work of Donald Schön and Martin Rein (1994) on policy conflict is insightful to understanding this two level process of creative planning fantasy. Writing from the perspective of American liberal policy analysis, Schön and Rein use the term 'frame' to stand as a synonym for the ideological perspectives, or narratives attributable to a master signifier, with which planners and policy analysts (and their institutions) must intrinsically identify and which inherently shape, or bias, their worldview. With regard to storytelling, the authors use the term 'generative metaphor' as the key transcendental mechanism underlying, or 'framing', the condensation of belief into new meanings where 'two signifiers from two heterogeneous semantic fields are substituted for each other' (Van Haute 2002, 16). For example: the city is like a human body, but it is a sick body, it lacks health and is in need of cure; the city's doctors are its spatial planners and they have the necessary prescription for the remedy – the medicine – to make it healthy again.

For Schön metaphors are more than a grammatical device. They are 'cognitive structure[s] which play[s] a significant role in the transference of concepts between two complex conceptual systems, either words or images' which are often intertwined to 'bring to mind new ways of considering things' or even 'radically modify our perception of a particular situation' (Casakin 2006, 254). Accordingly, for Schön, a generative metaphor 'can lead to novel perceptions, explanations, and inventions' (254). They can be potent creative devices when deployed in the appropriate rhetorical context (Jacobs and Heracleous 2006, 210). For example, this might be a metaphor of likening entrepreneurs in a local economy to a bed of mushrooms. This metaphor has entrepreneurs ready to pop up as soon as water (as perhaps a further metaphor for financial incentives) is added to their bed of rich fertiliser – the existing skilled labour force or other attributes of the local economy (see Rowe 2009).

Planning storytelling may use generative metaphors to unstitch the suture of master signifiers and to slide alternative orientations and value frames into a debate. As Bracher (1993, 49) suggests, a narrative 'does not have to engage *directly* a master signifier, image or fantasy; such engagements can also be indirect'. In such engagements, 'a familiar constellation of ideas is carried over to a new situation, with the result that both the familiar and the unfamiliar come to be seen in new ways'. In such a way, the wicked problem of urban poverty is recast, or rebadged, as an issue of blight and physical dereliction. Subsequent regeneration policies that promise a solution then tackle the buildings rather than the poverty of the people in the buildings (Schön and Rein 1994, 26). We can see that 'all metaphors engage in a similar twofold effect of commissioning certain paths for identity and desire and decommissioning others' (Bracher 1993, 51).

Metaphoric substitution can release new strata of meanings when deployed in 'strategic dislocation and recombination' (Boothby 2001, 127). Yet in a Lacanian context, Schön and Rein's generative metaphor can never be a complete description, for no 'matter how much we may try to express it fully, the object can never be totally integrated into the symbolic' (Van Haute 2002, 121). The symbolic always has a lack, a looseness of fit, where the selective deployment of metaphors can be used to slip new meanings and hence prescriptions into a narrative or story. We may use metaphors in our creations of illusions of certainty and security, but it is a metaphor's very lack of exactitude – its very uncertainty of meaning – which allows its looseness of fit to permit the sliding of meaning from one context to the next. Moreover, in this sliding of meaning, a 'metaphor is never neutral', '[i]t always highlights some elements of a phenomenon while hiding others' (O'Malley *et al.* 2008, 169).

> Things are selected for attention and named in such a way as to fit the frame constructed for the situation … They carry out the essential problem-setting functions. They select for attention a few salient features and relations from what would otherwise be an overwhelmingly complex reality. They give these elements a coherent organization, and they describe what is wrong with the present situation in such a way as to set the direction for its future transformation. (Schön and Rein 1994, 26)

The naming and framing of narratives 'exercise force over a group of people by engaging, directly or indirectly, signifying circuits common to the ego ideals, the body images, or the fantasies of members of the group' (Bracher 1993, 51). As Kochis (2005, 32) observes, the inherent attributes or implied 'entailments of a metaphor are particularly important when they dip, covertly, into the realm of ideological assumptions, that is, the cognitive processing of the entailments is not conscious, but can occur at levels of implicitness not readily accessible to examination'. Kochis continues with the example of the metaphor *of a level playing field*, which not only implies equity of opportunity and fairness, but more implicitly the implied role of government to guarantee equal access for all members of a community to the shared attributes of that polity.

Shared fantasies and metaphors play a crucial role in shaping identification within a discursive frame. In this regard, planning is not predicated on unbiased rational expertise and science, rather 'planning is irrational because it is creative, insofar as it influences people's preferences, shapes their perceived needs and expectations, and finally produces new values' (Ferraro 1995, 316). Through this slippage of signifiers in metaphor and fantasy creation – persuasive storytelling in spatial planning – 'subjects are pressured to relinquish previous desires (including identifications) and embrace new ones – or alternatively, to invest all the more completely in old ones' (Bracher 1993, 51-2). We suggest that this shifting of desires is especially valid if subjects wish to increase their 'perceived' confidence in the 'certainty' of achieving their needs and expectations.

## To Give Certainty of Belief

One of the fundamental strategies of rhetoric, or ideology, is to claim that the 'facts speak for themselves'. Yet the 'facts never "speak for themselves", but are made to speak by a network of discursive devices' enchained and propagated by relevant modes 'of hegemonic articulation' (Žižek 1999a, 64-5). Acknowledging and identifying with desirable planning icons such as those of 'a globally competitive city', 'congestion freeing public transit', 'a green, clean environment', or their metaphorical equivalents such as a 'Green Heart',[3] gives these master signifiers ontological substance and presence in our social reality. They are valid constructs of belief even if epistemically they may be fictitious aspirations with little possibility of attainment beyond being imaginary or symbolic illusions and/or fantasies of hopeful achievement.

The traditional liberal interpretation of policy conflicts 'treat controversies as disputes among actors who hold conflicting interests and use their respective powers to promote their interests, thereby initiating a win-lose political game' (Schön and Rein 1994, 29). But it is the ideological belief sets that the actors and the public identify with 'that determine what they see as *being* in their interests and, therefore, what interests they perceive as conflicting' (Schön and Rein 1994, 29). As such, their 'problem formulations and preferred solutions are grounded in different problem-setting stories rooted in different frames that may rest, in turn, on different generative metaphors' which are imbedded in the workings of master signifiers and their supporting narratives (Schön and Rein 1994, 29).

---

3   To use Van Eaten and Roe's (2000) Dutch metaphorical exemplar.

The spatial planning literature, at least that predicated on communicative or collaborative planning (Healey 1997; Innes 1996), generally attempts to mediate these alternative ideological frames into a shared consensual perspective (Hillier 2003a). Harper and Stein (2006) argue it is core to dialogical planning that practitioners facilitate understanding and trust between diverse but rational actors. We contend that this is another dimension of illusion. Rather spatial planners, acting in the interests of their institutions of governance, tend to have the upper hand, over most other actors and thus tend to according shape the overarching agenda, or 'frame' in the interests of their policies and plans (Gunder and Searle 2007; McGuirk 2004, 2005). Here spatial planning practitioners, intentionally, or otherwise, attempt to sell their institutionally derived fantasies as certainty of outcome to the public. They make the selected facts speak on their behalf.

Ideological frames of perception 'are not free-floating but are ground in the institutions' and knowledge sets 'that sponsor them' (Schön and Rein 1994, 29). Planners, as 'those supposed to know,' impose their profession's and institutions' identifications and beliefs on their communities 'who are supposed to believe' via their plans and policies. 'No one today *really* has to believe; our institutions do it for us' via the exteriorisation of belief in our 'larger cultural practices and technologies' (Dean 2001, 628).

However, robust social constructs of belief often prove difficult to create. At best, these ideological beliefs often occur only after substantial and sustained effort of emotive repetition (essentially advertising, or its variant), which ties the affects of desire of the populace to be influenced to the 'signifying chain' that is being proposed (comprised of emotive generative metaphors, master signifiers and their spatial planning narratives). This might be achieved by repeatedly articulating a 'lack', what this means, and its promised resolution – so that traces of the original primordial loss of maternal certainty, wholeness, and security are also tied to the 'sublime object' being put forward (Laclau 2005, 111-113; Žižek 1989). Or, similarly, it might be induced by promising the achievement of a series of traits in which the majority of the populace will be able to fulfil an authentic desire, or longing, such as the sense of positive identification fostered by living in a 'world class' city that is perceived to be 'globally competitive' (Žižek 1999c, 184). We suggest that this also occurs in the ideological formation of spatial planning beliefs when given added legitimacy through claims of scientific validity. For example, the research shows that the only effective action to resolve the deficiencies and make the city 'world class' and 'globally competitive' is to do ____ (fill in the blank). Accordingly:

> Interpretation as persuasion and reciprocal strategic reassurance is the proper job for planners ... rhetoric is the ability to persuade people to act according to new values suggested by the planner as a public speaker [where] planning rhetoric addresses mainly the future. (Ferraro 1995, 318-9)

Flyvbjerg (1998, 228) coins the term *realrationalität* to describe the process where 'rationality' and 'rationalization' are used 'for the purposes of power … to define reality' and central to public acceptance and belief in plans and policies of governance. 'When subjects act *as if* they believe, they maintain an order of appearances, a set of practices carried out for the sake of societal obedience' (Dean 2001, 644). Foucault would call this behaviour 'governmentality of the self' (Gunder and Mouat 2002, 130).

Fantasy and stories deployed within ideological frames facilitate self-governmentality by guiding acceptable choice. A classic example is the strategic deployment of traffic-light colours in planning consultation documents.[4] Here the only 'rational' solution is coloured or highlighted in green, the 'do nothing' option is generally amber and the undesired alternative, at least for the policy's proponents, is almost always illustrated in red. Concomitant with this type of activity is the rhetorical trope of persuading 'people to choose accessible courses of action by suggesting and discussing inaccessible (i.e., rationally irrelevant) alternatives' (Ferraro 1995, 317). This kind of manipulative approach '*closes the actual span of choices … and maintains the false opening*', the illusion that excluded actions could have occurred (Žižek 1997, 29 – emphasis in original). In other words, 'fantasy renders and sustains the structure of the forced choice, it tells us how to choose if we are to maintain the freedom of choice – that is, it bridges the gap between the formal symbolic frame of choices and social reality by preventing the choice which, although formally allowed, would, if in fact made, ruin the system' (Žižek 1997a, 29). Accordingly, this process of giving lip service to 'the external ideological ritual, and not to the depth of the subject's inner convictions and desires, is the true locus of the fantasy that sustains an ideological edifice' (Žižek 1999b, 91).

Yet the very fantasy of this policy consensus of social unification, or metaphorical 'wholeness', which tends to produce ontological security, must not be without concern. In contrast to the fantasy of consensus, Hillier (2002, 267) argues that 'within planning practice what should differentiate democratic from other forms of decision-making would be the legitimisation of conflict and the refusal to eliminate it through the establishment of an *authoritarian* harmonious consensus.'

But, sadly, this latter authoritarian 'coercion' of 'correct' public belief is often the role of planning policy analysis and process. Further, this negating of choice through manufacturing agreement and stifling resistance to the one 'correct' voice may be one of planning's most pernicious elements. We suggest that this should be a concern even if that 'correct voice' provides a necessary human illusion of certainty towards the unknown future, or other perceived issue of lack, or even if it underwrites the very ontological purpose of spatial planning that gives it much of its popular support. For in Lacanian thought, the very creation of a social fantasy

---

4  As well as to indicate a range of appropriate behaviours from food health to sustainable behaviours (see: Defra 2008).

that provides the illusion of certainty precludes a 'transition to a more imaginative and creatively engaged psychic economy' and a potentially more imaginative social reality that may empower a polity to actually 'renegotiate how' its members 'relate to the world' (Ruti 2008, 486).

Central to this concern is the traditional role of planning to achieve, or act in the name of a public 'good', or *the* collective good. This will be explored further in the next chapter, where we will argue, following Lacan (1992), that there can be no one supreme good, and that this illusion may indeed be the ultimate fantasy.

# Chapter 3
# Prescribing the *Good*

The question of the Sovereign Good is one that man [*sic*] has asked himself since time immemorial, but the analyst knows that it is a question that is closed. Not only doesn't he have the Sovereign Good that is asked of him, but he also knows there isn't any.

Lacan 1992, 300

## Introduction

The notion of creating the perfect city, or simply a 'better' city, or even a 'good' city is not new. Throughout the history of planning the profession has idealised the 'good city', and especially the utopian city (neighbourhood or region) of our dreams and fantasies, as an object which the discipline should strive to create in answer to the normative question, how should we live together in society (Bruton 1974; Friedmann 2002)? In this context spatial planning has been conceptualised as a practice of social guidance and reform driven by 'some notion of the better good, the notion that cities could be made better' (Bridge and Watson 2000, 506). As Campbell and Marshall (1998, 117) indicate, the choices which planning practitioners make are fundamentally about questions of good or bad, right or wrong. However, these are questions of normative value and relativity that preclude absolute clarity, although practitioners often treat the chosen values as truths and unquestionable cultural imperatives (Allmendinger and Gunder 2005). Consequently, we suggest that spatial planning, for all its successes in striving for a better good, will inherently fail to achieve a perfect or utopian city; a city free of dysfunction, social marginalisation or other trauma.

In this chapter, we seek to challenge the normative prescriptive role of strategic spatial planning practice. In effect, we challenge what has traditionally been regarded as the essence of strategic or 'forward' planning: the plan as a statement of what the city *ought* to become, of what *ought* to happen, with 'the master plan as a product, a discrete guide to a fixed form of future development' (Dyckman 1964, 224). A vital aspect of such 'strategic dreams' of idealised urban potential has been the 'governing away' of spatial manifestations of social pathology (Osborne and Rose 1999, 740).

We suggest that in the context of perceived urban deficiencies – lack – the role of planning practice has often been to apply a socio-spatial resolution to urban problems. This is often predicated on the medical metaphor of the city as either being healthy or sick, synonymous with good or bad. After all, few would argue that it is not good to be healthy! This is a metaphorical cure derived from some normative perspective, or theory, as to what defines a city as being healthy or good (Neuman 2005a).

What constitutes the good has been an enduring debate within the planning and related literature (Amin 2006; Campbell and Marshall 1998; Campbell and Fainstein 2003; Friedmann 2000; Healey 2005; Sandercock 2003c); as well as within wider critiques of the modernist project itself (Harvey 2000; Sack 2003). The socio-psychological dimensions of urban existence in modern culture have been explored from the earliest part of the last century (epitomised perhaps in the work of Georg Simmel (2000 [1905])) in attempts to produce socio-psychological insight and prescription for a 'better' community, or society, located within the context of a built spatial environment. The cities proposed by Howard, Wright and Le Corbusier were all utopian solutions to resolve both the spatial and social ills of the early 20th-century industrial city, in a belief that town planning had the capacity to change people's lives substantially for the better by transforming the urban environment (Bruton 1974; Hunt 2004).

In the 1960s, commentators such as Dyckman (1964, 232) lamented 'the fact that contemporary city planning has lost sight of functional links between its utopian goals and the apparatus of enforcing its programs'. The 'utopian goals' were not questioned, rather there was a lack of regard for the processes by which such goals were to be achieved. Over the past 25 years or so, the conceptualisation of planning as a self-contained bureaucratic function has tended to be superseded by that of a broader 'activity of governance required to make sure that all the services people need in a city are provided when and where the need occurs' (Gleeson and Low 2000, 12). Goals are still implicit in the above definition, and use of the words 'make sure' suggests a degree of control to give certainty of future services. While spatial planning now tends to emphasise enhancement of human and environmental well-being (Osborne and Rose 1999), through managed co-ordination of stakeholders' economic, social, environmental and aesthetic visions for the future, rather than just explicit statements of lack, strategic planning documents may still use the metaphor, or trope, of the urban environment as an ailing, dysfunctional, or unfit human body in need of therapeutic cure (Baeten 2002; Gunder 2003b; Hoffman *et al.* 2000).

Strategic planning practice has traditionally offered such resolution through rational scientific technologies in pursuit of a dream of a healthy city or region. This is a dream wherein residents may achieve happiness or goodness in life if only urban ailments and blights are cured. In this therapeutic condition urban ailments are viewed, again, in terms of a lack; for example, a lack of a sense of community (WAPC 2005), a lack of a physically safe environment, of economic vitality, of environmental sustainability (Gunder 2003b, 288-289); lacks which planning practice and its remedies seek to overcome and 'make better'.

In this chapter we consider the impossibility of the idealised, utopian city where 'good' for all can be achieved. We then provide an appreciation as to how humans' personal striving to be perceived by the Other as good, shapes both our very concepts of self and our wider material behaviours which, in turn, shape our empirically observable social world. We move on to problematise what constitutes 'good' urban behaviours, at least as defined by contemporary agencies of government and governance, and we further develop how these are behaviours shaped through the media and other arenas of socio-political life. In doing so, we have regard to the fantasy constructs deployed to shape 'our' desired cities – what ought to be – but, generally deployed without stating for whose benefit!

## The Good City and the Delirium of Utopia

> Planning as ideology formulates all the problems of society into questions of space ... [W]hat are represented are healthy and diseased spaces. The planner should be able to distinguish between sick spaces and spaces linked to mental and social health which are generators of this health. As physicians of space, he [*sic*] should have the capacity to conceive of an harmonious social space, normal and normalizing. (Lefebvre 1996, 99)

In this section we give a brief overview of conceptualisations of the 'good' from Plato to the present, and how notions of the 'good life' are intrinsically linked to those of the 'good city'. Platonic and Aristotelian conceptions of the good are centred on accounts of proper human functioning, of practical wisdom and good judgement (*phronesis*) (Flyvbjerg 1992). Plato, in *The Republic* (1992), makes claims about how typically 'good' and 'bad' cities would be arranged economically and politically, whilst acknowledging their utopian counter-factuality (Burnyeat 1992). A Platonic consideration of the good directly inspired the utilitarian writings of Jeremy Bentham and John Stuart Mill, and thus indirectly influenced the fundamental spirit of rational comprehensive planning as seeking to achieve the greatest good of the greatest number (Friedmann 1987). For Plato and rational comprehensive planners even in the 21st century, moral actions are guaranteed by 'correct' knowledge of the 'absolute good' or utopian ideal (MacDonald 2005). Like Friedmann, we seek to challenge such absolutist notions of city-making.

The concept of utopia has traditionally been regarded as 'a blueprint for a desired world which is ... located in present day concerns' (Parker 2002, 10). It is 'the expression of the desire for a better way of being' (Levitas 2007, 290). For Zygmunt Bauman modernist utopian thought is dependant on a belief in collective progress or betterment and a faith that this can be achieved, correspondingly:

> Utopian dreams need two conditions. First, the overwhelming ... feeling that the world was not functioning properly and had to be attended to and overhauled to set it right. Second, the confidence in human potency to rise to the task, belief that 'we, humans, can do it' – being armed as we are with enough reason to spy out what is wrong with the world and find out with what to replace its diseased parts, and with enough strength to graft such designs on human reality. (Bauman in Jacobsen and Tester 2007, 316-317)

Utopian thought embodies a movement in time-space towards something 'better', ideally 'where goodness reigns and everyone lives in harmony' (Hardy 2000, 55). Utopian space is an 'imaginary enclave within real social space', where 'the very possibility of Utopian space is itself a result of spatial and social differentiation' (Jameson 2005, 15). Accordingly, everyone's idea of utopia will differ; some conceptualisations only slightly, whilst others will be inevitably conflictual (e.g., the ideal worlds of drug barons and narcotics officers). All are dreams of some form of organised 'order'. Whilst planners and politicians may not discuss how to realise Plato's *Republic* or Thomas More's (1965 [1516]) *Utopia*, they have discussed, and continue to discuss, contemporary dreams or fantasies of good cities. From Fourier to Saint-Simon and Comte, through Howard, Geddes, Lloyd Wright, Le Corbusier and CIAM and the British New Towns movement, to the theoretical work of David Harvey and Leonie Sandercock and the physical dreamings of Robert Moses in New York and the New Urbanists such as Andres Duany, Elizabeth Plater-Zyberg and Peter Katz, authors' imaginaries have been (explicit or implicit) visions of a better world where 'the ills of the present day are banished to another space and time' (Pinder 2002, 233). As Pinder explains, in most visions, aspects of space are privileged under the assumption that social transformation will follow. Planners have thus therapeutically sought to improve the behaviour of individuals through environmental design in search of a 'city of salvation' (Pinder 2002, 233).[1]

Planning practice has long sought to be therapeutic in its resolution of the city's ills (Rose 1994), though as Osborne and Rose (1999) indicate, there has been a distinct shift in application of the term. The passage from Lefebvre (1996), cited above, epitomises a more medically-implicit metaphor of ailing urban areas, traceable back to the institutionalisation of town planning in the late 19th and early 20th centuries as a direct result of widespread outbreaks of cholera, typhoid and so on: 'sickness is a pathology of space that may be governed away by such means as pure water, sew[er]age, disposal of refuse, and the like' (Osborne and Rose 1999, 742).

Illness and the courting of death as a preliminary to healthy re-vitalisation and/or the temporary avoidance of death through the sustaining of health, are powerful metaphors (Hillier and Gunder 2005). Hence the frequent use, in strategic planning documents, of 'hypochondriac geographies' (Baeten 2002b) of the urban environment as a sick, dysfunctional, or overweight and unfit human body in need of therapeutic cure (Hoffman *et al.* 2000; Lefebvre 2003, 157). This is the cure which spatial planning purports to provide via provision of instrumental means, or strategies, to create the utopian fantasy of the healthy city or region. The fantasy is a dream where all residents may attain empowerment, happiness and comfort in their enjoyment of the good life if only a perceived lack can be overcome, be

---

1    The utopian city is a theme extensively explored in planning and related spatial literature (e.g., Baeten 2002a; Boyer 1983; Fishman 1977; Hardy 2000; Harvey 2000; Katz 1994; Lynch 1981; Schaer *et al.* 2000).

it one of economic competitiveness, social harmony, efficient mobility, or other identified general urban ailment or specific blight.

In such situations, therapists (planners) claim to have expert knowledge and expert technique free of ideological bias (Baum 1995), while humans have been socialised in modernity to trust professional experts and therapeutic doctors' authority (Rose 1999, 132-3). Therapy also addresses the fundamental ethical question of who we are and how we should live. As stated above, such questions have informed the prescriptive idea/l of the 'good city', the 'good environment', the 'good planning process', and so on (Gunder 2005b). Arnstein's (1969) famous 'ladder' of citizen participation locates therapeutic participation as only one step above manipulation. For Arnstein, therapy is a form of domination by professional elites emphasising a lack of citizen power. In Arnstein's understanding of 'planning as therapy', participation is deployed to calm citizens and to 'make them feel better'. At best it allows the public to 'let off steam' with little regard by the organising planners for the citizens' dreams, visions and desires, and, especially, for their dissatisfactions.

Utopias are unachievable ideal objects that stimulate and tease us with their desirability, yet seldom if ever, materially or otherwise, successfully deliver. There is always non-fulfilment of what is desired: 'a dream pursued and found vain, wanting, and destructive' (Raban 1974, in Pinder 2002, 233). The very language that describes any desired utopia inherently fails to be complete: it always lacks something in its prescription and our inherent desire to fill this lack perpetually creates further desire (Lang 2003, 249). Utopias are one manifestation of Žižek's (1989) sublime object of ideology, which, though remaining out of sight or falling short of full symbolic conceptualisation, still has a profound impact. In this way, a material object/goal is 'elevated to the status of the impossible Thing' (Žižek 1989, 71). Yet, achieving the utopian ideal (the impossible Thing) could entail destruction of the very living organism whose condition it is supposed to improve.

Lacan's position is that we accept such utopian fantasies because they obscure the agonistic reality of difference and lack that constitutes the human condition and that they provide an illusion of certainty, wholeness and social harmony towards the unknowable future (Stavrakakis 1999), as developed in the previous chapter. This is constituted in society's most fundamental desire for security, inclusiveness, and completeness (Žižek 1993). From birth we are 'thrown into the world, we try again and again to reconstitute the sphere of the maternal haven in the guise of family, ethnic community' and wider social order (Žižek 2002a, lxix). Here Lacan (1992, 1994) is key, for his fundamental teaching is that we can, and must, traverse this fantasy of trying to achieve a utopian wholeness. This is an illusion that wider society – what Lacan (2006) and Žižek (2005a, 373-374) often refers to as 'the big Other' – actually cares for us and can be relied on to protect us, and the potentially discriminatory fantasies this desire for 'oneness' constructs. Indeed, our desire for completeness results from a 'misrecognition' of our fundamental subjectivity. This is a subjectivity constituted on an unfulfillable lack – a void or hole – arising from our infantile relationship to our primary care giver that both creates and *lies* at the core of the human subject. In what follows, we offer a further engagement with another dimension of Lacan's theory of early childhood development in order to provide further understanding of self-identity and also of the constituting nature of the 'big Other'.

## Self-Identity and the 'big Other'

> For Lacan the Other represents not simply language understood as a system of signs or signifiers but also the ontological consequences of linguistic subjectivity … Lacan conceives the effects of language as both enabling and privative; the loss instituted in and through language is ontological … [with the] nonetheless logical implication that if the subject has lost something then the linguistic Other – the big Other – has taken it. (Dean 1997, 919)

We believe that Lacan's (1988a, 1988b, 2006) conception of what he terms the 'mirror-stage', 'imagio (imaginary) stage' and 'entry into the Symbolic,' or 'big Other', and its role in the formation of self-identity[2] offers a further valuable tool in facilitating comprehension of wider social reality and the role which spatial planning plays in it. The 'big Other' (often written as just 'Other'[3]) is one of the most complex concepts in Lacan's work (Evans 1996, 132). The big Other is not an 'other' which I can identify and engage with. Rather it is an abstract 'Other' that resides beyond social interaction. The big Other 'remains always radically exterior, beyond the horizon of any conceivable inter-subjectivity … [it] is the vanishing point that provides the co-ordinates for inter-subjectivity despite that it itself cannot be "subjectivized"' (Hook 2008, 54). It is the missing subject of the passive voice sentence. The missing subject that nebulously exists, without symbolisation, as the causal factor that still makes things happen; e.g., the plan commenced. It is the '*always already present* principle of authority, that underlay's the subjects very engagement with the symbolic' (Dolar 1999; Hook 2008, 60 – emphasis in original). It is the symbolic domain in its entirety: all the words and constructs, all the unwritten rules that govern all social interactions, or socio-political games (Fink 1995, 5; Hook 2008, 55). It is the guarantee of the symbolic order, even if it does not actually exist (Žižek 2005a, 373). Moreover, the big Other functions as the guarantee of the master, or empty, signifier, whose meaning is yet-to-emerge, it makes the symbolic field complete as a 'closed order' (Žižek 1996, 144-145). It fundamentally constitutes the enforcement of social reality, as we know it. This is especially so, if we wish to act and appear as 'good', for we

---

2   The essence of understanding Lacan revolves around his theories of early childhood identity creation, within which all human desire and action is grounded – see Chapter 2.

3   In this book we use the term 'big Other' to address this concept. We also use the concept of 'Other' (without the 'big') to stand for an aggregate of those who are different from oneself.

try to give it what we think it desires of us – to do good and act well in the world. In other words, we try to perform as we are socialised to do from an early age in our conformity with this big Other, through language and all that this conformity in trying to be 'good', entails.

The conscious 'Cartesian ego'[4] is considered in Lacanian theory to be a self-construct of the mind, which initially develops in the imagination as the 'ideal ego' as a consequence of the infant's emerging awareness of itself as a conscious subject that is apart from the rest of the world. This 'ideal ego' is initially only an image-orientated consciousness, which is then subsequently captured by the symbolic – language – to emerge as the 'ego-ideal' when the infant begins to gain the ability to speak and state its needs (Lacan 1988a). However, this conscious ego-ideal is unable to articulate its own being's unconscious subjectivity and desires through the use of language, or even to clearly and completely enunciate its actual material wants and needs (Lacan 1988b). The base of psychological conflict for Lacan is this 'radical incommensurability between the biological human organism and the socially, linguistically constructed human subject' situated within the symbolic network which constitutes society (Bracher 2000, 190).

For Lacan (2006) the young child does not have a sense of self that regards itself apart from other objects. Identity as a subject (in relationship to other subjects, who comprise society) is gained through three stages. First, the *mirror-stage*[5] where the infant sees its image in the mirror and begins to identify and constitute itself as an emerging subjectivity in its own right. Lacan (2006) suggests that between the age of six and 18 months, a child learns to 'master' the image of itself in a mirror. Once it realises that the image is 'empty' (2006, 75), the child can play with its specular image, experiencing the relationship between its own gestures and the movements reflected by its image. The child commences to identify itself as the image in the mirror.

Lacan understands the mirror-stage as a constructed identification: 'the transformation that takes place in the subject when he [*sic*] assumes an image' (2006, 76). As Lacan (2006, 78) writes, the mirror-stage is 'a drama' for the subject who is caught up in the 'lure of spatial identification'. It manufactures the succession of 'fantasies' that extends from a fragmented body-image to 'the finally donned armour of an alienating identity, which will mark his [*sic*] entire mental development with its rigid structure' (78). Lacan further states that 'this moment at which the mirror stage comes to an end inaugurates ... the dialectic that will henceforth link the I to socially elaborated situations' (2006, 79).

After the mirror-stage occurs the *imaginary stage*, where the subject's identification with the imaginary 'other' in the mirror results in a permanent

---

4    Descartes' construct of the rational, emotion free mind of radical doubt, often expressed as 'I think, therefore I am', but more accurately quoted as 'I doubt, therefore I think, therefore I am' (see Žižek 2006, 86).

5    A metaphor for a much wider set of perceptions of awareness of the subject (Dor 1998, 95-96; Fink 2004, 108).

distinction or split between the self and the image. The subject seeks unification between the two; another tragic desire for wholeness that will continue for life. This fundamental drive for unity with one's image (and not just with Mum) is what further helps generates all other 'desires', including ideals, jealousies and conflicts. As a consequence, Lacan (2006) defines the human subject as a split subject, split between self and image, but also split from its biological existence and raw desires by the need to engage with, and within, the predetermined symbolic reality of culture constituting the third stage of subjectivisation (and don't forget Mum!).

This final stage of subjectivisation is that of the *symbolic* when the child is socialised into an already existing language, culture and the full external identity of signifiers, as well as all the formal and informal laws in society which say 'no'. But this is not without cost. The individual must adapt to an already existing social reality, it must 'totally' conform to an external foreign system imposed upon itself so as to be able to articulate its needs and wants. But, there is no such thing as 'total'! Completeness is impossible. Inherently there will always be a remainder that does not perfectly fit what can be put into these pre-existing words and language. Articulation in the symbolic will always be lacking in completeness; there will always be a loss, a misfit between felt affect and what can be said about it.

The split subject will be further separated from its non-symbolic bodily and unconscious desires in this inability to fully articulate its perceived desires in words or actions. There will always be a remainder unsaid; not to mention, actions not permitted as acceptable behaviour. The subject is 'given a specific identity, a particular signifier to mark it out as an individual' and is socialised via 'the word of the Ancestor, the word of God or the rule of an Institution', but this is always incomplete, always lacking in what is not identified (Curtis 2001, 121). Through institutions such as religion, the family and education, together with their specific influences via professional and organisational guidance – the priests, doctors, teachers, or professional officials, the 'one who knows' – actors develop socialised individual and group identities and beliefs: master signifiers constituting their ego-ideal. It is through these incomplete identities that they also engage with the world and eventually with the practices of spatial planning, either as planners or as non-planners; those that are planned.

We enter into the symbolic, what Lacan calls the 'big Other', via the acceptance of a 'code of accepted fictions' (Žižek 1999d, 11). First, when our parent, or guardian, gives us direction as to what is 'good' and 'bad' in our behaviour. We want to be wanted by these adults, or at least not punished or sent to our rooms – so we generally tend to try to give them what we think they want. Then, as our educational and related institutions train us, many of us realise that in order to obtain a 'good' grade we must give the teachers the answer we think that they want by returning the teachers' truths and values as though they were our own!

Accomplished students do so whether they agree with the teachers, or not, and it is this way in which we acquire our norms in spatial planning, or in other areas of education, as well as in wider socialisation (Baum 1997; Gunder 2004).

It makes for an easier life! This is because an important part of our ego-ideal, our identity, is derived from being perceived by others as being a 'good' person. By extension, we generally strive to be a good person for each of our master signifiers of identification, by doing what 'good' planners, or partners, or citizens, and so on are expected to do. We use our knowledge of how 'good' planners, or residents, should act – as defined by the norms of the profession or wider society – to actually act. Phrased differently, we act in a manner that we think that others expect 'good' planners or residents to act – we conform to the expectations of society (Gunder and Hillier 2004).[6]

Finally, we direct ourselves, guided by, and perhaps following, the examples set by our friends, partners, employers and the media, in relationship to what we consider the 'big Other' – symbolic reality in its totality – would desire of us. Accordingly, the big Other may be defined as 'objectivised knowledge – the symbolic substance of our being, the virtual order that regulates intersubjective space' (Žižek 2001a, 254). It is 'the force of dialectical mediation-appropriation' (Žižek 2001a, 153) such as behavioural ideals encouraged by law, codes of conduct, ground-rules governing behaviour and so on, written, or often just learned through the experience of doing: what the French sociologist, Pierre Bourdieu (1998) called *habitus*.

While personally lacking faith in a dominant community belief and norms as to what constitutes good action or behaviour, or that of one's professional identification, residents or planners may well give the external appearance of this core belief and espouse the appropriate message and action – for this is what 'good' residents, or planners, are expected to do (Gunder and Hillier 2004). To phrase it in Hook's (2008, 52) words: 'I myself need not believe for there to be a believing of which I am part'. Further, in outward appearance, that is, what is measurable as the empirical materialisation of our social reality, there is little difference in the actions of the 'true believer' or those of a sceptic. If 'good' planners are expected to support sustainable public transport, provided that they publically support this value in their articulation of professional planning, it is inconsequential, at least to their practice as 'good' planners, if they commute to work in a gas guzzling SUV. Both the sceptic and the true believer act in a similar manner in response to the demands of the 'big Other' which includes one's profession's master signifiers and their contested norms of what defines 'good' professional behaviour (if not personal practice, in this example). The ideological construct of our social reality is thus constituted not only by the actual materialisation of what the social actor may actually believe, but just as likely, what he/she thinks is expected of him/her to materialise as belief (Žižek 1997a, 21).

---

6 Just as we generally conduct ourselves as 'good' US-Americans, Canadians, Australians, etc., should act by trying to comply with the wider values of our societies. This includes for many of us the cultural imperative to fulfil the desire to be successful, happy, healthy and to express these accomplishments in a 'normal' materialistic manner (McGowan 2004).

The Lacanian subject is a person who is situated in a network of complex relations of need and demand with many others (family, colleagues, boss, etc.). The big Other binds subjects to this structure. It gives identity and purpose through signs and practices, which at times may be ambiguous and conflicting. The big Other is exterior as well as determinative (Caudill 1997). Community life, including planning belief and action, is carried on through the enigma and power of the big Other; the symbolic order consisting of 'chains' that bind and orient, even while sometimes at odds with each other (Caudill 1997, 63). The status of the Lacanian big Other is that of 'belief (trust), not that of knowledge, since belief is symbolic and knowledge is real'[7] (Žižek 1997a, 107). We generally wish to be 'good' and are willing to seek direction in acquiring correct belief. The subject has been socialised to readily look for and accept therapeutic direction in their materialisation of correct, hence normalised, beliefs and resultant behaviours. This is central to contemporary governance.

## For Your Own Good: A New Form of Therapy

Pupavac (2004-2005) identifies a specific shift towards a different kind of approach to direct management of populations towards the end of the 20th century. There has been a marked shift in planning practice, as in many other professional disciplines, from an emphasis on highly regulated city-spaces and land uses (and a *relative* lack of regulation of individuals) to highly regulated individuals whose desires are therapeutically directed 'in the most appropriate and productive fashions' (Rose 1999, 90). This direction is often not explicit, but often somewhat indirect, or at a distance – what Foucault (1991) would call governmentality – where agencies of governance seek 'docile citizens that accept the norms and expectations of government as part of the ethical governance of themselves' (Gunder and Mouat 2002, 130). We suggest that implicit in this self-guidance is the perceived, or symbolic, gaze of the 'big Other'; inducing us to be 'good' and conform to what we think society wants of us, because we want to be seen to be 'good' citizens. Under this approach, government, spatial planning and related processes of governance, rather than just emphasising negative aspects of lack – illness or dis-ease – now stress the positive attributes of attaining and maintaining good health by encouraging the public to make the correct 'good' choices. In this regard Levitas (2007, 295), observes an 'apparent shift in the use of the term "utopia" itself, to signal a more concrete, systematic account of the social conditions for the fulfilment of human happiness – a more or less defined outline of a good society – rather than an attempt to express what is missing'.

---

7    One believes through the belief of the other, belief is always somewhat reflective and relies on a fundamental trust that others believe (Žižek 1998c, 3).

Spatial planning policies promulgate 'new ways of planning life and approaching predicaments, and disseminate new procedures for understanding oneself and acting upon oneself to overcome dissatisfactions, realise one's potential, gain happiness and achieve autonomy' (Rose 1999, 90). Bauman attributes this to a contemporary utopic process predicated on 'self-improvement' where we can become 'someone else', e.g., through cosmetic surgery, new clothes, new car, new house, etc. Here the 'dream of making uncertainty less daunting and happiness more plausible by changing one's ego, and of changing one's ego by changing its outer wrapping, is the "utopia" of liquid modern times; the "deregulated", "privatized", and "individualized" version of the old-style visions of a good society' (Bauman in Jacobsen and Tester 2007, 319).

Consequently, rather than the state imposing traditional authoritarian commands on its subjects, the contemporary state encourages the subject to participate (both in the mainstream economy, via employment, and in influencing the allocation of resources in disciplinary areas such as health and spatial planning), to choose, to consume appropriately and hence to enjoy a 'good' life (Gunder 2005b). In complex and subtle ways, through the joint efforts of the therapist (e.g., the 'doctors' of planning) and the client (local actants), problems are re/mis/shaped according to certain frameworks or repertoires (Rose 1996), of often a metaphorical nature, as discussed in the prior chapter.

Distinct planning techniques are often regarded as embodying 'good' therapeutic practice. In Australasia, and elsewhere, new urbanist design currently epitomises the urban therapeutic. Such design techniques include crime prevention through urban design, which is also believed to engender neighbourliness, community building, social capital, and hence, sustainability. Individuals need to learn techniques to internalise behaviours such as looking after the welfare of others and the environment through neighbourhood vigilance and increased social interaction; using public transit for sustainability; and, undertaking healthy obesity-reducing activities, such as walking to access services and facilities (Dixon and Dupuis 2003; Middlemiss 2008; Quinn 2006; Stegall 2006; Talen 2002). This new therapeutic paradigm effectively seeks to create new subjectivities able to cultivate self-competencies leading to a 'better life' and a 'better city' (see Levitas 1990). Sandercock (2004, 139), for instance, writes that planning can effect social transformation through 'a successful therapeutically orientated approach to managing our coexistence in the shared spaces of neighbourhoods, cities, and regions' where it may empower a 'capacity for collective growth'.

Development of such self-competencies is theoretically empowering both for the citizens and for professional spatial planners. In so doing, planning practice obtains an ethical legitimacy. It gives the appearance of being both democratic (as people are empowered to make choices for themselves) and therapeutic as it is in the interests of those over whom it is exercised. Such an approach requires careful critical analysis, however. Its ideas leave themselves open to Foucauldian critiques of self-serving and self-deluding artful governmentality (Gunder 2003a;

Hillier 2002). Further, they are still fantasy constructs seeking a desirous utopian city. They constitute what is today's dominant reality of the visions of the good city located within competitive globalisation (Gunder 2005b). They define a community – or so their proponents believe – necessary to attract the 'correct' dynamic and innovative, talented knowledge-people through a romanticised nostalgia for rescuing 'something expansive, utopian, essential, dispersed in the past' (Bloch 2000, 189). Yet, as Bloch (2000, 188) comments, these 'mostly infantile wishes fill the abyss of what we dream', serving mainly to suffocate immanence and stifle a potential for moving forward.

### The Good, The Bad and the Ugly: Australasian Fantasies of Designer Cities

Spatial planners are taught to cure our urban woes. Planning education not only supplies epistemic knowledge and practices, it also shapes students' dispositions to those of the profession by supplying a range of ideal, or ideological, prescriptive labels or signifiers to negate, or normalise, those spaces that are dysfunctional and diseased, and to facilitate communities in the creation of harmonious and healthy social spaces. Social and environmental justice, sustainability, Smart Growth, new urbanism and many of the other words we explore in this book are typical prescriptive signifiers (or 'plagues of fantasies' for Žižek (1997a)) that are inculcated in students to create a 'better', even a utopian, world (Gunder 2004, 303). These 'solutions' are inherently ideological, rather than technical in their prescriptive content (Gunder 2003b), even though it is planning technologies that shape and normatively determine how our built spaces 'ought' to be. Each of these prescriptive planning signifiers, and especially the utopian trace embedded within them, constitutes an unobtainable transcendental ideal which influences our planning and wider urban behaviours, whilst at the same time such singularly focussed processes induce us to 'construct and share illusions and fantasies ... that we are somehow achieving this impossible task' (Gunder 2005b, 193).

In the previous chapter we documented the importance that metaphor plays in shaping urban policy. This metaphor of urban health and fitness is particularly powerful, for as each subject knows, the failure of an individual's health has a potentially fatal outcome – death! Hence there is a strong normative desire to want to 'sustain' our environments and urban spaces in a healthy manner. These normative judgements lay the ground for ideological articulation with regard to urban spatial form (Schön and Rein 1994).

Consider the following statement published by a Regional Council with a core remit to provide planning and transportation direction through the management of urban growth for a population of 1.4 million residing within the 5,000 square kilometre area of Auckland, New Zealand.

Smart Growth is Smart Living.

Ensuring our cities remain economically competitive in the twenty-first century will be challenging. A visiting speaker from the United States advises against urban obesity … Many US cities are overweight – bulging at the edges and unfit as a result. Cities that follow a land-use diet of selective intensification are likely to have a competitive edge. (Auckland Regional Council 2004, 1)

The policy prescription is one of urban containment through nodal and corridor density intensification (outlined in Chapter 2). This is not the first time a trope of lack of fitness has been deployed by this particular authority. Five years earlier, a then-Regional Council planner wrote an article metaphorically titled *Auckland's Internal Growing Pains* with one of the Council's consultants.

If cities are people then Auckland is in the period of early adulthood. It's done a lot of its growing up, got much of its bone structure in place, now it's starting to 'put on the beef'. But is it doing this in a sustainable manner? Is it putting on too much fat and not enough muscle? (Waddell and Pollock 1999, 9)

The health metaphor again sought to illustrate Auckland as lacking fitness. Clearly, Auckland needs to shed the fat of urban sprawl and become a lean, mean, hence healthy and attractive young-looking city. Fat is lost and muscle created through self-control and exercise. Intensification is the mechanism to achieve this fitness goal of sustainability. The Region needs to discard the flab of metropolitan sprawl and develop into a fit and healthy, that is, competitive and desirable, city. Each resident must play a part in the city-region gaining this desired state.

Inherent in contemporary projects of urban governance is the notion that everyone has the obligation to contribute, in this case, to the prospect of sustainable urban fitness, for 'rights in the city are as much about duties as they are about entitlements' (Osborne and Rose 1999, 752). To ensure that the public act in an appropriate, dutiful manner, policies include mechanisms of public education, travel demand management (ARC 2003) and school, youth, community and industry awards promoting correct behaviours in facilitating 'fit and lean' outcomes that are environmentally sound (ARC 2005).

Concerns to promote better conditions of life in many Western urban cities (such as in Auckland) centre on a particular reading of the good as 'the best quality of life' for a small group of residents (Findlay *et al.* 1998) or non-resident entrepreneurs. To this end, Richard Florida's (2000; 2002c) widely influential work focuses on provision of amenities, environmental quality and social tolerance; all factors which can be 'changed for the better, given the correct urban policies' (McCann 2004, 1911). Behind these visions of the good city lies the driving force of economic growth and the assumption that places with high quality of life (and urban design) for the professional classes will economically out-perform their competitor cities (Zöllner 2004). Furthermore, there is an emphasis on strategic spatial planning as a product, a resulting spatial form, rather than as a process.

Economic and civic spatial boundaries are set and closure is achieved. There is likely to be little toleration of other alternative strategies or visions of the future.

To this end, the Urban Design Alliance of Queensland (UDAL), Australia, has developed an Agenda for the achievement of 'desirable' urban qualities. The Agenda proposes that 'cities and towns must be: sustainable, liveable, viable, responsible; and memorable', whilst 'good urban places must be: connected, accessible, meaningful, legible; and humane' (both quotes from Snow 2004, 24, bullet points removed). A similar agenda was implemented in New Zealand under the rubric of the New Zealand Urban Design Protocol (MfE 2005). This is a protocol that 'aims to make towns and cities more successful' through quality urban design (4). The document states 'we need to ensure that our towns and cities are successful places' (2). The protocol further states (11) that 'successful towns and cities are competitive, thriving, creative and innovative' and 'attract dynamic and innovative knowledge workers, entrepreneurs and companies' since 'they appeal to talented people because they offer a high quality of life' and so on. We draw attention here to the imperatives articulated by use of the words 'must' or 'need to ensure' and the empty signifiers of the listed terms and ideas, which, as Snow points out, have to be 'approached correctly'. We suggest, moreover, that such representations reveal more about 'bourgeois urban desires, fantasies and fears than about the city itself' (Baeten 2002b, 109) and worry that such powerful ideological fantasies will further serve to sustain the power of urban elites to the detriment of the already-disadvantaged.

There has been largely unproblematised acceptance of the criteria developed by Florida, as will be discussed in subsequent chapters, and further implemented by organisations such as UDAL or New Zealand's Ministry for the Environment, leaving little room to question the definitions of, means to achieve, or consequences of terms such as 'viable', 'responsible' and 'meaningful'. It is difficult to suggest that such motherhood statements are not 'good things' and there is little scope for discussion of alternative visions and stories. Nevertheless, Leonie Sandercock (2004, 136) has stated that even in such a world, 'an underlying commitment to some notion of the good city or good society is ever present'. Žižek, however, would give a principled refusal of any supposition of any knowledge of the good or ideal. A Žižekian ethic would rather be to question the difficulties we have with what we take to be our 'good' and the rivalries, masteries and identifications such a supposition carries with it (Žižek 2001a, 167). The crucial issue then becomes one of ideology and the questions arise: the good city or society for whom? And with what implications for those excluded?

The inherent subjectivity of notions of the good is increasingly recognised. Mannheim (1960) and Rawls (1993b) both indicated that different subjectivities make overall assessments of the good problematic. Sack (2003, 20) also points out that what is often held to be a good use of place depends on whether the place is effective for the project supported by a particular group. For instance, 'places of poverty, opium dens' and so on, 'can all be thought of as contributing to the diversity and complexity of the world' (Sack 2003, 25). 'Good' Israeli planning practice displaces traditional Arab settlements that lack official Israeli land titles, to allow the development of new Jewish communities (Yiftachel 1995). The good is a highly debatable term and largely a matter of perspective.

## On 'Ought' and Other Normatives

Perceptions of the good rapidly transform into normative prescriptions of 'ought'. Mannheim (1960, 234-236) provides a detailed explanation of how the normative 'ought' inherently drives decision-making. Indeed, traditionally 'there is a built-in "ought" in the very idea of planning' (Cussen 2000, 130). Witness the recurrence of 'must', 'should', 'need', 'ensure' and other imperatives in the urban design statements cited above.

The 'ought' is where the therapeutic becomes manifest in the notion that 'we *must* make [reality] better' (Sack 2003, 269, emphasis in original). We, however, have reservations about the assumed linkages between the utopian, the good or the healthy city and the production by spatial planners of a master plan or set of blueprints derived from, and as, an imaginary fantasy. Accordingly, we challenge the implications of strategic spatial planning as seeking 'the perfect balance between the "ought" and the "must"' (Bauman 2003, 16). That planning practice has always possessed a normative element does not necessarily imply that it is imperative to do so.

Far from curing the ills of the diseased city, many utopian attempts at social engineering through planning practice have produced dystopian consequences. These range from 'sink' estates and 'no-go' areas in British 1960s residential tower developments to insurrections in urban resettlement areas in Indonesia, the social exclusion of gated communities in the US or Australia and, more generally, against the reconstructed urban forms symbolic of globalisation and exclusion. In attempting to construct a desired good city, 'experts' or dominant groups may presume they know what is best, ignoring or silencing other alternatives. Utopianism is characterised by intolerance (Grey and Garsten 2002), especially of individual or minority opinions and needs, as all too often, the fantasy takes over and coercion to comply occurs. Authors are increasingly recognising that 'despair and hatred are the emotions involved in utopian thought' (Amis 2002, 18). In this context Bauman (2003, 16) observes that utopias are 'visions of a closely watched, monitored, administered and daily managed world ... a world in which prediction and planning would have staved off the play of chances ... the world of sages – whose job was to secure the benevolence of the rulers and the happiness of the ruled'.

Moreover, David Harvey (2000, 167) asks, whether the utopianism of spatial form that gets materialised can be anything other than 'degenerate. For instance, the ideals of free market economic rationalism have resulted in historical upheavals of urban docklands as capital has constructed, destroyed and reconstructed waterfront landscapes differentially in its image. Materialisations of ideal forms involve the authoritarian creation of fixed and exclusive boundaries or closures of space (such as the geographical area of a strategic plan or the zoning of residential estates with a minimum lot size to exclude affordable housing), time (the duration of the plan) and ideas. Harvey indicates that closure is both fundamental and unavoidable and suggests that attempting to evade closure simply embraces 'an agonistic romanticism of perpetually unfilled longing and desire' (Harvey 2000, 183).

Is non-fulfilment of planning therapeutic visions of the utopian good necessarily as melancholy as Harvey, Žižek and other critics would propose? The work of Leonie Sandercock (2003c; 2004) suggests not. Sandercock's is an explicitly utopian vision of 'therapeutic planning' (2003c, 162) completely different from that envisaged by Arnstein (1969). For Sandercock (2004, 138), 'the word *therapy* evokes an essential quality of community organisation and social planning' which enables citizens to speak the unspeakable, to talk of fear, loathing and hatred as well as of hopes and desires. In so doing, participants may develop processes of transformation, both of themselves and of their built environments 'in ways that reflect cultural diversity and the subjective sense of belonging' (2003c, 151). Sandercock (2004) recognises her explicit use of therapy in its psychological sense, acknowledging the importance of networks of relationships and of affect in many planning disputes.

The key to Sandercock's therapeutic planning is the possibility of transformation. 'Just as in successful therapy there is breakthrough and individual growth becomes possible, so too with a successful therapeutically oriented approach to managing our co-existence in the shared spaces of neighbourhoods, cities and regions, there is the capacity for collective growth' (2003c, 164; 2004, 139). This statement, however, reflects utopian and perhaps delusionary connotations of Freirean-inspired empowerment which have been problematised and largely critically rejected in recent social work literature (see Forrest 2000; Pease 2002). Sandercock's therapeutic planning also concentrates on procedure rather than spatial form. It tends to assume that if the practice is 'good' then the outcome will also be 'good'; something which does not inevitably follow.[8] We do not wish to disparage Sandercock's 'utopian impulse' (1998, 1) too much, however, as we believe that strategic spatial planning practice requires some element of hope-full looking forward and processes by which we might collectively work towards social and physical transformation to create our desired places.

---

8   For further discussion of this point see Levitas' (2003) exploration of different meanings of utopian process. Levitas distinguishes between process as the historical transition to utopia (process *to* utopia), process as utopia in itself (process *as* utopia) and processes of social change within utopia (process *in* utopia).

## Desirous Places

In the previous chapter we documented how planning actors and their affiliated partners gained public agreement via the rhetorical use of culturally shared 'master signifiers', their related metonymies and metaphors, and their resultant frames of perception and norms. We demonstrated how each signifier becomes linked to associations in the public's unconscious that induced a conscious expression of desire for a particular set of values or specific consequential actions. In the present chapter we have attempted to indicate how we are guided towards the 'good'. We are directed first by the institution of our immediate family as young children, then by our teachers and finally by society's media and its professional experts who are presumed 'to know'. All are constructing for us what we 'ought' to interpret as the good and what counts as 'good' actions, behaviours and solutions, so that we moderate ourselves to give the 'big Other' what we think it wants of us.

Yet the big Other is not to be trusted. The big 'Other is at the same time lacking, a domain of presumption and fiction, and yet, it nonetheless remains the anchoring point that a given society relies upon to maintain its coherence' (Hook 2008, 61). Accordingly, effective deployment of rhetorical tropes to prioritise specific values and notions by media and other dominant influences constituting a voice of the big Other (such as professional experts and their institutions of governance) can induce or seduce subjects to both strengthen or change their desires and identifications (Bracher 1993, 51-52). For example, would anyone openly admit to a wish to live in a city that is losing wealth and happiness to other locations because it lacks the fitness to compete?

> In Lacan, the construction of reality is continuous with the field of desire. Desire and reality are intimately connected ... The nature of their link can only be revealed in fantasy ... when harmony is not present it has to be somehow introduced in order for our reality to be coherent. It has to be introduced through a fantasmatic social construction. (Stavrakakis 1999, 62-63)

In this manner, 'man [*sic*] does not adapt himself to reality; he adapts reality to himself' (Roudinesco 1997, 114). Professional and business elites employ ideological fantasies as to what constitutes an enjoyable and satisfying city in order to hide the dysfunctions and unpredictabilities that are inevitable in all social spheres. Social reality 'is sustained by the "as if," the fantasy of what things are like' (Dean 2001, 627). Rationalisation, or *realrationalität* as Flyvbjerg (1998) calls it, exists between the everyday activities of social life and the universal ideals or values of what ought to be.

The belief that planning is not political, but technical 'allows the myths of objectivity, value neutrality, and technical reason to persist, and thereby fosters a certain delusion about planning practice' (Sandercock 2004, 134). Sandercock continues: spatial planning as a perceived techno-scientific process 'helps to redefine political debate, producing new sources of power and legitimacy, changing the force field in which we operate'. Lefebvre suggests that planning is based on a strategy of mixing scientificity and rationality with ideology. 'Here, as elsewhere, scientificity is an ideology, an excrescence grafted onto real, but fragmentary, knowledge' (Lefebvre 2003, 166). In particular, Lefebvre argues that quantitative expertise including the technology of spatial planning is largely a myth, 'an ideology that operates under the cover of this myth of technology' (Elden 2004,145).

In achieving the good, healthy city, our symbolic systems need anchoring points or points of fixation of meaning, even if 'empty', to quilt social reality and its actants. As Levitas (2007, 290) observes: 'there is indeed a place for utopia in contemporary ideology'. These are the master signifiers of belief and identification for our communities, city and countries and ourselves, which constitute our hopes for the future. Crucially, it 'is of utmost importance ... that these Master Signifiers emerge precisely at those points where meaning can never be fully determined' (Hook 2008, 62). They are always meanings-yet-to-come of the good, guaranteed by the big Other, and accordingly able to consolidate the social field and its constituting subjects towards that which is yet to be: the future (Žižek 1996, 144).

In these first three chapters we have dealt with the Lacanian symbolic and imaginary registries of conscious thought, language, identification and affect. Yet for Lacan, there is a third registry of reality beyond that of the symbolic or image. Lacan calls this the Real, which we attempt to introduce and engage in the next chapter.

# Chapter 4
# The Haunting of *Risk*

## Introduction

> The narrative of risk is a narrative of irony. This narrative deals with the involuntary satire, the optimistic futility, with which the highly developed institutions of modern society – science, state, business and military – attempt to anticipate what cannot be anticipated ... we do not know what it is we do not know – but from this dangers arise, which threaten mankind!
>
> Beck 2006, 329

We take the discussion of the desire for certainty, health and 'goodness' further in this chapter, drawing on Ulrich Beck's (1992, 1998, 2006a, 2006b, 2008) concept of risk society. We start with a discussion of scientific empiricism[1] and social constructionism[2] as alternative ways of constituting learning in the social sciences, including that of spatial planning. We then discuss and critique Beck's concept of risk. The subsequent section then expands the constructionist position into a discussion on representation and non-representation, which draws on the Lacanian Real, which we will discuss in some detail in relationship to Henri Lefebvre's (1993, 1991, 2003) concept of urban space. Derrida's concept of hauntology is in turn briefly engaged with, to further argue spatial planning's very ontological being as the papering over of the fear of risk, uncertainty and perhaps, ultimately, of our very death, in the unknown future. We contend that risk is a fear of the undecidable and unknown, which inherently haunts society as a spectre seeking exorcism.

We argue that planning should not necessarily seek to maintain its 'priestly' role of exorcism by providing the illusion of certainty toward the future. We contend that planning (and wider society) tends to avoid, or repress, emerging

---

1 Empiricism, also called 'empirical realism' or 'positivism', is the traditional scientific method of empirical observation, hypothesis testing via narrative explanations of causality and statistical modelling of reality (which is in this worldview observable, but exists external to humanity) to allow predictive forecasting (see: Hacking 1981; Laitin 2006).

2 The constructionist position is that knowledge in the social sciences is a construct, or artefact, that is shaped, evolved and made within human cultures (see: Berger and Luckmann 1966). The constructionist approach is concerned with 'how policies work in practice and the creations of norms, embedded belief systems and knowledge' (Armstrong and Wells 2006, 266).

issues constituting risk until a solution is available for prescription. This is not without cost. We conclude by arguing the need to accept uncertainty and to actively strive to engage with emerging 'risky' issues, rather than avoid or negate them, even though spatial planning and its institutions may be unable to provide definite resolution to the new concerns.

## Social Constructionism versus Scientific Empiricism

> Just as, a century or so ago, the idea of *progress* helped to name an optimistic era, so today *risk*, by its very pervasiveness, seems to be the defining marker of our own less sanguine historical moment. (Jasanoff 1999, 136 – emphasis in original)

In the wider social science literature, two perceptions of risk tend to dominate conceptualisations of the term (Cutter 1993; Evanoff 2005; Healy 2004; Jasanoff 1999; Lidskog *et al.* 2006; Snary 2004). The first perspective, empiricism, which has tended to dominate governmental and scientific discussions of risk, espouses a 'positivistic scientific theory of knowledge and a bureaucratic-rationalistic policy orientation' (Jasanoff 1999, 137). Risk, in this view, is something that can be measured, observed, mapped and, hopefully, controlled. In this perspective, risk is considered to exist only when it can be assigned a probability of occurrence. Otherwise it is regarded as uncertainty (November 2008, 1524). An institutional failure to manage risk is therefore either a consequence of the available knowledge and capability being disparate to the institution's mission, or a 'lack of political will to take unpalatable action' (Jasanoff 1999,137).

The second perspective is a social constructionist one, where risks 'do not directly reflect natural reality but are refracted in every society through lenses shaped by history, politics, and culture', and/or focused by the narratives of the 'specialised languages and sets of practices' 'which serve to channel power in society' (137). In this context '[r]isk is not an objective condition, but a social construction of reality, which starts with the question of how people explain misfortune' (Hoogenboom and Ossewaarde 2005, 606). As suggested by this quotation, predictable or unpredictable occurrences, uncertainty and even the unknowable can all be accommodated in a social constructionist perspective on risk.

Risk, in this mode of interpretation, is inherently an ideological construct addressing a lack of understanding that in turn seeks an authoritarian response, that purports to control this unknowable, or unpredictable '*Thing*' – what is missing – and provides, at least the illusion of certainty, solution, or control, over this unrevealed threatening spectre. That is: what is lacking, missing, empty is filled, covered over, contained, or given the illusion of safety and certainty as developed in the previous chapters.

Consequently, Tierney (1999, 223) observes that 'political power, organizational agendas, and economic interests drive the science of risk assessment' and that any effective cultural understanding of risk requires that the relationship of power and risk to be explored. As Bruno Latour (1993) amply demonstrates, power, politics and science are inherently and always intertwined when addressing the unknown '*Thing*'. In this regard, the invention of facts is not, however, a discovery of the things that are 'out there'; but 'an anthropological creation that redistributes God, will, love, hatred, and justice' in light of, and through the filtering and interpretation mechanisms of empirical observation (Latour 1993, 83-84).

Risk is a virtual threat (November 2008). Kristeva (1982, 1) regards risk as epitomising the *abject*: 'a threat that seems to emanate from an exorbitant outside or inside, ejected beyond the scope of the possible, the tolerable, the thinkable' so that 'the one haunted by it [is] literally beside himself.' Further, a response to this cultural fear, or haunting, and its desired resolution, results in the constant seeking of an impossible absoluteness of knowledge to provide, or at least give the illusion of, certainty towards a safe tomorrow – a core tenet of planning. Moreover, this seeking of comprehensive knowledge and/or construction of illustrating narratives that, at least, give the illusion of certainty of knowledge, underlies and empowers both the positivistic and constructionist perspectives put forward by Jasanoff as well as underlying spatial planning's central ontology.

We contend that human societies increasingly reside in a life-world of fear and anxiety largely constituted by a loss of trust in our own ability and that of our national institutions to both ultimately know and deliver a better world. As Beck (2006a, 2008) has observed, this is exemplified by repeated public sector mistakes and failures – not to mention those of the global private financial sector – and compounded by ever-increasing media awareness of the incapacity of our institutions to provide a predictable and secure state of existence: Gidden's (1991) ontological security. Overwhelmed 'by complex institutional logics and technologies that we [i.e., the lay public] do not understand, we experience a lack of faith in our own agency; exhausted by the failure of bureaucratic and political attempts to make the world a better place, we lose faith in the power of humans to solve problems' (Lavin 2006, 259). This occurs while we still maintain a traditional vision of the world as a stage that has been largely shaped by human will and ability in the struggle for continued existence and progressive betterment. Moreover, this illusionary vision and expectation of our institutions to provide for continued societal security, if not outright progress and betterment, persists, despite daily experiences of the general failure of institutions to successfully address the underlying causes that induce this constant fear and anxiety induced by the unknown (Lavin 2006, 261).

At best, the responses of traditional institutions of government, including those of spatial planning, displace this fear rather than address and conquer it, resulting in a constant state of ongoing ontological anxiety and distrust. There is fear both of the 'absolute threat of extinction', and the corresponding 'relative threat to self-preservation and self-enhancement' induced by our perceived lack of security and control (Hendrix 1967, 64). For many, this state of fear and anxiety with regard to ontological security is inherently a condition of the current state of contemporary existence, without hope of resolution and escape; what Beck (1992) refers to as the risk society (Ungar 2001). This anxiety is further compounded by a 'dislocation, disintegration and disorientation associated with the vicissitudes of detraditionalization' as a consequence of the 'collapse of inherited norms, values, customs and traditions' often perceived as a direct consequence of globalisation, or as Beck argues: the emergence of the cosmopolitan state (Beck 2004, 2005b, 2006b; Ekberg 2007, 346).

## Planning for Ulrich Beck's Risk Society

> Today, in the era of 'risk society', the ruling ideology endeavors to sell us the very insecurity caused by the dismantling of the Welfare State as the opportunity for new freedoms. (Žižek 2008b, np)

Oren Yiftachel (2006) argues that spatial planning theorists do not need to talk just about what planners do, but also to theorise about planning's implications for wider society. Perhaps planning theory's focus on spatial planning practice explains why there has been, relatively limited engagement until recently with the sociology of the 'risk society' and related social constructionist orientated interpretations of risk in the planning theory literature.[3] Gleeson (2000) addressed Beck's conceptualisation of the risk society in his wider debate on reflexive modernisation. Gunder (2003a, 249) drew on Beck's conceptualisation to explain wider society's disillusionment with positivist science. Similarly, Davoudi (2000, 129) referred to its reflexive value for critically shaping the educationalist needs of a reflexive profession supportive of sustainability. Numerous other planning theory articles and books have touched on Beck (often together with the British sociologist, Anthony Giddens) and give a passing reference to reflexive modernity (see, for example: Allmendinger 2002a; Flyvbjerg *et al.* 2003; Hasson 2005; Healey 1997; Howe and Langdon 2002).

---

3   Of course, risk management and related areas of environmental, earthquake, flood, fire, public safety and similar catastrophe management are well represented in the planning literature and, in itself, constitutes its own specialised sub-field (see, for example: Nixon *et al.* 2006; Wamsler 2006). Also, well represented in the literature is the concept of economic risk (see: Flyvbjerg *et al.* 2003), which relates back to the neo-classical work of Frank Knight (1921) and the early (pre-economic) philosophical work of John Maynard Keynes (1921) on probability, risk and uncertainty (also see: LeRoy and Singell 1989; Runde and Mizuhara (eds) 2003). Geographers have also considered the notion of risk (e.g., Bickerstaff and Walker 2002; Bickerstaff *et al.* 2006, 2008; November 2008); while planning scholars, especially Coaffee and Murakami Wood (2006, 2008) and Murakami Wood and Coaffee (2007) have recently begun to engage the concept.

Beck (1999, 3) defines risk as 'the modern approach to foresee and control the future consequences of human action ... an (institutionalised) attempt, a cognitive map, to colonize the future'. Further, risk is a 'systematic way of dealing with hazards and insecurities induced and introduced by' the processes of 'modernization itself' (Beck 1992, 21 – emphasis removed). Does this not resonate with practices of modernist spatial planning in its striving for certainty towards the future? Indeed, we suggest that the concept of risk, and society's responses to it, underlie spatial planning's ontological premise within modernity.

Ulrich Beck was one of the first social scientists to identify the 'strange paradox in modern society; that risk might in fact be increasing due to technology, science and industrialism rather than being abated by scientific and technological progress' (Jarvis 2007, 23). Beck's concept of risk includes 'problems that are difficult, if not impossible, to understand and resolve scientifically' and that are often external to traditional areas of individual or institutional responsibility (Bickerstaff and Simmons 2008, 1315). Beck's (1992, 22-24) theory of risk advances an argument for a 'second modernity' of reflexivity premised on five interrelated theses of risk. Firstly, that the concept of risk and the power that it engenders is different from that of material wealth and its traditional power. Modernity is dependent on the knowledge and judgements of experts. Accordingly, for Beck, the pivotal players in risk society are the experts: legal, scientific and mass media practitioners, including spatial planners, all of whom gain both social and political empowerment via their expertise and dispersal of the social definition and construction of knowledge.

The second thesis is that risk affects people differently: '*social risk positions* spring up' (1992: 23). Beck argues that, as a consequence of globalisation, risk breaks up the traditional categories of class and national jurisdictional protection. For example, he claims that pollution is international and the wealthy have little, or no more, protection from air-pollution, a pandemic of bird flu, or radiation (e.g., after Chernobyl) than the poor. Beck contends that we all reside in a global risk society and much of Beck's (2004, 2006a, 2006b, 2008) later works are concerned with how we might globally and collectively engage with risk: what he terms cosmopolitan realism.

Thirdly, the diffusion and commercialisation of risk displaces capitalism to a higher state. Risk provides 'the insatiable demands long sought by economists' as it displaces traditional finite consumer needs and wants with 'a *bottomless barrel of demands*, unsatisfiable, infinite, self-reproducible where, the economy becomes "self-referential", independent of the surrounding satisfaction of human needs' (Beck 1992, 23 – emphasis in original). Risk is central to the issues of ecological modernisation and sustainable development, where environmental need is deployed as a potentially expanding source of corporate profits (as will be discussed in Chapter 8).

Beck's fourth thesis is that everyone, regardless of wealth, is affected by risk. For all, the 'commonality of anxiety takes the place of the commonality of need' (49). Accordingly, knowledge about risks, for Beck, is of more political significance than economic power. This leads to the final thesis that once risk is socially recognised, it becomes politically explosive. Risk society has the potential to overrun traditional areas of the private sphere, requiring new areas of regulation, but regulation predicated on the worst state catastrophes, inducing a *'reorganization of power and authority'* (24 – emphasis in original). To summarise Beck's thesis of a second modernity: 'the ethos of wealth creation that characterized industrial modernity has been overshadowed by an ethos of risk avoidance, class consciousness has been displaced by a risk consciousness and the increased awareness of living in an environment of risk, uncertainty and insecurity has become a major catalyst for social transformation' (Ekberg 2007, 344). Or to state it more succinctly, 'the "bads" churned out by the capitalist behemoth come back to haunt their progenitors' (Mythen 2007, 797).

We disagree with several elements of Beck's theory. Beck privileges the role of experts, but we ask, what of the role of politicians? We are particularly concerned with how political processes are utilised to highlight certain aspects of risk and obscure others. The rhetoric justifying the invasion and occupation of Iraq, i.e., the need to eradicate the risk of Saddam's certain weapons of mass destruction, is one sad example of the manipulation of risk to justify unrelated political ends. We are also concerned that while economic class and wealth cannot protect one from all environmental and other risks, capital certainly helps in the provision of security, access to knowledge, and, if all else fails, in the ability to move away from a risk-prone situation. This has been well documented in New Orleans after hurricane Katrina, not to mention in the wider environmental justice literature (Bullard 1990, 1999; Agyeman 2005; Throgmorton 2008; Žižek 2008d, 95).

Beck's thesis for a second reflexive modernity is not without challenge and question for others as well. For example, Latour (2003, 40) questions Beck's authoritarian stance, his 'God's-eye privileged position', in understanding and explaining his view of society as the one universal 'truth' of social reality, and suggests that this is perhaps naïve in light of contemporary social constructionist thinking. This viewpoint suggests that there is no one correct perspective; rather, that diverse worldviews and their explanatory narratives compete for accountability among alternative interpretations. Elucidatory narratives and categories of risk are dynamic and change according to events (November 2008). Accordingly, Beck's 'risk society' is but one narrative among many to describe society. Even Beck's very focus on 'society' may be suspect:

> It has become clear over the years that the existence of society is part of the problem and not of the solution. 'Society' has to be composed, made up, constructed, established, maintained, and assembled. It is no longer to be taken as the hidden source of causality which could be mobilized so as to account for the existence and stability of some other action or behaviour. (Latour 2000, 113)[4]

---

4   A critique equally appropriate for the Lacanian 'big Other', which often acts in its hidden causality in a manner synonymous with that of 'society'.

Additionally, Atkinson (2007) takes Beck to task for negating the concept of social class by presenting a world of equally shared risk, which falsely creates a worldview of individualised fluidity without social stratification or disparate inequality. Similarly, Lacy (2002) challenges Beck's dismissal of critical Marxist and related critique, especially his failure to engage with the detrimental effect of capitalism on the environment, as well as Beck's lack of any alternative societal prescription that might retain the positives of modernity's progress while expunging its negativities of exploitation and degradation. Fressoz (2007) argues that many of the characteristics and concerns of *Risk Society* have not newly emerged in contemporary modernity, as argued by Beck, but also occurred in, and as, a consequence of 19th-century industrialisation. Similarly, 'natural hazards', which Beck attributed to anxiety in pre-modernity, are as prevalent today as in the past, e.g., the 2004 Indian Ocean tsunami (Furedi 2002; Mythen 2007).

Martell (2008, 131) questions 'the lack of empirical evidence' in many of Beck's propositions, particularly his later prediction that a global consciousness will emerge to address the concerns of environmental degradation and climate change. Irwin (2001) argues that Beck is too critical of science and the scope that it provides for developing new methods and technologies of societal progression. Indeed, some argue that risk can be a positive and rewarding human experience, allowing change and social development by challenging convention and authority (Boyne 2003; Furedi 2002; Lupton and Tulloch 2002). Others challenge Beck for distorting the concept of risk and its analysis and making unfounded assertions about low-probability events, including extrapolating 'too readily from worst-case scenarios and overstat[ing] the globalizing tendency of risk' (Mythen 2007, 800). Other critiques are predicated on a positivistic scientific perspective. This perspective defends the validity of statistical prediction, the availability and usefulness of preventive measures and science's perceived accuracy in appraisal and valuation of harmful or catastrophic events, not to mention, scientific ability to avoid bias and/or be aware of its implications (see, for example: Campbell and Currie 2006).

Yet, as Beck's (2006a, 2006b, 2008) later thinking expounds, there is an inherent irony embedded within the concept of risk, which sits particularly at odds with the fundamental concept of risk analysis that critics, such as Campbell and Curries, defend. This is, that 'the experience of the past, encourages anticipation of the wrong kind of risk, the one we believe we can calculate and control, whereas the disaster arises from what we do not know and cannot calculate' (Beck 2006a, 330). The implications of Beck's (1992) five theses of the risk society in a globalised world are perhaps well illustrated by the unexpected, if not unpredicted, emergence of organised terrorism focused on the first world and the consequential American led 'war against terror' arising after 11 September 2001 (Beck 2002, 2003, 2005a; Coaffee 2006; Spence 2005).

For Beck (2006a, 335) 'in the face of the production of insuperable manufactured uncertainties society more than ever relies and insists on security and control'. Yet at the same time as the 'magnitudes of risk, become so great by becoming international or global in scope and inter-generational in space, the prospects for the orderly control and distribution of risk across and within populations becomes both impossible and meaningless' (Jarvis 2007, 30). Consequently:

> Neither science, nor the politics in power, nor the mass media, nor business, nor the law or even the military are in a position to define or control risk rationally. The individual is forced to mistrust the promises of rationality of these key institutions. (Beck 2006a, 336)

Moreover, consistent materialisations of external threat, be it medical such as SARS or pollution, combined with repeated 'regulatory failures, together with the educational revolution – where a large segment of the population has been university trained – have made citizens more likely to critically evaluate the knowledge claims made by science' and governments (Lidskog *et al.* 2006, 95). Furthermore, risk, the pressures from globalisation and ecological degradation, has now become 'incalculable, and beyond the prospects for control, measurement, socialisation and compensation' (Jarvis 2007, 32). How can institutions act effectively when their claim to knowledge of effective risk control and institutional legitimacy, not to mention the very context of scientific 'fact' itself, is progressively under challenge as an inherent construct of society and culture?

Latour (1993) argues that a 'modern constitution' ontologically separates cultural and social values from the non-human, or scientific, 'fact'. Yet, as Latour and our prior chapters demonstrate, our narratives have never been rationally modern; that is, free of embedded values. Symbolic representations – words and the 'facts' they signify – are generally devoid of their constituting embedded meanings and values, signifiers in their deployment take on relevant and contemporary signification (Healy 2005). Words seldom convey their initial source of context; the specific circumstance of the creation of the signifier. Meaning shifts and context are inherently lost. Further, the basic Lacanian tenet is that words never convey the speaker's entire truth and complete intended meaning; they always lack comprehensive content (Lacan 2007). In this regard, so-called knowledge resides in individuals in the form of words, or signifiers, and is then conveyed incompletely in symbolic speech and writing between actors. However, 'reduction to signifiers or symbols facilitates the "purification" of representations into the material or cultural/symbolic realms and the many categorizations attaching to these, such as: "fact" and "value", "content" and "context", "expert" and "lay", "object" and "subject", etc.' (Healy 2005, 242). Moreover, the very human context of these initial categorisations is absent in the deployment of words.

> Representational thinking results from the erasure of the processes and practices enabling, generating and reproducing cognitive representations. This erasure legitimates representationalism because with it these representations then simply mirror the world. 'Facts' speak for themselves for precisely this reason. They are granted autonomy – status as 'things in themselves' – by denying the human effort and artifice involved in their manufacture. (Healy 2005, 242)

This presumptive status of facts as autonomous is intensely ideological, however. Facts can never construct themselves, or speak for themselves. Once initially constructed to allow representation in the face of new circumstances or discovery, 'facts' are then always selected and made to speak via selective structures of discursive argument, not to mention, metaphorical or metronomic slippage, put forward by human agents (Žižek 1994b). Yet, sometimes this process of symbolic representation breaks down when some new event occurs and existing representational language cannot cope with representing this rupture in the symbolic. What happens when the appropriate words to describe this new '*Thing*' – facts, values, or other – have not yet been constructed in language and given shared meaning? What happens when the unknown occurs and words fail? This is what Badiou (2005) calls a truth event.

Governments and their agencies of regulation have had considerable difficulty in understanding that there are some dimensions of risk, fear, hazard, or simply the new, not directly predicated on conditions directly attributable to either natural or known causes in the environment, or in society. In this regard, 'even the dominant framings of environmental' or cultural 'problems do not represent neutral readings of reality', indeed 'a policy-shaping conceptual framework such as risk builds upon underlying social modals of agency, causality, and responsibility' (Jasanoff 1999, 140). These are conceptualisations removed from the discussion, however. Here, existing words may fail. In addition, some unknown 'facts' are still to be identified and signified into words, regardless of the loss of the context and content of their creation; other unknowable 'facts' may never exist in the symbolic by the impossible nature of their affect.

How can one put into words the feelings of rage, humiliation or anger of members of a minority group who experience discrimination, or those of citizens of a country being invaded by a more powerful nation, or of surviving members of a community destroyed by a catastrophe, such as the Lockerbie disaster or the Indian Ocean Boxing Day tsunami (Thrift 2008)? Further, how can one articulate experiences impossible for human perception or intuitive understanding? What occurs, for instance, at the heart of the sun, at the core of a nuclear blast, or the birth of a universe? The 'language' of mathematics can be used to 'describe' such situations, but Badiou (2005, 2008) suggests that there are even limits to the articulation available in mathematics. Finally, we ask, how can one articulate events that we cannot even conceive? These are un-articulatable unknowns. Could an 18th-century person have the capacity to imagine, yet alone describe, a nuclear explosion? We suggest not. Accordingly, Santilli (2007, 175) notes:

> a culture must seal itself off from what it cannot acknowledge as real or meaningful, and that we shall call the realm of horror ... the horror with no name, which a culture bars from entering its symbolic domain, is not entirely absent. It literally haunts the edges of the culture, as an indeterminate menace and potential.

Indeed, aspects of repressed and forgotten horrors, if ever they can be known in the first place, reside in what Lacan (2006) calls the Real; they haunt us from outside human imagination[5] and our symbolic interchange. It is from the non-space of non-representation that the affect of fear and anxiety arises and causes psychic pain (Thrift 2008). This is a pain that we try to avoid, 'because our most primal fear is of the unknown', of this *Thing* that haunts us (Lavin 2006, 256). This is a fear that may be captured by political words and images to channel our anxiety into anger and rage against an Other, perhaps as a scapegoat, to hide and obscure the failure of our politicians and governments to deliver on our demanded certainty. Accordingly, if our governments do not 'create fables to feign knowledge' about this unknown, and often even unknowable, spectre, we often create our own fables (Lavin 2006, 256).

Ideologies of certainty paper over, or often negate, dismiss and obscure the fact that we reside in a risky, uncertain and not necessarily known reality. Rather than attempting to engage these initially unsymbolised or poorly articulated, but emerging issues, where old words tend to fail and 'solutions' as such, cannot emerge, our institutions, including the public information media, often simply try to negate them. In this regard, even after the Kyoto Agreement in 1997, climate change might be considered a prime example, at least for several countries (Carvalho 2007; Krogstrup and Svendsen 2004; Soroos 2001).[6] Yet, beyond overt ideological distortion serving self-interest, such as previous US government denial of ecological problems (Orr and Ehrenfeld 1995), or the neutralisation of risk denial theories as justification for risky and defiant individual human behaviours (Peretti-Watel 2003), we suggest that there is a need for enhanced understanding of how and why new contentious issues emerge. Particularly, we suggest, we need to understand why institutional responses so often commence by attempting to seal off, or negate, these initially poorly articulated, but haunting issues. Perhaps one way to do so is to acquire a better understanding of what resides outside the symbolic. Lacan refers to this as the Real.

---

5    Although we attempt to capture their 'preontological and precategorical domains' in art, or horror-art, 'consisting of literary fiction and films' (Santilli 2007, 177). This is the stuff of sci-fi and horror movies such as *The War of the Worlds* or *The Night of the Walking Dead*.

6    Even countries which engage policies to address climate change still tend to expand their energy-intensive infrastructure, such as motorways, airports, or coal-fired power stations, and continue to promote growth of their consumption economies. At the same time, these countries often grudgingly promote energy conservation, carbon taxes, more sustainable cities and the like, to partially mitigate their consumption effects that serve to exacerbate global warming (Gunder 2006).

## Outside of Representation: Beyond the Symbolic and Image – The Real

> For Lacan the Real, at its most radical, has to be totally de-substantialized. It is
> not an external thing that resists being caught in the symbolic network, but the
> fissure within the symbolic network itself … for Lacan the Real – the Thing – is
> not so much the inert presence that curves symbolic space (introduces gaps and
> inconsistencies in it), but, rather, an effect of these gaps and inconsistencies.
> (Žižek 2006b, 72-73)

Lacan (2006) observes that the human subject understands reality and the objects within it via three registries: the imaginary, the symbolic and the Real, with the latter residing outside any means of representation by images or symbolism. This Real is virtual. It 'precedes language,' and 'is best understood as *that which has not been symbolized*, remains to be symbolized, or even resists symbolization; and it may perfectly well exist "alongside" and in spite of a speaker's considerable linguistic capabilities' (Fink 1995, 25).

The newly born infant perceives the world undifferentiated, as Real (Boothby 2001). Wholeness is being with the primary care giver; incompleteness is being without Mum. Gradually the child's senses develop and a process of differentiation occurs into other discrete things. Things begin to exist to manipulate and play with, as well as to take Mum away from the child. The child's ideal-ego forms having passed through the mirror stage of self-awareness and identity, at first in a registry of differentiated images and then upon engaging with the second registry of the symbolic, by learning to give and articulate names – signifiers – to these things. Central to Lacan's teachings is the pre-existing primordial third registry, one that we cannot put into words, yet has had affect upon us since our first engagement with the gestalt of our initial post-birth world. This is for Lacan the registry of the Real.

The *Imaginary* is 'the world, the register, the dimension of images, conscious and unconscious, perceived or imagined' (Sheridan in Lacan 1977, ix). It is the visual register such as that of the child in the mirror stage that relates to their visual image in space. It is vision, which confirms the separation of subject from object. Within the Imaginary, 'space is hierarchically organised and structured in terms of a centralised, singularised point-of-view by being brought under the dominance of the visual' (Grosz 1990, 38).

However, Lacan (1992) distrusts visual representations. He uses the term 'misrecognition', suggesting that there is misrecognition of the gap between the subject and its image of itself. For instance, we mistake the represented persona for the whole person, or the two-dimensional zoning map, or photograph, for the place represented. This was a problem quickly realised in early post-war British spatial planning where inflexible County, Town and Comprehensive Development Area maps as stand-alone policy instruments or mechanisms, proved incapable of dealing with the socio-economic and environmental complexity of human settlement development (Bruton and Nicholson 1987, 21). As Steve Pile has commented, image-orientated geography (or planning, or architecture) is the medium of deception. It 'offers "ground truth" but cannot be trusted' (1993, 135).

The *Symbolic* relates to language; words are signifiers. Yet, it is impossible to comprehend everything. The point of Lacan's psychoanalytic teachings, however, is that it ought to be possible for us to comprehend our lack of comprehension, to learn from this and to come to terms with it (Gregory 1997). There is always something missing in our speech and writing, a lack or gap between our words and exactly what 'truth' or meaning we are striving to assert (Verhaeghe 2001, 41), between our representation of something or someone and the subject itself. As introduced in the previous chapter, infants are forced to assimilate into an already existing realm of language and culture to make their needs known. Children must completely adapt themselves to the 'big Other', and not this 'big Other' to them. Consequently, the human subject is a divided or split subject. Human subjects have both biological existence in the natural world and identity in this symbolic world. Subjects exist *outside* of their signifiers and their stories of identification, beyond their socially constructed categories of human perception and symbolism.

This outside constitutes the third registry of the Lacanian *Real*, in which we and other objects exist, but which we cannot articulate fully due to the lack, or gap, that resides in the symbolic. The repetition of difference (words) can never cover the Real and, as Hillier (2003a, 45) notes: 'attempts to describe the Real are destined to simply distort it.'

The Real is why we fail in our specific definitions of such abstract concepts as quality, amenity, freedom, or the good. It is why urban design or landscape aesthetics must ultimately rely on opinion (Bourassa 1991; Scott 2003). It is why different groups agonistically struggle with each other as they all seek to impose their definitions of 'the good' or 'freedom' – what ought to be – on others (Laclau 2000). All too often we blind ourselves to this irreducible gap between symbolic/imaginable reality and the Real. Yet, fundamentally, it is this traumatic attempt to encounter the Real that initiates a process of incomplete symbolisation and the 'ever-present hegemonic play between different symbolisations of the Real' (Stavrakakis 1999, 74). It is this 'play' which leads to the emergence of politics between the different symbolic viewpoints of what the 'world' does and should look like and to the political institution of new fantasies (decision/accepted viewpoint, etc.) in place of dislocated ones, as to 'what ought to be'.

The logic of lack – incompleteness in the symbolic – and the Real, perhaps becomes clearest when applied to the idea of consensus. There is always an excess of meaning which escapes signification. Spatial planning attempts at inclusive consensus formation are predestined to fail. Consensus is incomplete. There is always something excluded; a Real that remains unsymbolisable. The Real remains open to a range of political master signifiers, which are utilised, in consensus-building processes to try to 'fill' or 'suture' (Newman 2001) this lack and to overcome its fundamental antagonism. However, as Newman (2001, 147) states, 'this is an impossibility: the Real of antagonism, which eludes representation, can never be overcome'. Further, dissatisfaction, conflict, antagonism and contradiction are not breakdowns of the system but rather lie at the heart of society and social change (Tajbakhsh 2001, 13).

Lacanian thought suggests that any conception of the socio-political institution of society as a harmonious totality or of a public sphere with complete information is no more than a fantasmatic mirage (Hillier 2003a). The ideals of comprehensive knowledge and a non-agonistic society of absolute consensus are the Lacanian impossible fantasy of utopian dreams rather than the actual lived social reality that we experience under our self-imposed conformity to what Lacan called the big Other, with its capitalised 'O'.

The Real will always exist despite the comprehensiveness of the symbolic. The Real is a rift, or void, where nothing can be said or defined and it resides as a logic of constitutive lack – a 'traumatic kernel or surplus which escapes signification' (Newman 2001, 147). 'It is an un-definable unthought outside of language, imagination and signification, an unattainable and un-definable void that we desire to fill – but cannot' (Gunder 2003a, 296). For Lacan the Real 'remains the same in all possible universes (of observation)' (Žižek 1999e, 1999c, 78). It just resides outside of the language and conscious fantasies that the symbolic and imaginary are capable of constituting. We can never say *exactly* what 'is' or what we desire comprehensively 'ought to be'. Here, 'what emerges via distortions of the accurate representation of reality is the Real – that is, the trauma around which social reality is structured' (Žižek 1999c, 79).

Of direct relevant to spatial planning, the French sociologist thinker of spatiality, Henri Lefebvre (1991, 38-9, 48-49) also conceives of the world and space as composed of a similar triple schema to that of Lacan's three registries. For Lefebvre these are the 'perceived', 'conceived' and 'lived' that can be historicised via dialectical terminology into three evolutional spatialities he calls *natural, absolute* and *abstract* (Blum and Nast 1996). The first is the space that is seen, generated and used – the registry of Lacan's image(nary). The second is a space of symbolic knowledge and rationality, the instrumental space of 'social engineers', 'urbanists' and 'planners' (Lefebvre 1991, 38) – the registry of Lacan's symbolic. The third space is the evolving qualitative space of 'less formal and local knowledges' of daily existence, which resist clear articulation (Elden 2004, 190). The scientific, or symbolic, traditional response of spatial planning practitioners to this third abstract space of being is to negate it. For Lefebvre, 'lived space is an elusive space, so elusive in fact that thought and conception usually seek to appropriate it and dominate it', but they cannot, for 'there's more *there* there' (Merrifield 2000, 174).

> The qualitative is worn down. Anything that cannot be quantified is eliminated. The generalised terrorism of the quantifiable accentuates the efficiency of repressive space, amplifies it without fear and without reproach, all the more so because of its self-justifying nature (ideo-logic), its apparent scientificity. In this situation, since the quantitative is never seriously questioned, [there is] no scope for political action … urbanism reflects this overall situation and plays an active role in applying ideo-logic and political pressure. (Lefebvre 2003, 185-6)

It should not be argued that Lefebvre's 'lived space' that lacks quantification is the same as Lacan's (1998, 2006) Real that resides in both the human subject and the material spatial world, yet is incapable of symbolisation. We agree with Blum and Nast (1996, 2000), however, in suggesting that Lacan's conceptualisation of the Real may well have influenced Lefebvre's notion of 'lived space'.[7] Rather Lefebvre's 'lived space' comes close perhaps to what Lacan refers to as 'knowledge in the real' (Žižek 2002b, 185). These are unsymbolic bodily knowledges of how to unconsciously perform life's many daily activities such as walking, driving a car, or passing time with a neighbour.[8] These are habits and techniques of the self that we 'just do' in our daily habits of lived space (Burkitt 2002; Howe and Langdon 2002).

While it can never fully contain the Lacanian Real, natural science seeks to suppress this boundary, this lack, by unsuccessfully attempting to cover over the Real with knowledge of the material world for 'this open boundary, mobile and real, between knowledge and the real, is what Lacan calls the subject of science' (Morel 2000, 68). Yet natural science is never complete knowledge, it fails in its striving for total articulation of the material world. Something always remains unsaid. There always remains a lack or void in knowledge. To totally fill this void and create a complete body of knowledge is modern science's 'holy grail'; yet, natural science can never achieve this absolute task (Verhaeghe 2002, 125), as most scientists, no doubt, readily acknowledge.

Applying social science to human subjects fails, as does natural science in the attainment of complete knowledge of the observable world. As developed in the previous chapter, human subjects often act inconsistently with regard to their true beliefs and desires. Rather, subjects act in a manner that attempts to give the 'big Other' what they think it wants through their 'correct' actions. Subjects materialise the ideology that constitutes social reality in their very words and observable actions. Unlike the Real of the material world, the Real of the human subject is untouchable. Observable actions of conformity may not only obscure conscious beliefs and wants, but the Real resides in the subject's unknowable unconscious and, only drives ego consciousness indirectly via desire and the fantasies that this desire produces (Žižek 2008a, 328-329). The Real of the unconscious – 'the real of the human subject which causes symptoms and discontent in civilization' – is an entirely different unknowable Real (Loose 2002, 281-2). The human subject's 'Real is the intrinsic division of reality itself'; consequently, to cover over this void induced by the Real, the subject is lured and deluded into ideological illusion within the imagined and symbolic realms of daily life in social reality (Zupančič 2003, 80). The human subject's Real is 'filtered, framed by fantasy, as though by a window' that at best, might only be partially accessed through psychoanalysis (Morel 2000, 74).

---

7   See in particular the footnote and surrounding text in Lefebvre's (1991, 136): *The Production of Space*.

8   What Giddens (1991) calls 'practical consciousness'.

Both Lacan and Lefebvre would agree that science and scientific method fails in their ability to fully articulate the qualitative components of human life. Further, the Lacanian position goes somewhat further than Lefebvre in suggesting that in attempting to address this unknowable Real, human subjects all construct and materialise ideological fantasies to paper over this lack of ability to articulate and know this *Thing* (Stavrakakis 1999; Žižek 1999c). For, as even Lefebvre (2003, 67) asserts, sooner 'or later radical critique reveals the presence of an ideology in every model and possibly in "scientificity" itself.' Lacanian theory argues that our very social reality and social interaction are constituted and composed of ideological fantasy constructs. The 'big Other', which we seek to please, is an illusion constituted on misrecognition, misunderstanding and ideological constructs of contradicting social logics (Žižek 1997a). Further, spatial planning, as a human discipline of governance, plays a significant role in shaping the creation of this social reality of misrecognition, particularly, as it relates to wants and needs and, especially, to desire, not to mention the community's engagement with the registry of the unknown: the Real.

However, the 'Real is not the Beyond of reality, but its own blind spot or disfunction – that is to say, the real is the stumbling block on account of which *reality does not fully coincide with itself*' (Zupančič 2003, 80). From this blind spot arises fear of risk. For Beck (2006a, 332), risk is 'the *anticipation* of catastrophe', an ominous anticipation that something bad is going to happen, even if this *Thing* which may occur is unknown. This unknown risk resides in the Real, external to the symbolic 'in a permanent state of virtuality, and becomes "topical" only to the extent that they are anticipated' (Beck 2006a, 332). These risks are not known; at best, they are 'becoming real' 'always events that are threatening' (332). Without representation, 'techniques of visualization, without symbolic forms, without mass media, etc., risks are nothing at all' (Beck 2006a, 332). Risk resides hauntingly in the Real, inducing a state of anxiety that 'some*Thing*' is going to happen, and requires illusion and fantasies of safety or security to cover its spectral presence. If technology, government or business cannot provide this illusion of security, some people turn to a 'higher' order, such as that of religion or faith, in order to create this sense of ontological security. This is a haunting, perhaps compounded by our own repressed individual fear that the only certainty that we all have to our future, is that we are finite, we will die (Hillier and Gunder 2005, 1061).

Consequently, articulatable risks are at best the incomplete illusions produced in symbolic representation to cover, or engage with, the symptoms of the Real that cannot be articulated – repressed or never known hauntings from that which must always lack words. For Crang (2000, 313) 'what they share is the haunting of urban fears and urban imaginaries' ... 'is the hole, a puncture' ... 'the traumatic kernel of the [R]eal [which] is inarticulable.' This haunting induces an experience similar to fear, 'but it is not the kind of fear one feels before a specific danger ... it is an anxiety about the instability and contingency of the world itself' (Santilli 2007, 184). For the Real 'is associated with an insubstantial, ephemeral nothingness, a fleeting non-presence haunting the constituted field of reality and rendering it "not whole"' (Johnston 2008, 147). In this regard, 'the primal nature of the concept of the [R]eal in Lacanian psychoanalysis (whereby the [R]eal is always-already experienced as virtual from the point of view of symbolic reality that is itself necessarily virtuality), illuminates the strange impossibility that surrounds Derrida's figure of the spectre (the spectre has a transitional body that represents both actuality and virtuality)' (Featherstone 2002, 370). This is a spectre of anxiety 'that is never quite absent in our daily existence' or 'entirely exorcised' by society (Santilli 2007, 184).

## The Spectre of Derrida

Much of Derrida's work is concerned with the aporia of undecidability,[9] a lack of certainty in the world, in areas of knowledge, forgiveness, action and responsibility (which will be discussed in further detail in Chapter 9). So much so that Bernstein (2006, 397) states that 'Derrida loves aporias ... [w]here many of us see problems, difficulties, perplexities to be resolved, Derrida sees aporias – impossible possibles or possible impossibles'. For Derrida, making a true decision requires both an ability to act and an acceptance of the potential radical uncertainty inherent in the future. True decisions require a leap of faith that opens a gap between the certainty of known knowledge and the consequential outcome that the decision will eventually produce (Barnett 2004, 517). Decisions are inherently haunted by undecidability (Derrida 2000a). We suggest that undecidability may be considered as one dimension of the Lacanian Real. There is always uncertainty: 'from the knowledge to the decision, a leap is required, even if one must know as much and as well as possible before making a decision' (Derrida and Roudinesco 2001, 92 in Egéa-Kuehne 2003, 278).

In this regard, 'radical uncertainty should be understood as related to our attempts to mould the world to our purposes ... we can talk of risk only when the occurrence of an event is linked to a decision; otherwise we talk of danger' (Pellizzoni 2004, 545). It is in the attempt to assert control over the environment, or society, by providing a 'solution' to the 'problem', that danger is resolved into risk. Pellizzoni (2004, 545) continues: 'the more we take risks, the more uncertainty shifts from shadow to saliency.' That is, 'ghosts haunt places that exist without them; they return to where they have been excluded from' (Derrida 2000b, 152).

> A decision once made does not, however, banish the ghost of the undecidable.
> It remains haunted by the decision not-made, by the possibilities rejected, by
> the courses not taken. Most of all, it continues to be haunted by the intransigent
> unforeseeability of the future. The future is spectral. (Bullen *et al.* 2006, 56)

---

9  Undecidability is something that does not conform to either polarity of a dualism or dichotomy, i.e., it is neither black or white, nor alive or dead. It is rather a liminal space of both/and.

Derrida (1994, 10) calls this repetitive return of the suppressed, forgotten, or never known, 'hauntology'[10] and suggests that it underlies all modernist constructs that purport to contain fact and certainty. What Beck (1992; 1999) calls the risk society of 'second modernity' haunts the dominant planning and related policy narratives, 'because they are not included or acknowledged' (Bullen 2006, 55) and give repeated grounds for contestation of their largely sedimented meanings. This haunting is manifest outside representation and the symbolic, in what Lacan refers to as the Real, as a virtual effect or affect (Featherstone 2002).

## Beyond the Haunting of Risk

> It was, and still is, the illusion of modernity to think that rational science, efficient economics and smart political programs could in time overcome and eliminate the horror of the human condition. What, in fact, modernity has often done is simply add to the horror of being, leaving us with the debris of its history. (Santilli 2007, 189)

In this chapter, we have considered the concept of risk, where risk is largely argued as a symptom, of modernity and progress, at least as articulated in Beck's sociology of risk. It found planning for risk to be a key attribute of the spatial planning discipline. Indeed, this attribute provides a key dimension of spatial planning's traditional ontological perspective: the illusion of the provision of certainty towards the future via an apparent transcendence of the veil of time. We have suggested that the very ontological nature of provision of certainty impairs the ability of spatial planning to engage with emerging issues. Planning is generally solution-led, and without a potential solution to frame an emerging problem, spatial planning, as currently practised, has great difficulty articulating or engaging the new.

We have explored the concept of symbolic representation and found that there are always dimensions lacking in words and texts. 'Facts' are devoid of context and ordered to speak for the actor in a selective manner; facts, or at least their deployment, are inherently ideological. Furthermore, sometimes words simply do not exist, yet the affects of a nameless '*Thing*' may still haunt and induce anxiety and fear. Articulations of risk are often symptoms or illusions produced in response to the lack of words, knowledges, blind spots, fissures and even impossibilities. Lacan, and other authors referenced in this text, refer to this state outside of representation as the Real.

We have briefly discussed Derridean undecidability and hauntology in the context of risk and the Real, and suggested that risk haunts spatial planning policy narratives and decisions as a virtual affect of the Real. Rather than a traditional search for certainty and control over the unknown, by providing the illusion of

---

10   Which has a similar pronunciation in French, as in English, to that of 'ontology'.

an ideal solution that shapes and controls the 'deficiency' or 'lack', we suggest that planning might seek to accommodate uncertainty as a core ontological state of a qualitative, rather than merely a quantitative, and hence readily measurable, world. This might be via a care-full consideration of and engagement with the idea of immanence, an engagement with the constant permanence and indwelling of the unknown that pervades and haunts reality, rather than the seeking of idealised utopian end states of complete closure. An acceptance of uncertainty and the limits of spatial planning's capability to control the unknown and unknowable, requires an acceptance of our haunted state of risk. We proposed that this acknowledgement of uncertainty and engagement with emerging 'risky' issues should be taken as a positive opportunity for involvement and engagement of spatial planning.

For example, perhaps an earlier and more active initial engagement with emerging concerns about atmospheric carbon dioxide build-up leading to what we now understand (with some degree of confidence) as climate change, might have resulted in an earlier, or perhaps even a more pre-empted resolution, or mitigation, of this now globally threatening problem.[11] We ask how many comparable spatial planning and related issues currently exist without being actively or adequately addressed, or even considered as worthy of engagement? This is, we suggest, largely a consequence of our traditional institutions tending to actively avoid engagement with things initially sensed and given initial voice through feelings of affect and dis-ease, i.e., a qualitative feeling that something is not right. Even when there is 'factual' awareness that a problem exists, institutions often do not become engaged, unless, as developed in Chapter 2, they can first prescribe a 'solution' promising control and certainty of outcome. Such solutions, if available, are generally constructed within a metaphorical framing of the policy issue that tends to draw only on established spatial planning 'best practice' or related knowledge. Without this orthodox solution-driven policy framing of what is deficient, risks are not generally overtly articulated, unless imminent catastrophe threatens.

A Lacanian perspective suggests that we should confront and traverse the core modernist fantasies produced by the desire for certainty. It suggests a move away from an idealist illusion that we can achieve some transcendent, if undefinable, end-state, be it sustainability, comprehensive multi-culturalism, or capitalist heaven-on-earth. Rather than creating ideologies of illusionary certainty and solution, spatial planning might be better deployed in actively acknowledging the Real: that some 'Things' simply escape capture in the symbolic. And further, that even the symbolic, itself, is inherently incomplete. We suggest that human existence is a process of imperfect trajectory and encounter with constantly changing environments, without certitude, and hence active engagement with risk – whether measurable, predictable and controllable; or constructed, arbitrary and even inherently incomprehensible – is all-important for this process. To act, to decide, does not give closure. Rather, it produces new uncertainties that continue

---

11   See Carvalho (2007) for an analysis of the role of ideology and the printed media in the UK in the public engagement with climate change between 1985 and 2001.

to haunt social reality. But we must still act in the world. Spatial planning, as well all those for whom it plans, might be better off to embrace this reality, though we recognise the political unpopularity of our advice.

Rather than risk being perceived as a fear of the undecidable, or unknowable, which haunts society as a spectre and induces anxiety, we argue the need to actively confront and even welcome a potential for the 'truly' new, as an opportunity for innovation and continued improvement of the means for city-making and engaging with the wider dimensions of societal change. Accordingly, rather than producing illusions of certainty, an active engagement and acceptance of the unexpected, unknown, and even unknowable may go some way towards exorcizing the anxiety, and often the very lack of action, that contemporary engagement with risk tends to induce. In this chapter, we have suggested that risk, uncertainty, aporia, and undecidability are present in any action and lie at the core of any social reality that knowledge seeks to uncover. We thus suggest an acceptance and engagement in spatial planning and related policy field of the impossibility of absolute certainty, solution and predictability that in turn, will allow us to engage the inherent unknowability of the Real that underlies both social and material reality.

In the next chapter we will engage with a key modernist fable of certainty: a belief in unlimited capitalist growth and progress. This is a fable that this chapter has called into question, but we suggest one that still resides in a dominant position underlying key determinants of contemporary societal rationality. We will explore this fable from two directions: firstly, from the perspective of enjoyment, law and its transgression; secondly, from the perspective of the spatial planning master signifier of 'Smart Growth.'

# Chapter 5
# Is *Smart Growth* Dumb?

## Introduction

*Smart*: Less than precise, especially of bombs. May cause collateral damage.

After Watson 2004, 344

In this chapter we examine the US-American spatial planning term 'Smart Growth',[1] in order to explore the concept of growth in relationship to spatial planning, predicated on the axiom that we exist in a world of finite carrying capacity.[2] The seeking of enjoyment, or what Lacan calls *jouissance,* will be central to this consideration. As Stavrakakis (2007, 181) observes, 'what sustains the social bond is not only symbolic power, but also affective investment'. To this end, *jouissance* provides a 'sophisticated angle on the discussion of emotions and affects' that is currently intriguing the social sciences (see, for example: Connelly 2002; Nussbaum 2001a; Thrift 2004, 2008). After an introduction to the concept of *jouissance*, we engage with the spatial planning paradigm of Smart Growth. We use this master signifier of US-American city and regional planning as a springboard to explore, from a Lacanian-derived perspective, the dominance of liberal capitalism. In particular, we will explore how the orthodox response to city-making as the accommodation of growth, is derived from, and driven by, the hegemonic values of wealth creation and maintenance of capital via spatial planning related laws and regulations. Indeed, we suggest that spatial planning sits at the very heart of this inherently political process.

> The very *raison d'être* of planning is bound up in the mutual accommodations of the political and the economic. The state is in need of the institutionalization of planning in order to prepare the ground for the development and reproductions of capitalist relations, and the needs for capital are that the interventions of the state are necessary for a smoother functioning of the market. Hence, modern planning makes its appearance as an institutionalized mechanism for the good of the general public. (Law-Yone 2007, 319)

---

1   Which is a term, generally, but not always, written in proper nouns.

2   Carrying capacity is the amount of global resources necessary to sustain a given population without resource reduction. Often called the ecological footprint, Rees (1992) has argued that to be sustainable each region of the world needs to live within its regional carrying capacity, with a net effect of achieving global sustainability.

In the later part of the chapter we introduce the Lacanian concept of 'traversing the fantasy' to explore this relationship of spatial planning to the imperatives of contemporary capitalism and its pernicious need for continuous growth and expansion, which we argue is largely driven by a will to *jouissance*. We conclude by setting the context for continuing this discussion in the subsequent chapter on competitive globalisation.

## Desire: *Jouissance*

> Desire ... is itself something that has to be constructed through fantasy, and these fantasies differ in their relationship to different circumstances. (Brent 2004, 221)

Central to Lacan's (1988a, 1988b, 2006) theorising is the role of desire in constituting the human subject. We suggest that desire is also a core dimension of spatial planning. Desire is constituted by a gap between need and demand: 'desire begins to take shape in the margin in which demand rips away from need' (Lacan 2006, 689). Actors desire satisfaction beyond that of basic need. This may be a satisfaction, which can seldom, if ever, be fully achieved, or often even permitted. As a result, actors' identities are partially constituted by a potential prohibition of desire through its representation in society's regulating laws (such as planning law and regulation) and the informal norms that give guidance as to how to behave as a 'good' citizen. The law may restrict the enjoyment of satisfaction, yet enjoyment is also often produced in its transgression. Lacan calls such enjoyment *jouissance*.

We suggest, along with Stavrakakis (1999, 2007), that the Lacanian conceptualisation of the human subject as a split subject provides a crucial insight for explaining a key dimension of socio-political conduct. For Lacan, the subject is inherently separated between the symbolic realm of conscious understanding – including a sense of self and identifications that we share with others in society; while divided/split from the ability to articulate or even understand the subject's own unconscious self – and its often strange drives and desires as motivated by *jouissance*. An awareness of unconscious human desire and *jouissance* opens new avenues beyond that of utilitarianism[3] as to why actors behave as they do in spatial planning and wider societal processes. For instance, this understanding provides insight as to why actors construct illusions about what constitutes their

---

3   Utilitarianism is a moral philosophy, based on the principle that the happiness, or satisfaction – the utility – of diverse people can be measured and aggregated in a manner so that it can be compared, generally in monetary terms. In utilitarian theory a societal optimum may be achieved in production, distribution and other policy decisions. In achieving this utilitarian goal Jeremy Bentham (1969) coined the phrase 'the greatest good for the greatest number.' Utilitarianism provides one dimension of the underlying logic of rational human behaviour in traditional economic thought.

perceived social reality and to obscure the undesirable, while at the same time they allow themselves to be seduced by other fantasy constructs into identifying with and acting out other potentially desire-fulfilling behaviours (Žižek 1989, 2002a). We exemplify this point by the mundane, but everyday reality for many of us – at least until the 2008 'credit-crunch' perhaps – who continue to use their credit cards and borrow, knowing that their income is already fully spent. Further, this understanding of desire and fantasy construction offers insight as to how ideological beliefs may be materialised into our daily planning and wider practices (Dean 2001; Stavrakakis 2007; Žižek 1997a).

As we have developed in previous chapters, the conscious ego in Lacanian theory is literally a self-construct, initially arising in relationship to the infant body's perception of the external world. This is a consciousness subsequently captured by symbolic language as the young child learns to articulate its needs and wants. As a consequence of language being imposed on us by our integration into culture, the conscious ego-ideal is barred and/or split from understanding its own being's unconscious subjectivity and often complex desires (Lacan 1988b). Lacan (1988b, 1998) also defines this barred subject as a stance, or position, adopted in relationship to the Other's unknowable desire – originally that of the infant to the (m)other – insofar as that desire arouses the subject's own desire. The subject adopts a stance against the traumatic encounter with the Other's desire as an experience of pleasure/pain – originally ourselves as terrified infants screaming for the unfulfilled desire of non-stop wholeness provided by our primordial experiences of Mother's milk and security. The lack of wholeness induced by our first separation from Mother's security is our most fundamental unconscious psychic trauma. But this is a trauma mixed with pleasure, the crying and screaming at the loss of Mum and the call for her return is mixed up in the pleasure of being complete in union with Mum, so that the two are intertwined (Fink 1995, xii). This is what Lacan calls *jouissance*.

*Jouissance* is a French word signifying bodily enjoyment or pleasure. But in the Lacanian lexicon it has an extended meaning. *Jouissance* also means a search for enjoyment that transcends the pleasure principle into what Freud refers to as the 'death drive' (Lacan 1994, 281; Žižek 2002a, 206). In this pre-symbolic realm of *jouissance* and the ongoing trauma of separation from the (m)other's desire, our most fundamental and profound memories are constituted; memories that forever reside in our unconscious, ever split and barred from direct conscious awareness by our symbolic self. They reside in the Real. All our experiences and memories, good or bad, of our first months of life are not forgotten. Rather, they were never formed as image or symbolic based memories, but continue to reside in our unconscious (as do later 'repressed' memories), influencing our ongoing desires.

Human development, entering into language and socialisation – that is having a place in the symbolic network constituting culture and society – comes at a cost to its participants. This is the cost of displacing *jouissance*; and the very conscious desire for *jouissance*, itself, because it is 'fundamentally indifferent – and often inimical – to the well-being both of oneself and of the other person' (Bracher

1993, 20). *Jouissance* is anti-social. It is inherently 'childish', and it is blatantly pathological in its drive for unachievable fulfilment. At the same time as our ego-ideal consciously shapes and tempers our external identity to try and conform with the norms of language and society, our 'unconscious goes its own way, taking no account of the interests of the living being and its adaptation to reality, and desire is borne along by signifiers that knead and shape our existence – even against our interests as living beings' (Van Haute 2002, 125). This drives us: it supplies the psychic energy that makes us act, often at odds with acceptable behaviour, i.e., beyond societal norms and law (Boothby 2001). From telling someone what we really think they look like with their new, expensive hairstyle, rather than indulging in an expected, more cordial, 'white lie', to transgressing laws, for instance by doing a cash 'deal' to avoid paying sales tax (VAT/GST), illegal soft drug use, or knowingly building a house extension without the necessary development consents, most, if not all of us, take pleasure in being 'rebellious', at least to some degree.

*Jouissance* is not pleasantness, however, 'but an unconscious clinging to that in being which does not wish one's own good, an unconscious masochism that is not utilitarian' (Ragland-Sullivan 1991, 64). Lacan's concept of *jouissance* is of a different order to pleasure. It answers to a different logic – 'a "logic" that takes precisely no account of what the subject can experience as "pleasant"' (Van Haute 2002, 225). *Jouissance* is an 'unconscious energy, difficult to displace, which invests displeasure with a pleasurable quality'. Accordingly, an understanding of *jouissance* 'is eminently qualified to shed light on our attachment to conditions of subordination and suffering, to the reproductions of structures of obedience and of ideological systems' (Stavrakakis 2007, 181).

We all experience the negative side of *jouissance* when we transgress a societal norm, or expectation, knowing that it is wrong, but we do it anyhow. It is why we sometimes stubbornly stick to a position, perhaps on a spatial planning issue, knowing that the position is untenable, but it gives us pleasure to be 'perverse' or 'obstinate'. Some unconscious internal force – a manifestation, a symptom, of our desire driven by *jouissance* perhaps for a forgotten or repressed key word, phrase, experience, image or belief (i.e., a repressed master signifier) may make us hold our ground even when we know in our conscious reflection that our position is unwinnable and even likely to cause us social or professional embarrassment, or worse. It is perhaps why a member of the public knowingly submits a planning development application that is wildly non-complying as to what is permitted, or even for what may be a prohibited use, in an urban regulatory plan; yet they have an expectation, a fantasy, that approval will be readily forthcoming. It is the subject's frustrated *jouissance* that subsequently drives the applicant into a frenzy of protest at the application's refusal, even though this outburst will be to no avail (Hillier and Gunder 2003, 2005).

Understanding our desire is impossible. This drive to *jouissance* resides within the Real, outside of the symbolic (Lacan 1998, 55). At best, *jouissance* and the Real express themselves in the symptoms which they evoke when we transcend cultural norms and laws construed by our constructed – signified – reality. We are always in a bind. To act freely is to be 'caught between acting on one's own fundamental fantasy – in this case the *jouissance* of masochistic resistance that defines the Real of desire ... – or accepting the subjectivization [symbolic identification] that is offered' by conforming to the expectations of society (jagodzinski [*sic*] 2002, xxx-xxxi).

The ego-ideal is often indecisive in our actions because of this unyielding contradictory position between what we symbolically think is expected of us by society, but do not actually know, and what we unconsciously desire to do. Can I? May I? Should I do it, or should I not? Absolute knowledge is always lacking. In this light, our quest for knowledge, according to Lacan, is motivated by 'some failure of pleasure, some insufficiency of pleasure: in a word, dissatisfaction' (Fink 2002, 34). This gap, or lack, in knowledge is never filled; so we are always driven to further fulfil our desire for security/certainty through the attainment of further master signifiers and their supporting sub-codes. Let's do more research. Let's develop a better policy. Let's do a new plan. The value of acquiring knowledge 'is renewed every time it is exercised, the power it yields always being directed towards' our *jouissance* (Lacan 1998, 96-97).

Spatial planning knowledge is one dimension of this quest. In North America, at least, it has led to contemporary spatial planning practice, embodied in values largely captured by the term: Smart Growth. After an explanation of this term, we will suggest that it is highly ideological in nature as it perpetrates an unquestioned belief in growth and capital accumulation, even as it attempts to environmentally mitigate the worst excesses of urban development.

## Smart Growth

> The word 'smart' carries a universally popular connotation. At first glance, who can rightly oppose the notion of 'smart growth', since its opposite would presumably be 'dumb growth'? (Miller and Hoel 2002, 16)

Smart Growth is a spatial planning and environmentalist led response to traditional US-American urban growth and the resultant car-based suburban sprawl it produces (Downs 2005). It is concerned with increasing urban density as a mechanism to accommodate urban growth; often referred to as urban containment. Smart Growth may be considered as 'a comprehensive strategy of regional sustainability that suggests economic efficiency, environmental protection, a high quality of life and social equity can be achieved through concerted and negotiated land use policies' (Scott 2007, 17). The concept of Smart Growth was developed in the mid-1990s in response to a US Environmental Protection Agency initiative (Krueger and Agyeman 2005, 412). It was first given legislative 'teeth' by the State of Maryland in 1997, where targeted financial incentives for development infrastructure and consumer residential location choice were used to encourage higher density development in specifically identified areas (Daniels 2001; Miller and Hoel 2002; Shen and Zhang 2007).

In contrast to the traditional appeal of sustainability for tackling environmental issues, such as those of carrying capacity and environmental footprint, Smart Growth tends to focus on basic quality of life issues at the local and metropolitan level (Tregoning *et al.* 2002, 341). Downs (2005, 368) attributes six common principles to Smart Growth together with three less universally advocated principles (7-9):[4]

1. Limited outward extension of new development in order to make settlements more compact and preserve open space. This can be done via urban boundaries or utility districts [in North America].
2. Raising residential densities in both new-growth areas and existing neighborhoods.
3. Providing for more mixed land uses and pedestrian-friendly layouts to minimise the use of cars on short trips.
4. Loading the public costs of new development onto its consumers via impact fees rather than having those costs paid by the community in general.
5. Emphasizing public transit to reduce the use of private vehicles.
6. Revitalising older existing neighborhoods.
7. Creating more affordable housing.
8. Reducing obstacles to development entitlement.
9. Adopting more diverse regulations concerning aesthetics, street layouts, and design.

Other commentators describe Smart Growth as a toolkit of good planning practices, espousing additional dimensions of social equity, liveable communities, local democratic determination, transport and consumer choice, ecological integrity and fiscal responsibility (APA 2002; Howell-Moroney 2008; Krueger and Agyeman 2005).

Downs (2005) argues, however, that there is limited general public support for Smart Growth. Rather, support originates from three diverse groups: non-government environmentalists, spatial planners and other local public officials, and innovative private sector real estate developers. With regard to the last group, Scott (2007, 21) identified one general contradiction of Smart Growth that arguably requires resolution, which is its 'promotion of social equity and inclusionary governance while exploiting market mechanisms' of capital accumulation for its pro-development supporters. Howell-Moroney's (2008) statistical analysis

---

4    All the principles resonate strongly with the dominant values of spatial planning, as well as those of urban design and new urbanism, in the US, as well as in the UK, Australasia and Canada (see: Bramley and Kirk 2005; Cheshire 2006; Day 2003; Friedmann 2005; Gow 2000; Gunder and Searle 2007; Leo and Anderson 2006; McCann 2007; MfE 2008; Sternberg 2000).

of Smart Growth adoption across the US shows a strong correlation between its implementation and regions with high rates of per capita growth, often in line with related growth-control initiatives and concerns for the implementation of housing affordability policies.

Smart Growth shifts the benefits and costs relating to urban spatial development. Under regimes of Smart Growth, urban fringe landowners are less likely to profit from traditional urban edge sub-division, whilst existing suburban or inner city land-owners are likely to gain unexpected property value increases in areas suitable for housing density intensification. Traditional expectations are upset, thus alienating conventional land speculators. Unfortunately, Scott (2007, 21) observes that ironically, while 'market forces are beginning to strengthen the hand of smart growth in terms of higher densities, mixed-use developments and transit-orientated development; however, they are also making social sustainability a more difficult proposition', due to higher housing costs of more desirable 'urban living'. This observation is statistically confirmed across the US (Anthony 2006). Nevertheless, Downs (2005, 369) observes that most 'Americans are accustomed to sprawl and its consequences', but not the implications and potential benefits of Smart Growth. Accordingly, 'faced with such uncertainty, they are reluctant to support such a major change.'

Smart Growth is most effectively implemented at the state, regional or metropolitan government level and has been argued to be an agenda facilitating formalised metropolitan government (Scott 2007). Since 'key Smart Growth principles require government action at the regional or state level, not at the local government level where most powers over land use planning now reside' it has fostered considerable local authority opposition as '"[h]ome rule" powers are among the most vigorously defended of any authorities entrusted to local governments' (Downs 2005, 369).

We suggest that the term 'Smart Growth' performs as yet another Lacanian master signifier. Consider the following quotations.

- Smart Growth is 'a recent buzzword that implies that all growth is good, if it is planned' (Jentsch 2006).
- 'Little by little, Smart Growth was becoming a recognised "brand", if not a household term, that conveyed a new sense of balance and energy in the fight against sprawl' (Tregoning 2002, 342).

As the term has gained popular acceptance, it has appeared to lose clarity of meaning or, indeed, meaningful substance. It acts as an empty signifier. Smart Growth comprises an 'array of very different policies, not all of which are necessarily compatible', introduced as responses to urban problems resulting in 'the use of a common label for approaches that are not fully consistent and may even be contradictory' (Ye *et al.* 2005, 301-302). Indeed, we suggest that Smart Growth could even act as a synonym for many of the explicit contemporary values and tools of wider spatial planning. What we have specific concern with is not the label itself, but the implicit assumption within the master signifier that growth can indeed be 'smart', in a finite world where the existing human population has already exceeded its carrying capacity – on average US-Americans, have each exceeded their sustainable carrying capacity more than fivefold (Rees 2002, 263).

We would suggest rather that the label 'dumb growth' might indeed be much more appropriate to such a situation, no matter how much the policy approach taken seeks to mitigate the adverse effects of the growth being managed. Growth, smart or otherwise, still occurs in the US and elsewhere, 'credit-crunch' or other economic recessions or downturns of the business cycle, notwithstanding. This growth is largely driven by a mechanism, or should we say imperative, of wealth accumulation for both the development industry and homeowners, rather than simply as a mechanism to meet the need for quality human shelter (Cladera and Burns 2000; Ewing 1997; McLoughlin 1992; Weiss 2002; Wolf-Powers 2005). Perhaps we need to challenge this imperative in light of its inherent environmental consequences, rather than simply thinking we can be 'smart' about continued growth, even if delivered through mitigating practices of spatial planning for urban intensification.

## When the Limits of Growth are Reached, Carry on Consuming!

How is it that financial markets and self-interest seem to prevail over human responsibility to others, the non-human environment and to future generations of humans? We suggest that Lacanian-derived theory can provide one understanding of this dilemma. Slavoj Žižek (1989, 28; 2002a) suggests that while most members of society understand the problematic characteristics of their social codes, norms, and values, they often continue to act as if they do not know the consequences of their actions. People 'disavow the existence of problems and inconsistencies in their reality', manifest, for instance, in terms of political alienation, labour exploitation, corruption, production of cultural or environmental trash, resource depreciation, global warming, and so on (Kovacevic 2003, 110).

Ideology, from a Lacanian perspective, is not a matter of a lack of knowledge or intentional deception. Ideological construction occurs when we attempt to form a comprehensive harmonious social reality in which we perceive ourselves as decent human beings, wanted by others, in order to fulfil our fundamental desire to be whole, complete and well-balanced. Accordingly, we try to shape our awareness of social reality as free of perceived conflict as possible. In doing so we allow ourselves to see only what we want to see, even though we have knowledge about the likely consequences of such selective 'seeing'.[5] Further, the fantasy-

---

5  For example: we suggest that most planning academics affirm sustainability strongly to their students, yet most, at least in the first world, are heavy producers of greenhouse gases in their behaviours, including leaving computers switched on, car use and long distance travel to attend academic conferences.

construction mechanism of ideological illusion is 'not located in the *knowing* but in the *doing*' (Brito 2008, 60 – emphasis in original), for Žižek (2008a) would argue that we in the global North may well know that our consumption behaviours are unsustainable, but we continue to consume, nonetheless. This ideology is not a fantasy-construct hiding social reality; rather it 'in fact serves to support it' (Brito 2008, 61). Our dominant ideology actively encourages us to continue to grow the economy via continuous consumption in a manner well beyond that of our sustainable carrying capacity. This is because our social reality continues to be predicated on ignoring the known physical constraints of a finite world even though they may be established as scientific 'fact'. Consequently, in order that we can continue to enjoy a generally shared consensus of a pleasurable and safe existence in our daily lives, we cannot afford to look too closely at the fantasy constructs that constitute our social reality, and especially at what we repress, or ignore, in our *doing*, even though we may actually know better.

It is this human ability to discount what may be perceived as dissonant, provided it is not so alien as to threaten the apparent solidity of our social reality,[6] which is emphasised by the contemporary ethical-political importance placed on individual consumer duties and responsibilities. Our desires – what we want – are learnt and assimilated from the Other, 'the subject's desire is the desire of the Other' (Žižek 2002a, 108). As such, desires are inherently a social construct and constantly reinforced by our dominant societal norms. We suggest that the social reality of competitive capitalist growth predicated on consumerist display of material wealth and accumulation – to demonstrate to ourselves and others that we are 'good' or 'successful' – is one such learnt set of desires. This is a set of values evolved through time and first learnt as young children from our parents, close family members and friends, arguably supplemented by our educational systems, and consistently reinforced by media-imposed values of belief and desire, which in aggregate constitute the illusion of the 'big Other' (Stavrakakis 2007).

As, summarised in Lacan and Žižek's core conceptualisation of ideology – outlined in prior chapters – the 'big Other,' acts as the aggregate, but virtual, 'all Others' to which we respond and to which we attribute direction and guidance in our actions. The big Other 'acts like a yardstick against which [we] can measure [ourselves]' perhaps personified as 'the "God" who watches over me ... or the Cause that involves me (Freedom, Communism, Nation) and for which I am ready to give my life' (Žižek 2006b, 9). It is the symbolic order that provides the rules and directions for self-regulation that reinforces a person's capitalist consumption and accumulation habits. But it is virtual, a 'subjective presupposition' that only 'exists only in so far as subjects *act as if it exists*' (Žižek 2006b, 10 – emphasis in original).

Lacanians would argue that 'the reason why the individual derives enjoyment from a strong libidinal attachment to commodities, exemplified by the ideological allegiance to the pursuit of property as happiness, is that commodities play

---

6 In which case we want to expel, or destroy it. Headscarves may be fine, but not niqabs (see Chapter 7).

the role of a fetishistic object' of desire (Kovacevic 2003, 110). Consumerism cannot be explained without taking the axes of desire and enjoyment seriously (Stavrakakis 2007, 228). Fundamentally, we attempt to fulfil our conceptualisation of our primordial maternal lack with commodities, but this merely induces greater 'loneliness' (Declercq 2006, 78) by leading subjects into dependency on desired objects. We can never sate our desire, 'it is caught in the rails of metonymy [substitution], eternally extending towards the *desire for something else*' (Lacan 2006, 431 – emphasis in original). Desire always lacks completeness and lures us to seek more: more consumption, a better car, a better house, a better city (Johnston 2005, 189); hence, the spatial planning role in this accumulation process. Consequently, under capitalism, 'the excess (the consumption of "useless things") becomes the rule, that is the elementary form of buying is the act of buying things we "don't really need"' (Žižek 2002b, 277). Yet, consumer happiness ultimately in Žižekian thought is not a class of truth. It is an ontological class of being. For what is missing, or lacking, and underpinning our desire resides in the Real, which is 'impossible to articulate in demand' (Stavrakakis 2007, 236). Consequently:

> 'happiness' relies on the subject's inability or unreadiness fully to confront the consequences of its desire: the price of happiness is that the subject remains stuck in the inconsistency of its desires. In our daily lives, we (pretend to) desire things which we do not really desire, so that, ultimately, the worst thing that can happen is for us to get what we 'officially' desire. Happiness is thus hypocritical: it is the happiness dreaming about things we do not really want. (Žižek 2002d, 59-60)

Past pleasures drive us to desire constant replication of our experiences. The seductiveness of commodity consumption is difficult to displace (Johnston 2005). Especially when it is re-enforced and facilitated by the marketing and advertising of products to 'stimulate and channel desire' via 'constructing a whole mythology around the product' so that we actual buy the product's promises of happiness, enjoyment, prestige, popularity and love, rather than the product itself (Stavrakakis 2007, 238-239). We need our prestigious homes to display our other commodities and demonstrate our happiness. Smart Growth is the way to achieve this ideal! As Žižek (2003, 145) observes, in relation to housing or any other commodity:

> a commodity is a mysterious entity full of theological caprices, a particular object satisfying a particular need, but at the same time the promise of 'something more,' of an unfathomable enjoyment whose true location is fantasy – all advertising addresses this fantasmatic space ('If you drink X, it will not be just a drink, but also …').

Matching this desire for consumption and the fantasies it generates, is the desire for the perceived ontological security of capitalist accumulation and life satisfaction, represented for most US-Americans and Australasians primarily through home ownership (Dupuis and Thorns 1998; Rohe and Stegman 1994). For Lacan

(1992, 229) 'the good is at the level where a subject may have it at his disposal ... it is the birth of power ... to exercise control over one's goods is to have the right to deprive others of them' not of its use value – the fulfilment of a need – but in 'its *jouissance* use' value. For most of us, renters aside, our greatest asset is our home and in 'making their lifestyle decisions, Americans are typically focused "on the house"', for houses 'and property are assets which have to be protected and defended' (Pallagst 2007, 12).

One key dimension of spatial planning is its role to protect, or give the illusion of protection of, property rights and values (Needham 2006). We suggest that Smart Growth plays a central role in this process, albeit by somewhat shifting the playing field so that landowners and speculators at, or beyond, the urban fringe, are largely disenfranchised from their traditional growth related profits. Spatial planning protects and regulates land values through zoning or similar legal mechanisms of land use control. Yet, as Dear and Scott (1981, 15) famously contended, spatial 'planning interventions are, by their very nature, remedial measures generated as reactive responses to urban land use and development pathologies' where planners 'are frequently able to control the outer symptoms of these pathologies, but they can never abolish the capital logic that produces them'.

We suggest that a Lacanian interpretation of this observation, seen through *jouissance*, gives an additional dimension, beyond that of mere utilitarian consumer satisfaction maximisation, to an understanding of consumer behaviours and their capitalist drives. The Lacanian position suggests that the commodity fetish is driven by an innate human seeking of an impossible return to a primordial maternal wholeness, whose very impossibility we try to placate and substitute via the search for material consumption and wealth accumulation. In particular, we suggest that such awareness allows examination of the symptoms of these behaviours and how they are manifest in spatial planning processes. Behaviours include the contemporary set of practices encapsulated under the master signifier, Smart Growth, or materialised in other manifestations of late capitalist desire for city-making and the resultant resource, environmental and psychic degradation they may incur. Traversing the fantasies producing these 'capitalistic logics' and an understanding of their causal underlying trauma-induced *jouissance*, may, perhaps, permit their eventual mitigation or negation.

Contemporary social reality is sustained because it underpins and meets the primal desire of most subjects in society for a relatively conflict-free, safe and assured happy future, even if it can only deliver this as a fantasy-scenario of material happiness. Spatial planning has an important role to play in the construction and maintenance of this fantasy of material happiness. In our contemporary society, the 'moral law' is no longer the imperative that acts as a limitation, stopping us from enjoying too much. Instead, the cultural imperative to consume and enjoy has become the new 'moral Law' in its own right, because 'the ultimate "transgression"' would now be a 'wish to pursue a life of moderation' (Žižek 2004b, 174). We suggest that Smart Growth plays a significant role in facilitating this imperative for consumption.

## Law and its Transgression

Law originates in desire (Lacan 2006, 689). Desire 'comes into being' when the 'Other intervenes to say *no*' (Bowie 1991, 162, emphasis in original). 'Every prohibition, in other words, is sustained by a secret investment in *jouissance*' (Vighi and Felder 2007, 149). The idea of planning control as driven by a will to *jouissance* implies a certain pleasure in either applying, transgressing or objecting to the letter of spatial planning law for the planner, the applicant and 'affected residents' as stakeholders. The will to *jouissance* can induce obsession. For instance, people sometimes hold intractable positions in the face of overwhelming authority, or might accumulate hundreds of shoes, or may wish to construct the most spectacular palatial home, regardless of zoning standards, or its effects on the environment and local amenity.

Lacanian theory suggests that a subject's *jouissance* is given freest rein when an act of desire contains a dimension of transgression. It is the 'little sin' that gives the most pleasure; it is the prohibition as such which elevates a common everyday object into an object of desire (Žižek 2004b, 177). The bio-politics of contemporary spatial planning are predicated on enjoyment – you will enjoy! – not the prior duality of repression/freedom of the Weberian[7] traditionalist capitalist master's injunction: 'No you cannot do that!' The achievements of traditional utopian goals were ones of freedom to act against the repression of the negative injunction. Contemporary injunctions are to enjoy, even if being watched by police CCTV cameras – or at least to sustain our happiness – regardless of what we actually desire.

A basic tenet of capitalism is to achieve growth, which is synonymous with wealth and enjoyment. Happiness and satisfaction are both symptomatic of the achievement of this want. Smart Growth is driven by this capitalist logic. It attempts to mitigate some of the worst externalities of urban spatial growth by minimising the adverse impacts and effects of sprawl whilst tying to maximise liveability, quality of life and social reproduction. These are attributes necessary for place-based competitiveness in the attraction of increased inward investment and in-migration and retention of talented knowledge workers (Krueger and Savage 2007, Yigitcanlar *et al.* 2008, 66); believed necessary conditions for vigorous and sustained economic growth (to be further discussed in the next chapter).

In this context, want driven by desire often becomes politicised as demand. A lack represents the symbolised desire of a group of individuals with the intention to impose their opinion over others. As Gunder (2000a, 5) writes, they impose

---

7   After Max Weber's (2002) analysis of the historical rise of capitalism where the traditional authority figure of the state, capitalist, or church attempted to command obedience and behaviours conducive to being productive workers. Weber (2002) demonstrated how the Protestant work ethic in early Northern European capitalism (rather than leisure or enjoyment) was the only way to attest the glory of God and achieve one's predestined place in the eternal and everlasting joy of Heavenly life.

'their own enjoyed delusions about reality via selected "distorted" knowledge and language ... a successful will to *jouissance* beyond just material greed'. This applies to having consumer choice. It also applies to the protection, or appreciation, of property values. This may occur either through countryside residential subdivision at the urban periphery inducing land value appreciation as well as promoting more outward sprawl, or via urban containment, intensification and Smart Growth which also increases land values through greater utilisation of land density (perhaps 40 dwelling units per hectare rather than just five or ten). Yet, those imposing their demands will continue to live in a state of uncertainty, with their desires not fully satisfied. Desire always leads to the desire for something else creating new demands and new desires (Lacan 2006, 431).

The pain of unfulfillable desiring, points out a key difference between a Lacanian analytical approach and a rational choice approach predicated on traditional economics. In a rational choice-based analysis, the identity of social actors is assumed to be that of self-interested utility maximisers whose desire can theoretically be sated. Moreover, core questions relating to the identities of agents, as well as their agency, remain unaddressed. There is a failure to recognise that interests are discursive constructions specific to time, culture and place. As Griggs and Howarth (2002, 106) indicate, this failure produces a logical fallacy, which is 'to read off preferences from observed behaviour and then use these very same preferences to account for the pattern of behaviour observed in the first place', as though a closed set. A rational choice approach ignores the unseen, the unsymbolised, the unconscious and the unknowable. It overlooks the Lacanian perspective of the split subject of conscious articulation but unconscious *jouissance*. Reliance solely on the visible leads into a trap of mis-recognition as we never know either our own unconscious desires or those of other subjects.

Lacan used the concept of Law in the widest sense to represent all shared societal norms and rules of behaviour, within society and constituent groups. In aggregate, he refers to law as one dimension of the big Other, with which we as individuals desire to conform and to please – by giving society what we think it wants, so we can belong (Sharpe 2001). The big Other, on another axis, may be defined as objectivised knowledge: 'the symbolic substance of our being, the virtual order that regulates intersubjective space' (Žižek 2001a, 254). The big Other is an impersonal set of rules and conventions, a symbolic order or 'code of accepted fictions' (Žižek 1999a, 1), such as behavioural ideals encouraged by spatial planning law, officer Codes of Conduct, ground-rules governing communicative action or consensus-formation and so on.

As developed in Chapter 3, the Lacanian subject is a person who is a network of relations of need and demand with many Others (family, colleagues, boss, etc.). We desire to be wanted so we attempt to give the big Other what (we think) it wants of us – to be 'good' – in our conduct and behaviour (Lacan 1988b). As such, it induces individuals 'to fit ... into places within the preponderant social order' (Sharpe 2001, 102). The big Other both gives internal identity and purpose through the signs and practices of the symbolic order, and is also the external source of rules and conventions that maintain the legitimacy of the belief in spatial planning, or other, prescriptive authority. Apollon (1996, 32) observes that 'the question of the foundation of the law as the legitimation of authority is a repressed question'. Moreover, such repression is necessary for the power of spatial planning to function. Apollon (1996, 32-33) continues that such power 'appeals to the sovereign use of violence, through the concern of the law that establishes that sovereignty'. The political or planning enterprise, as a management device, cannot be separated from the exercise of power against those managed, as it must guarantee both the permanence and the legitimacy of the authority's representation. The law thus becomes Other. Spatial planning rhetoric, such as that of Smart Growth, is then carried on through the enigma and power of the illusion of the big Other; the symbolic order consisting of 'chains' that bind and orient (Caudill 1997, 63). Yet spatial planning, or other laws, regulations and norms are actually constructed, over time, by human induced and directed processes and practices.

Consider, for example, the formal process of recommending for, or against, spatial planning permission in a traditional Council Committee or Commissioner report on, say, a matter of urban intensification. The statement: 'It is recommended that …' seldom stands alone until resolved into policy by the Committee or Commissioners. The recommendation is generally the concluding statement of a several page report. Most reports, after an initial description of the development application, consider the appropriateness of the development with regard to the Council's statutory requirements. These include the application's compliance with local, regional, state and/or national legislation and any spatial planning policy guidance (if appropriate). The application's appropriateness, or lack of it, is further justified and legitimised with the deployment of a selective mix of 'scientifically based facts or policy standards' (e.g. agricultural land quality of the site, open space standards, or dwelling unit density targets required, etc.); established case law or local policy precedents; normative submissions from affected parties for, or against, the application; and other selected material considerations (Hillier 2004).

Crucial to guiding the political decision-makers effectively towards a resolution supporting the recommendation are the careful choices made by the spatial planner as to which statements on formal law, regulation, precedence, fact and opinion are *selected* for inclusion in the report, as well as their careful *ordering* within the text.[8] The facts never speak for themselves. As Žižek (1994c, 11, emphasis in original) points out, the assertion that they do is 'the arch statement of ideology – the point being, precisely, that facts *never* "speak for themselves" but are always *made to speak*' through the construction of an appropriate strategic argument to achieve a desired result.

---

8   An in-depth description of the considerations of 'laws', good practice, norms, political sensitivities, judgements based on character insights of the Councillors, and so on, that go into the crafting of an effective Committee report could constitute a book of its own (see Hillier and Gunder 2005, for a more detailed exploration of this process).

Spatial planners may be regarded as gatekeepers of the law, be this the law of sustained urban sprawl, Smart Growth, or even, no growth – although, the latter sits at odds with society's embedded desires in the dominant ideology constituting capitalist social reality to consume and accumulate. Spatial planners give or deny permission to act according to their interpretation of some symbolic order or 'code of accepted fictions' (Žižek 1999d, 11), now often labelled: Smart Growth and legitimated for the spatial planners implicitly by this fictitious big Other. The 'law, predisposes social subjects to accept and obey what seems to be emanating from the big Other, from socially sedimented points of reference invested with the gloss of authority and presented as embodying and sustaining the symbolic order, organising reality itself' (Stavrakakis 2007, 169-170).

### Traversing the Fantasies of Consumer Behaviour: Beyond the Housing Market?

As Lacan (2006, 819) repeatedly asserts, the big Other, as such, does not exist, for 'there is no Other of the Other.' The big Other is an illusion, a fantasy construct. Consequently, 'from the fear of losing our anchorage in the big Other, we should pass to the terror of there being no big Other … the fact that there is nothing to fear is the most terrifying fact imaginable', for we then have to take responsibility for ourselves (Žižek 2008a, 434). It is our shared master signifiers, their contested meanings and our desire to be loved by others which construct our lifeworlds and worldviews, not some mysterious big Other. Central to Žižek's critique of ideology, then, lies 'the invitation to traverse our ideological fantasies and to confront the Real that structures our desire' (Vighi and Felder 2007, 155). The exposure that there is no big Other, but only ourselves, is one such traversing.

We suggest other necessary traverses. These include the illusions that an 'invisible guiding hand' of the capitalist market ensures a collective common good, especially when we reside in a global economy in a world of finite environmental, social and now seemingly economic carrying capacity. Or that science can provide all necessary solutions without failure or the creation of new risks, as discussed in the previous chapter. As Žižek (2008a, 421) observes:

> Capitalism only works in precise social conditions: it implies trust in the objectivised/'reified' mechanism of the market's 'invisible hand' which, as a kind of Cunning of Reason, guarantees that the competition of individual egotisms works for the common good. However, we are currently experiencing a radical change … What looms on the horizon today is the unprecedented possibility that a subjective intervention … catastrophically [disturbs] its course by triggering an ecological catastrophe, a fateful biogenetic mutation, a nuclear or similar military – social catastrophe, and so on. No longer can we rely on the safeguarding role of the limited scope of our acts.

Indeed, this is Beck's society of risk, but much more so, where fear must surely turn to trembling (after Kierkegaard 2006)! For there is no safe 'invisible hand' of the market, there is no 'big Other' watching over us, and we have already exceeded the planet's environmental carrying capacity. So what can we do? Should we carry on consuming without limit or constraint? Perhaps the threat is simply too great: we cannot comprehend it, so we do not. 'I know very well (that global warming is a threat to polar bears, arctic foxes, bees and even to humanity), but nevertheless … I cannot really believe it' (after Žižek 2008a, 445). 'One person alone cannot make any difference'. 'Others don't do anything, so why should I?' We cannot rely on either our common sense or on science, in its promises of certainty and hope of solution, both fail in their comprehension. So we can carry on and go shopping, including unconstrained house buying, or we can accept that these illusions are capitalist fantasy constructs materialising unconstrained consumption in their unquestioned belief and behaviours.

But there is finite global carrying capacity. If we are truly smart about it, we have to accept this reality. We cannot continue to enjoy economic growth, at least economic growth and progress dependent on continuing unconstrained consumption of finite resources, such as land and materially-derived commodities. Nor can we expect science to resolve any emergent problems that this consumerist behaviour creates, whether global warming, environmental degradation, or other adverse effect. There is no correct approach to continued consumption. Simply advocating Smart Growth only facilitates these fantasy constructs, by giving the impression that we are doing something 'smart' about the problems of growth and consumption. We suggest that these fantasies must be punctured, even if this means somehow confronting our *jouissance* and changing the Real underpinning our fundamental desires.

## Beyond the American Dream: The Global Dream to Consume and Enjoy?

Desire as driven and experienced in the loss or gaining of enjoyment (*jouissance*) is central to Lacanian theory (Blum and Nast 2000, 199; Žižek 1989; 1999c). *Jouissance* is what illustrates any object standing between the Real and ourselves so that the object can catch our interest and 'delude us with its seemingly compelling significance and impose its ideological imperatives upon us' (Kay 2003, 54). Contrary to the classical definition of ideology where illusion is but distorted knowledge, for Lacan, ideology is not 'an illusion masking the real state of things but that of an (unconscious) fantasy structuring our social reality itself' so that our ideological beliefs are materialised in all our social actions within society (Žižek 1989, 33).

Something catches our interest as a significant political, economic, or related master signifier of ideological belief and identification when it approaches what Lacan calls (1992) 'the Thing' which acts as a pressure point of the Real against the imaginary/symbolic registries. The pressure of the Real is sensed and expressed as an object or concept that has the effect of a transcendental illumination or incarnation of impossible *jouissance* that is utterly compelling, say, the desire for a particular solution, or even utopian ideal, that addresses a known problem, or lack, in both ourselves and perhaps the urban fabric (Žižek 1989, 132). It is sublime, accordingly it overwhelms, yet cannot be fully envisaged due to its intensity, hence Žižek's (1989) title: *The Sublime Object of Ideology*. In other words, something captures our interest and awe as a desired solution, but we cannot look too closely at the object due to its intense and overwhelming nature. Hence, we are attracted to 'solutions' like 'Smart Growth' as the answers to our known problems, even though we cannot look too closely at their prescriptions, as this might destroy the illusions that they spin and the *jouissance* that this provides.

*Jouissance* is one of the four structuring elements[9] of social discourse, or social interactions, links and relationships, where synchronic language meets diachronic speech to evoke an effect on the Other (Lacan 2007, 15). Zupančič (2006) associates Lacan's (2007) theory of the Four Discourses (discussed in the next chapter) with the Marxian theory of commodification and surplus-value via Lacan's concept of surplus-enjoyment (*plus-de-jouir*). Lacan (2007, 177) contends that surplus-value and surplus-enjoyment are historically equivalent, especially in the situation of the Master's – the king, the priest, the father's – authoritarian injunction of 'No!' in the emergent early phase of modern capitalism. In contrast to the historical authority and rationality of the Master's repressive command, late capitalism is structured under a rationality of knowledge constructed by the university and then implemented by the bureaucracy of governance. Now knowledge and technology, rather than the Master's injunction, achieve agency, expressing a logic of governmentality and expertise (including that of planning) that does not prohibit enjoyment. Rather this agency channels *jouissance* 'in ways that produces a "bio-politics" of an alienated subject that has no option, but to enjoy and be satisfied' (Hillier and Gunder 2005, 1053; McGowan 2004; Žižek 2004b; Zupančič 2006). Accordingly, 'strategies of domination will gradually shift their emphasis from the prohibition of the passions to their regulations and control, promoting certain desires … in order to suppress others … even to the point of instituting enjoyment as a social duty (in late capitalist consumer societies)' through the manipulation of *jouissance* (Stavrakakis 2007, 183).

As Žižek (2005b, 127) observes, internationally, '"today's" politics is more and more the politics of *jouissance*, concerned with the ways of soliciting or controlling and regulating *jouissance*'. For Žižek (2005, 2008a) *jouissance* is central to contemporary global governance, not in restricting behaviours, but in the imperative, the ultimate injunction to rule our lives, you will ENJOY! For consumption and enjoyment are central to the dominant imperative of global capitalism, wealth creation and accumulation. Further, the 'class-and-commodity

---

9   With the other three elements being: knowledge, desiring subjects who do not know their unconscious desires, and master signifiers that constitute each subjects' identifications, as we discuss in more detail in Chapter 6.

structure of capitalism is not just a phenomenon limited to the particular "domain" of the economy, but the structuring principle that over determines the social totality, from politics to art and religion' (Žižek in Butler *et al.* 2000, 96).

Such injunctions are exacerbated further in the current milieu of consumerist post-democracy personified by the master signifier: global capitalism. 'Post-democracy is founded on an attempt to exclude the political awareness of lack and negativity from the political domain, leading to a political order which retains the token institutions of liberal democracy but neutralizes the centrality of political antagonism' (Stavrakakis 2003, 59). In response to the dominant 'logic' of global competitiveness, technocrats and experts including spatial planners, shape, contextualise and implement public policy in the interest of the dominant hegemonic bloc. This is constructed and legitimised under the logics and knowledges of scientific narratives, with an objective to remove existing or potential urban blight, 'dis-ease' and disfunction detracting from local enjoyment and global competitiveness (McGuirk 2004). Of course, the hegemonic network, or bloc, initially shapes the debate as to what constitutes desired enjoyment and what is lacking in global competitiveness. In turn, this defines what is blighted and dysfunctional and in need of spatial planning remedy. Such ideas are predicated on a logic – or more accurately a rhetoric – that a lack of a particular defined type of enjoyment, or competitiveness, is inherently unhealthy for the aggregate social body.

> Planners, programmers, and users want solutions. For what? To make people happy. To order them to be happy. It's a strange way of interpreting happiness. The science of the urban phenomenon cannot respond to these demands without the risk of validating external restrictions imposed by ideology and power. (Lefebvre 2003, 141)

As a consequence, technocrats, in partnership with their 'dominant stakeholders', can ensure the impression of happiness for the many, while achieving the stakeholders' specific interests. As we illustrate in the following chapter, this is now very much a global issue.

# Chapter 6
# Pressures of Competitive *Globalisation*

## Introduction

Globalisation:
1. International economic integration through liberalised trade and technology that allows rapid flow of information and goods.
2. An unstoppable force already of inestimable benefit to billions of people and with the potential to enrich everyone.
3. '... the imposition on the entire world of the neo-liberal tyranny of the market and undisputed rule of the economy and of economic powers, within which the United States occupies a dominant position' (Pierre Bourdieu).
4. An ideal of shared wealth, limitless innovation, world government and no more war.
5. Another word for corporate greed, exploitation and destruction (particularly of the environment).
6. It depends on your point of view, but also on where you live.

Watson 2004, 167

In this chapter we build on material in Chapter 5 to argue the influence of competitive globalisation on city-region policy management in areas of urban spatial planning and, especially, its sub-set of economic development. In this regard, the 'fusion of competitive city-regionalism and liveability issues [i.e., Smart Growth] ... have been politically powerful' (McCann 2007, 189; Scott 2007). We introduce Lacan's (2007) theory of the four discourses and pay particular attention to the role of two discourses, that of the master's and the university/bureaucracy's, both of which, we suggest, are central to spatial planning policy formulation. In doing so, we further concentrate on the way the Lacanian conceptualisation of enjoyment – *jouissance* – is deployed by capital markets and agencies of governance to create desiring policy-makers (and not merely desiring citizens) who respond appropriately to the requirements of global capitalism.

At the metropolitan or regional policy level, relevant to implementation of Smart Growth, spatial planning policy and that of economic development 'have been closely entwined', with key economic development debates rising 'to public prominence through the [spatial] planning process' (Counsell and Haughton 2003, 225). This trend is often referred to as the 'New Regionalism' (Ward and Jonas 2004). 'Entwined' issues include, for spatial planning: the allocation of employment land, the recovery of brownfield sites, labour market housing allocation and/or quality, urban form, environmental protection, cultural and physical infrastructure, social inclusion and public amenity. All of the above tend to be associated with an overarching debate of maintaining or improving the globally competitive status of the city-region to encourage inward investment, often deploying some variation of the rubrics 'world or global city' (Albrechts 2006; Boudreau 2007; Forester 2006; Gibbs and Krueger 2007; Gunder and Searle 2007; McCann 2007; McGuirk and O'Neill 2002; McGuirk 2007; Parnell and Robinson 2006; Robinson 2008; Saito and Thornley 2003).

One of the more influential reflections on the theory of economic development practice can be attributed to the spatial planning theorist Robert Beauregard. In a book chapter in *Theories of Local Economic Development,* Beauregard (1993, 267) sought to 'expose the constitutive rules of economic development as practised in the United States' by governments and not-for-profit organisations. He did so by considering the boundaries and categories of useful ideas, conventions and knowledge then deployed in economic development practice. We suggest that these identified boundaries and categories are insightful as to what they then contained – and some fifteen years on, what they did not consider – for understanding contemporary economic development and related spatial planning policy and practice: particularly, the role of enjoyment, or *jouissance*, in this process.

After briefly reviewing Beauregard's paper, we summarise the contemporary dimensions of economic development which have emerged over the last fifteen years, perhaps best epitomised by the expressions 'global city' and the 'rise of the knowledge economy'. We will then introduce the reader to Lacan's (2007) discourse theory as a means of further considering the role that enjoyment has played in framing some of these new narratives of economic development. In particular, we consider the ways that enjoyment and desire produce a requirement for the 'expert that knows' and how this need and desire for the knowing expert underlies, and sometimes blinkers, contemporary orthodox economic development policy formation and approaches, not to mention, those of spatial planning. We conclude by asking the question: in whose interests is enjoyment actually articulated and achieved?

**Beauregard and After**

Unsurprisingly, Beauregard (1993) found that local economic development in the United States was primarily concerned with generating inward capital investment for an area to achieve efficient and timely growth, principally so that the area's prosperity did not fall behind that of other regions. Other quantitative and qualitative concerns, such as the actual quality of jobs created, appropriate democratic processes deployed and equity questions were, at best, secondary political or ideological matters of little consequence to economic development policy and practice. Beauregard (1993, 274-5) concluded that this 'partitioning of reality' by economic development resulted in 'theoretical distinctions' that focussed on 'dominant economic institutions of capital', privileged investors, included but subordinated the state, emphasised 'growth over institutional capacity' and offered 'a linear notion of time mediated by political and economic cycles'. Further, these distinctions failed to resolve 'a variety of spatial contradictions between political territoriality and economic space, local intervention and global influences, and landscapes of production and those of consumption and reproduction.'

Accordingly, economic development practitioners concentrated on marketing their local economies for inward investment. Rather than empirical data and analyses of the local economy, it was boosterist stories of investor success, both local and from other areas, that tended to dominate this 'place marketing', particularly when drawn on rhetorically to paint an image of future progress and unsurpassed achievement. Public economic development policy and practice were developed and universalised through attempting to repeat previous successful feats. Correspondingly, the standard economic development response became that of 'ideological formulations, the participating of economic development into routine activities and special projects, and a tolerance for [resultant] epistemological conflict' (Beauregard 1993, 280).

Some 15 years on, much of what Beauregard observed still rings true in both economic development policy and practice, within both the US and elsewhere in the English-speaking world. The greatest change may be in the stories of success used, their context, and how they have come about, rather than the process itself deployed. In particular, changes include: governance, rather than government-funding; facilitation of private–public partnerships; the evolution of world hierarchies of place and sectoral cross-industry clustering; the importance of talented knowledge workers, not to mention bohemian indexes (Florida 2002b), or knowledge cities (Yigitcanlar *et al.* 2008); and the rise of these new, largely academically-derived economic development policy 'success' narratives, themselves (Boland 1999, 2007). The strongest trend is the continuing rise of the importance of globalisation for both the nation state and footloose multi-national capital and the resultant emergence of a new regionalism, focussing on the importance of globally competitive city-regions with direct spatial planning implications. Such a globalising process culminates in what Žižek (1997c, 43) refers to as 'auto-colonization', where 'we are no longer dealing with the standard opposition between metropolis and colonised countries; a global company as it were cuts its umbilical cord with its mother-nation and treats its country of origins as simply another territory to be colonized.'

In this chapter we wish to add another consideration to such theorising: the now important role that enjoyment plays in underpinning these new dimensions of local economic development policy and practice.[1] This is a direct underpinning of assumptions such as an enjoyable place and 'cool' population corresponds to strong economic growth. In the chapter we will also argue, drawing on Lacan, that

---

1    There is another significant dimension to economic development that has arisen in the last 15 years: the importance of sustainable development. We do not address sustainable development here, however, but examine this particular master signifier in Chapter 8.

it is the search for enjoyment, or *jouissance*, by economic development decision-makers, policy drafters and practitioners which also underpins the acceptance of contemporary economic development initiatives. These initiatives fill in the lack – what is missing – for these decision-makers and specialists, by providing the illusion of a solution for local economic competitiveness, as exemplified by their near universal acceptance.

## Contemporary Dimensions of Competitive Globalisation

While Beauregard (1993, 274) made reference to globalisation, it was with regard to the contradictions inherent in attempting to mimic the global economy at a local scale. Globalisation, and the transformations that it has subsequently induced on the nation state and local governance, was not then a significant consideration, particularly in relation to competitiveness between city-regions. In addition, at the start of the 1990s, the importance of the 'knowledge economy' was yet to become a key concern of economic development. These considerations emerged as 'foundational concepts in economic development theory' in the second half of that decade (Amin 1999, 2002, 2004a; Boland 2007, 1022; Brenner 1999; Duffy 1995; Jessop 1999, 2000; Lever and Turok 1999). In particular, competitive advantage and the fostering and development of competitive industrial knowledge clusters have become important economic development tools at the regional and local levels, with Michael Porter's (1995, 2000, 2003) work being especially influential in this area (Amin 2002; Turok 2004). The use of rankings of places/cities with regard to their 'competitiveness' (Huggins 2003; Malecki 2007), or as 'world cities' (Beaverstock *et al.* 1999), together with rankings of local quality of life (McCann 2004, 2007), has also gained importance. Such fairly spurious rankings are often criticised as comparing 'chalk with cheese'. Cortright and Mayer (2004, 36) observe, economic development-related rankings 'conceal more than reveal when they conflate a disparate set of industrial sectors into a single amorphous category'.

A key component of the materialised 'competitiveness', often concomitant with quality of life, has been the knowledge base, or knowledge clusters, of an area and the ability of this 'knowledge economy' to induce innovation, creativity, and economic expansion; not to mention, resurgence for areas in decline (Florida 2002c; Landry 2006; Porter 2003; Storper and Manville 2006). It is now argued that economic development 'is driven by cities' ability to attract creative people '… which will, in turn, attract investment and stimulate economic growth' (Boland 2007, 1022).

Richard Florida (2002a, 743, 2002c, 2004) suggests that local innovation, entrepreneurialism and economic growth are dependant on the residence of talented knowledge workers – human capital – which in turn is 'associated with regional openness to creativity and diversity.' Beyond traditional employment and investment opportunities, the quality of life, including amenity, lifestyle and range of leisure opportunities available are necessary elements for city-regions to attract both talented people and businesses. Florida (2002a, 744) asserts that 'talent is a key intermediate variable in attracting high-technology industries and generating higher regional incomes.' Like firms, regions also compete with each other to attract largely foot-loose highly-skilled talent. Key to maximising this success for Florida is the provision of a perceived high quality of life and the city-region's willingness to accommodate personal diversities in value-orientation, lifestyle, nationality and ethnicity. Hence, one emergent dimension of contemporary spatial planning globally is the provision of 'liveable cities', meeting the aspirations of inward investors, not just those of traditional financial capital, but, crucially, those with human capital in terms of talent and creativity (Douglass 2002; Friedmann 2005; McCann 2004).

As Florida (2002a, 754) states: 'talent does not simply show up in a region; rather, certain regional factors appear to play a role in creating an environment or habitat that can attract and retain talent, or human capital.' Rather than employers, or companies, being the prime organising units in a local economy, it is the quality, amenity and diversity of a city-region's urban spaces that now fulfil this role of attractor. Florida (2002c) calls for city-regions to have strategies, not only for business, but also for people. He goes further to suggest, that one dimension of this desirable location is predicated on a base of 'bohemian' enjoyment seekers. Drawing on empirical evidence, Florida (2002b, 68) notes that 'places that have a high concentration of bohemians (or alternatively a high concentration of gay people) reflect an underlying set of conditions or milieu which is open and attractive to talented and creative people of all sorts (including those who work in high-technology industries) and thus create a place-based environment that is conducive to the birth, growth and development of new and high technology industries.'

Boland (2007), as well as Storper and Manville (2006), expose the naïveté of some politicians and local policy makers who blindly accept, without fully understanding, these recent narratives as representing the only means for achievement of economic development success. Boland (2007, 1023) identifies the impacts which Michael Porter and Richard Florida especially have had on economic development. Theirs are important global voices, particularly with regard to the importance of creativity, the clustering of talent and the competitive advantage that knowledge is supposed to provide in contemporary economic success. Boland (2007, 1032) argues that these, and other academic expert voices, have played an important role in legitimising and giving weight to a contemporary local economic development 'policy bias towards city-regionalism, competitiveness, the knowledge economy and place marketing'; so much so that they have resulted in 'a situation where cities adopt the *same* economic development toolkit'. Rather than local innovation in development of economic development policy that identifies and optimises local competitive differences, the contemporary uniformity of such 'cloned' or 'karaoke' policy often results in the very lack of competitive innovation and originality.

Compounding this lack of focus on site-specific uniqueness and creativity, local officials and politicians often do not actually understand the implications of their chosen policies, the links of causality, or lack of them, which underlie specific ideas. As Storper and Manville (2006, 1252) observe: 'correlation is not causation and, while Florida is doubtless aware of the difference, it seems at least that some of the policy-makers who read his books are not.'

Further compounding this near-universal adoption of economic development orthodoxy, just as Beauregard (1993) observed 15 years before, economic development is still largely predicated on place marketing for inward investment of capital. However, this is a capital expanded to include human as well as financial investment. Inward investment is still largely achieved via stories of success and projections of the 'right' image, or 'brand', that attempts to differentiate a particular city from the rest, all predicated on the dominant ideas, or orthodoxy, of what turns a local economy into a successful 'competitive global or world city'. Notwithstanding 'the aspirations to create local uniqueness, place marketing frequently results in' an even greater promotion of a universal sameness that is almost inter-changeable between various diverse cities (Boland 2007, 1028).[2]

### Time for Lacanian and Žižekian Theory

In the rest of this chapter we suggest that a desire for, and seeking of, satisfaction and enjoyment – i.e., *jouissance* – underlies the adoption of many of the dominant economic development and related spatial planning narratives, policies and practices associated with the rubric of 'global competition'. This Lacanian approach includes a basic tenet that the symbolic, or language, always fails in attempting complete and comprehensive articulation and this, in turn, frustrates the actor's enjoyment (Lacan 2006, 2007). Not everything can be said – something is always lacking – and there is always an empty remainder, a void not capable of capture by language. Moreover, driven by a desire for the satisfaction of fulfilment and completeness, actors then use fantasy construction, rationalisation and the deployment of empty words – master signifiers without explicit meaning – to 'paper over' and obscure, but also to some degree symbolise 'around', this frustrating lack or unsymbolisable remainder[3] (Žižek 1989, 1997a, 2008a).

Of specific relevance to this chapter's focus on the economic development dimension of spatial planning is Jones and Spicer's (2005) deployment of Žižekian and Lacanian theory, especially that of the master signifier, to explain the failure

---

2   Which might be argued to reinforce arguments for Beck's (2006b) Cosmopolitan vision of a progressively uniform global economy which accommodates cultural difference and which is dominated by blocks of largely interchangeable city-states/regions.

3   At best, each of these empty signifiers is used to 'palpate what it cannot conceive; it gestures at what it cannot grasp', for each word, at best, can only cover over what is lacking in symbolic representation (May 2005, 82).

of 'entrepreneurial studies' in the business organisational literature to come to terms with and succinctly define itself. Here 'the entrepreneur is a marker of this lack; the entrepreneur is indefinable, and necessarily so; the entrepreneur is an "absent centre"' (Jones and Spicer 2005, 236). The empty and undefinable word 'entrepreneur' papers over this one example of the void in the symbolic. Rather, than narratives of entrepreneurship being stable and coherent representations focused on a universally agreed core meaning, they are composed of 'paradoxical, incomplete and worm-ridden symbolic' structures that posit 'an impossible and indeed incomprehensible object at its centre' (Jones and Spicer 2005, 236). This is a void of understanding and meaning – signification – that all actors with an interest in entrepreneurship strive to seek for and comprehensively fill, in order that they can understand this valued sublime 'concept' of explicit commercial and economic development success. They do so to gain the multiple levels of pleasure and enjoyment that having access to the 'secret' of entrepreneurship would provide. However, they continuously fail in their search, including even failure to identify what is lacking – what remains outside of articulation – about this core concept of economic development success.

Drawing on this understanding of lack, rationalisation and fantasy construction, Žižek argues that the 'more we pride ourselves on being "free thinkers in a free world"', 'the more we blindly submit ourselves to the merciless superegoic command ("Enjoy!") which binds us to the logic of the market' (Vighi and Feldner 2007, 146). Particularly poignant for economic development, is that this desire for satisfaction and enjoyment resides at multiple levels. Firstly, the enjoyment provided by the desired ideal 'guaranteed' to yield economic development success and, secondly, the wider desire to enjoy as expressed and materialised in our prevalent consumer habits. Both conflate each other under the rubric of economic development to create an environment constituting our materialised social reality, which is largely reflective of our collective desires – a desire for fulfilment, in turn synonymous with enjoyment. This loss or surplus of enjoyment – *jouissance* in the Lacanian lexicon – is one of four elements central to Lacan's (2007) Theory of the Four Discourses.

## The Four Discourses

> Symbolic exchange is what links human beings to each other, that is, it is speech. (Lacan 1988a, 142)

> What I seek in speech is the response of the other. (Lacan 2006, 247)

Drawing on the structuralist, anthropological and linguistic traditions of authors including Saussure, Levi-Strauss and Jakobson, together with the metapsychology of Freud, Jacques Lacan (2007) proposed a theory of discourse which sought to identify and analyse the underlying elements within language that permit both culturally formative and transformative actions (Sturrock 2003). This is Lacan's (2007) theory of the four fundamental structures of discourse: the discourses of the master, the university/bureaucracy, the hysteric and the analyst. Each represents, respectively, four fundamental social effects:

1. governing/commanding,
2. educating/indoctrinating,
3. desiring/protesting,
4. analyzing/transforming/revolutionizing. (Bracher 1993, 53)

We suggest that the four discourses can be useful in providing an understanding of planning debate, authority/expertise, and the *realrationalität* of planning process.[4]

Lacan's theory is based on four elements: the master signifier ($S_1$); the network of signifiers that is knowledge and constitutes the often contested meaning(s) of a master signifier ($S_2$); the product that is both excluded and produced by knowledge as loss or surplus of *jouissance* (*a*); and the split subject (\$), split between unconscious and conscious existence (Bracher 1993, 53). In each of Lacan's four discourses, these elements – $S_1 \to S_2 \to a \to \$$ – rotate through different placements in the following structural relationship, or model of discourse, illustrated in Figure 6.1 and explained in the subsequent text.

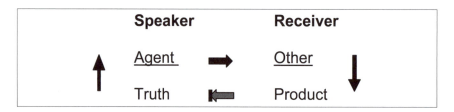

**Figure 6.1    Lacan's model of discourse**

The positions on the left of Figure 6.1 visualise the active factors of the speaking subject; the Agent driven to speak by his/her desire as Truth. The positions on the right of the figure visualise the active factors of the hearing subject. The observable, or conscious, elements of the Agent and the Other in the speech act are located on the top, above the bars. The bottom or lower positions are those of 'the covert, latent, implicit, or repressed factor'; the internal factors at the unconscious level of the split subject within each actor that drives the speech act or is created by it (Bracher 1993, 54). The position of agency and dominance is located in the top left. It is that of the speaking Agent and is the overtly active component of the

---

4   Lacan's discourse theory differs from that of Foucault, because it is fundamentally premised on an understanding of desire, rather than of power (Fink 1998).

discourse. The internal element of 'Truth' driving the dominant Agent exists in the concealed place on the bottom left; 'the factor that supports, grounds, underwrites, and give rise to the dominate factor, or constitutes the condition of its possibility' (Bracher 1993, 54).

The 'Other' on the top right is engaged by the factor within the receiver called into acceptance by the interpellation of the communication. It is what makes you turn your head when someone calls out 'hey you' and you somehow know that you are the 'you' being hailed. Knowledge 'passes easily when the subject adopts a passive attitude towards discourse and empties itself of any existing knowledge that might interfere with the new knowledge taken in' (Alcorn 1994, 43). This is facilitated by 'positive transference: one learns where one loves' (Verhaeghe 2001, 44). But this has a cost. By permitting themselves to accept the message, receivers, consciously or not, internally create the Product at the bottom right of the figure – a Product that generally has little to do with the Truth of the Agent initiating the discourse (Verhaeghe 2001). This Product should then induce the receiver to respond to the Agent of the speech act, i.e., to feed back to the speaker seeking more of the driving force of Truth underlying the original message. But this feedback is largely blocked (illustrated by the stopped grey arrow), as is the original communication to a much less extent, because the receiver has existing beliefs that induce misconceptions, and language inherently lacks completeness for perfect communication. For if there were perfect communication, we would never need to repeat ourselves (Lacan 2006)!

In speech, every human subject deploys all four discourses, but, fundamentally, each type of discourse always 'starts with an *agent* driven by a *truth* to speak to *another* with as a result a *product*' (Verhaeghe 2001, 41). It is never possible, however, for the speaker to transmit a complete message. Something is always lacking. The Agent's speech is always driven by desire constituted as Truth. Yet this is a truth that 'cannot be completely verbalised, with the result that the agent cannot transmit his [*sic*] desire to the other; hence a perfect communications with words is logically impossible' (Verhaeghe 2001, 23).[5] 'Both the impossibility and incapability are the effect of the radical heteronomy of the truth: part of it lies beyond the signifier and belongs to the realm of' the Real and *jouissance* – outside of language and the symbolic (Verhaeghe 2001, 41). For example, this might be a repressed trauma from childhood that makes the Agent dislike a particular colour, sound or similar largely irrelevant attribute of an object, or activity; so that the agent opposes an action concerning the object, without really understanding why they feel that way.

---

5   Which, if a valid assumption, demonstrates the impossibility of Habermas's ideal of undistorted speech, which underlies communicative rationality and the planning theories derived from it (Hillier 2003a).

*The Master's Discourse*

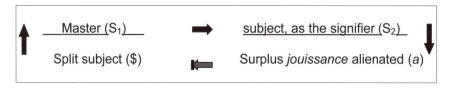

**Figure 6.2    The Master's Discourse**

The Master's Discourse demands to be the first one discussed, and this is illustrated in Figure 6.2. The masters are the unquestionable authorities. They seek no justification for this imperative, dogmatic, power: it just is. Masters are not concerned with knowledge in itself, rather with certainty. 'I AM = I AM KNOWLEDGE = I AM THE ONE WHO KNOWS' (Ragland 1996, 134). The masters are satisfied provided everything works and their authority is believed and maintained. The authoritarian masters command that hearing subjects learn and organise their knowledge ($S_2$) in a way that supports the masters' own beliefs and values ($S_1$s) whilst repressing and restricting contrary knowledges, desires and fantasies at odds with the ($S_1$s) of those the masters (Bracher 1994, 121). For this to work 'the other has to sustain the master in his [*sic*] illusion that he is the one with the knowledge … the pupils [or residents, citizens, etc.] make the master' (Verhaeghe 2001, 27). The masters' weakness is that they are unconscious of their own desires, the actual reasons for asserting their master signifiers ($S_1$s), for the hidden Truth of the discourse is that of the divided subject.

The Master's Discourse directly attempts to mould the receiver's ego-ideal, as 'one reads or hears such a discourse, one is forced, in order to understand the message, to accord full explanatory power and/or moral authority to the proffered master signifiers [$S_1$s] and to refer all other signifiers [$S_2$] (objects, concepts, or issues) back to the master signifiers' (Bracher 1993, 64). Globalisation, sustainability, Smart Growth, economic competitiveness or entrepreneurship (or any alternative $S_1$) are important 'truths' because the master says they are and the speaker is the master who knows! Those governed in obeying the master forgo *jouissance* as the loss of enjoyment or frustration, not to mention loss of spontaneity and creativity, produced by their obedience and conformity to the demands of the master.

Regrettably, as desirous as the ability to assert total authority might be for some spatial planning or economic development practitioners, the Master's Discourse can seldom belong to the enlightened practitioner. 'The [professional expert] is by no means in the position of the Master: knowledge ($S_2$) and the Master ($S_1$) are mutually exclusive' (Salecl 1994, 168). In contrast to the master's orders, often made by politically elected officials, the spatial planning or economic development practitioner (at least under contemporary Western capitalist political economy and governance) are rarely in positions to command, because 'scientific' knowledge must provide explanation and justification for their assertions from legitimising epistemic evidence. Practitioners, or even most planning academics,[6] are seldom the Agents of the Master's Discourse, rather both are more often the Agent of the University/Bureaucracy's Discourse, where the Master's assertion of $(S_1)$ 'lies' as the Agent's own Truth and the practitioner or teacher's interpellations of knowledge $(S_2)$ shape the governed, or the student, as an alienated subject within the symbolic order.

*The University/Bureaucracy's Discourse*

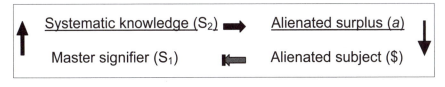

**Figure 6.3    The University/Bureaucracy's Discourse**

In Figure 6.3 the speech act produces the alienated subject ($) of the university educational system and contemporary governance (Bracher 1993). For example, in attending planning school, students place themselves in a spatial planning or economic development (if taught in a planning programme) knowledge system $(S_2)$ that constitutes the professional body of knowledge for the discipline. By doing so, the knowledge-receiving students are eventually transformed into spatial planners and economic development practitioners. Yet, as students gradually acquire the identifications of professional practitioners they become alienated from their own original desires and beliefs and are eventually obligated to reproduce, reinforce and apply their received knowledge and practices on the public – those who are governed. Under this discourse, planning educators seek to produce new practitioners who are inspired Agents of the academics' own master signifiers and supporting knowledges. The more systematic knowledge is received, the more students are transformed into 'normalised' spatial planners, symbolically regulated by these norms, knowledges and practices; whilst at the same time they become progressively more alienated from their own unconscious desires and any passionate response, or challenge, to the received 'wisdom' (Verhaeghe 2001, 43; Žižek 1998a, 107).

Fink (1995, 132) observes that there is 'a sort of historical movement from the Master's Discourse to the University Discourse, the University Discourse providing a sort of legitimation or rationalization of the master's will.' Educators can

---

6   Unless they are *professing* a 'truth', e.g., you must be sustainable, you must be equitable, you must believe in economic growth!

seldom, if ever, compel the student to believe. They can only represent the master signifier's ($S_1$) truth as its Agent by asserting the $S_1$'s sub-codes of knowledges, norms and beliefs ($S_2$). 'The teacher is therefore polite in the relationship not to the pupil but to the knowledge of the Other, to which he [*sic*] is a responsible subject' as 'a representative of *socially recognised* knowledge' that 'forms the very frame structuring our perception of reality' (Salecl 1994, 168).

Educating and/or governing Agents in this discourse are driven by the Truth of their belief in their master signifiers. These are the $S_1$s that guarantee knowledge – the anchoring points under which the knowledge sets reside. Initially, Lacan argued that the University/Bureaucracy's Discourse was that of scientific research, where 'knowledge' in its own right is the master signifier ($S_1$) (Fink 1995). Lacan's later thinking shifted to consider that this discourse uses systemic knowledge to justify any master signifier. For instance, the political leader, or the economic development guru, (either acting as master) says that we must become a world class city, so, this is why we must and how we will achieve this imperative! In this regard, the University/Bureaucracy's Discourse entails the use of systemic knowledge for rationalisation by the Agent of the speech act. Here the receiving subject is interpellated by any knowledge, or assertion, attempting to justify the master signifier ($S_1$) of the dominant Agent of the discourse. This might not be only that of the academic or bureaucrat, but also the Agent of the dominant societal perception of social reality itself, the very ideologies that construct our social reality. This discourse suggests that objectivity, 'the classical requirement of science … [is] mere illusion' (Verhaeghe 2001, 31). As a consequence, Lacan's latter 'view of genuine scientific activity correspond[s] to the structure of the hysteric's discourse' (Fink 1998, 34). The Hysteric's Discourse will be discussed in the next chapter, as will that of the analyst's, but first, we deploy the discourses of the master and of the university/bureaucracy to pursue an understanding of the role of enjoyment under competitive globalisation.

### Enjoyment Provided by the One's Who Know

Desire as driven and experienced in the loss or gaining of *jouissance* is central to our social reality (Žižek 1994a, 1999c, 2006a). Just as a seductive (or well advertised) consumer item makes us feel incomplete unless we buy it, this desire for enjoyment also allows an abstract idea, such as Florida's (2002b) bohemian index, or the search for the secret of entrepreneurship, or the concept of 'Smart Growth', to catch our interest and fascinate. Any idea can 'delude us with its seemingly compelling significance and impose its ideological imperatives upon us' to believe in and identify with that idea (Kay 2003, 54). If only we do the following – whatever that might be – we can live in a world-class city of talented knowledge workers; or know the 'secret' of becoming a successful, hence rich, entrepreneur; or continue to grow rich and accumulate smartly, forever.

Contrary to the classical definition of ideology where illusion is but distorted knowledge, Žižekian ideology is not 'an illusion masking the real state of things but that of an (unconscious) fantasy(s) structuring our social reality itself' so that our ideological beliefs are materialised in undertaking, or doing, our social actions within society (Žižek 1989, 33). We act in a certain way because we think that is what the 'big Other' expects of us. It is what we should *do*, to be loved and wanted, to be desirable to the Other. Further, these social fantasies of desire fill out the voids of our deficient social structures by covering over any incompleteness, or dis-ease and dis-satisfaction, through the provision of giving us opportunities to identify with a fulfilling illusion – our local economy will be successful, because our bohemian index is rising, or whatever – hence giving us a sense of security and enjoyment. In Lacan's (2007, 15) and Žižek's (1994a, 2002a, 2006a) theorising, *jouissance* is one of the key elements of the social bond constituting society and the social interactions, the links and relationships that society constructs where language evokes an effect on all others, which, aggregated, constitute society. Indeed, for Žižek (2006a, 309) politics and public policy, including economic development and spatial planning, are directly and primarily 'concerned with ways of soliciting, or controlling and regulating' this enjoyment.

A concept that has the effect of a transcendental illumination or incarnation of impossible potential enjoyment in terms of a significant economic development or spatial planning related idea (often predicated on another ideological belief) may well catch policy-drafters' and decision-makers' interest. Such stories of 'success' can be identified with; therefore, they *must* be identified with. They are compelling, overwhelming; hence, they become Žižek's (1989) sublime object that calls out to us to be a new but elusive truth that somehow induces in us some promise for ideological transcendence, even if it seldom, if ever, delivers.

For each political decision-maker or policy advisor, in Lacanian thought, 'there is an *ideal economy*, an economy in which needs *would* be met, desires *would* be satisfied, proper human and social development *would be* achieved[:] *If only* …' (Byrne and Healy 2006, 243). Therefore, for this ideological belief to function, there has to be *someone else who knows*, who can deliver this 'truth' via the Master's Discourse and hence 'embody the deeper meaning' to this idea or ideal system (Sharpe 2006, 111). With regard to economic development, especially, it is the policy gurus, the Porter(s) and Florida(s), the intellectual *Masters*, the *ones who know* the desired answer, who provide what is missing and fill in this lack that will make the ideal of success come true.

Or at least that is the hope, for, at best, the fantasy that the guru, the master, has the answer which 'protects us from the anxiety of the lack, and it gives a name to – it symbolizes – the thing that blocks us from getting what we desire' (Byrne and Healy 2006, 243). In Jones and Spicer's (2005) analysis, the empty 'thing' that business practitioners try to grapple with is the essence of entrepreneurship. In a similar vein, the crucial aspect for the desiring agent seeking the essence, or secret, of successful economic development, spatial planning (or any field of complex endeavour) is that it 'functions through the constitution of this lack (of knowledge, social capital, resources, etc.), which as a void gives body to all sorts of fads, theories and rationalisations' (De Vries 2007, 37). The 'ones who know' provide the utopian fantasies that will offer resolution (Stavrakakis 2007, 261). The desire for economic development, or spatial planning, to be successful thus continues, even in its continued failure to achieve that desired success.

### The Reification of Enjoyment: You Will Enjoy, Not Transgress!

As we noted in the last chapter, Zupančič (2006, 169) associates the Marxian theory of commodification and surplus-value with Lacan's (and consequently Žižek's) theorisation of enjoyment through the Lacanian concept of surplus-enjoyment (*plus-de-jouir*). Lacan (2007, 177) contends that the surplus-value of capital and surplus-enjoyment are historically equivalent, especially in the situation of the traditional Master's authoritarian, religious or secular, injunction of 'No!'. Marshall (2007, 110) suggests that, since the 1980s, corresponding to a shift from government to governance, the decline of the welfare state and the rise of globalisation, we have progressively moved from societies of capitalist prohibition to a present-day global society of commanded enjoyment, where literally nearly anything is possible due to technology 'and the prevalence of the market in all facets of social life'. Catlaw (2006, 270) observes that for public policy administrators the 'challenge, in light of contemporary circumstances, is not to find new ways of inhibiting enjoyment, as neotraditional views would advocate, but of finding ways of making enjoyment possible'.

Global '[c]apitalism is instated in conjunction with the university [/bureaucracy's] discourse, its twin and double' (Dolar 2006, 136). The voice of the master of unquestioned authority is still necessary, but only as the underlying truth or foundation of the University or Bureaucratic Discourses deployed (Boucher 2006, 275), particularly, in the production of knowledges about how to maximise enjoyment. This then shapes the important role of the favoured policy gurus in providing the overarching 'truth' to economic development and spatial planning. What is crucial under the capitalist dimensions of globalisation is 'a new sort of command ... involving the imperative to know rather than to obey' (McGowan 2008, 57).

In contrast to the historical authority and rationality of the state's repressive command to not enjoy because it gets in the way of doing productive work, late capitalism is structured under a rationality of 'scientific' knowledge deployed by the state and local government, or perhaps the governance of a public-private partnership, through the bureaucratic provision of policy initiatives. These are policy initiatives that in their 'judgements, evaluations, summarise, and assessments' 'suture the subject' in the 'bureaucratic colonization of normative space' (Boucher 2006, 286), representing the development of Lacan's (2007) University or Bureaucratic Discourse. Today, knowledge and science – or at least the appearance thereof – is necessary to rationalise and legitimise the agency of policy action, rather than the

State or other authority's arbitrary injunction giving permission and negation. This is achieved by expressing a logic of efficiency and expertise (including that of economic development and spatial planning) that does not prohibit enjoyment, but rather channels enjoyment in ways that produce a 'bio-politics' of dissatisfied subjects that have no option, but to seek enjoyment and satisfaction (Marshall 2007; McGowan 2004, 2008; Žižek 2004b; Zupančič 2006).

Individuals 'no longer submit to an exploitative labour market because of some imposed belief – "work harder and your reward will be in heaven" – but because there is no belief, nothing other than the axiom of capital – the desire to buy more, work more, earn more, have more' (Colebrook 2006, 86). That is the imperative to have more enjoyment, more happiness, because it is good for you, your community and the nation! Florida (2002b, 57) argues (drawing on Frank 1997) that successful clustering of creative economic activity is dependent on a blending of business and bohemian cultures constituting 'enjoyment and self-actualization over work' to create a state where 'capitalism has absorbed and integrated what used to be thought of as alternative or cool' into an 'into mainstream economic activity.'

At the beginning of the 21st century, 'the power of capitalism does not lie in its repression of our pleasures, but in its coding of all those pleasures into money *and* in producing a surplus value of that code: for we are now enslaved, not by being *denied what we want*, but of being manufactured *to want*' (Colebrook 2006, 133 – emphasis in original). As we observed in the previous chapter, the worst possible 'transgression' occurs when one negates consumption in attempting 'to pursue a life of moderation' (Žižek 2004b, 174).

## Globalised Happiness Whether You Want It or Not

Slavoj Žižek claims that, 'a nation *exists* only as long as its specific *enjoyment* continues to be materialised in a set of social practices and submitted through national myths that structure these practices' (Žižek 1993, 202). Whilst winning cycling or swimming Olympic medals might bring a nation state and its enjoyment into existence, Žižek argues that the barely challenged international narrative of global capitalisation and the fantasies it now induces also structure the enjoyment of nation states and their many city-regions (Stavrakakis 2003, 63; Žižek 2004b, 61). These are attainments of enjoyment without goal or direction, apart from simply pride and attainment of material pleasure as measured by national GDP.[7] As Žižek (1997c, 45) observes, the 'true horror does not reside in the particular content hidden beneath the universality of global Capital, but rather the fact that Capital is effectively an anonymous global machine blindly running its course'. As we noted in the previous chapter, the invisible hand of the market fails in provision of a 'public good' if, at a global scale the effects of capital are sufficient to damage the world, if not ultimately to destroy it.

---

7   Gross Domestic Product.

Even the ruling British Labour government,[8] in contrast to its more socialist origins, has placed 'economic globalisation' as 'the most significant factor in shaping Labour Party thinking since the early 1990s' (Allmendinger 2003, 326). In New Zealand, Australia, Canada, the UK and, no doubt, the US, key national, as well as local, economic development policies and supporting spatial planning policies seek to ensure that 'our' diverse city-regions are globally competitive (Gunder 2006). As McGowan (2004, 193) observes:

> we trust fully in the staying power of global capitalism ... The universe of global capitalism is, or so we think, here to stay, and we best not do anything to risk our status within it. Hence, we pledge our allegiance to it, and we put our trust in it. This is the fundamental mode of contemporary obedience to authority ... Global capitalism seems an unsurpassable horizon ... because we don't want to lose it – and the imaginary satisfaction that it provides.

Unfortunately, illusion hides behind this global fantasy of capital where 'the basic feature of' this dominant cultural imperative 'no longer operates on the level of ideals and identifications, but directly on the level of regulating *jouissance*' (Žižek 2004b, 113). This is a global capitalism, indeed, where surplus-value is synonymous with surplus-enjoyment, supporting the injunction: 'you must enjoy!' In this light, the role of public policies, including those of economic development and spatial planning, is to facilitate *jouissance* by providing the 'correct' space – healthy, vibrant, competitive, fit and attractive – where enjoyment, especially for talented, foot-loose, knowledge workers, can be effectively materialised and maximised under the imperative of global capitalism. The 'need' to attract and retain play-full bohemian and talented knowledge workers is central to this imperative of enjoyment. It is mandatory to plan spatially for this key crucial community of creative talent, regardless of other cost, if one wants one's city-region to become and to remain globally competitive!

Consequently, local public governance and the policies of economic development and spatial planning which facilitate this necessary environment of vibrancy and 'fun' are 'nothing more than an ideology that claims to be either "art" or "technology" or "science," depending on the context' (Lefebvre 2003, 159). This ideology gives the illusion of rational scientific practice in the public interest. It does so by drawing on the 'truths' of the academic masters of success – the gurus who know – the Porter(s) and Florida(s) and their related ilk.[9] However, this is an ideology that obscures, by selectively deploying only selected 'facts' and also by leaving things unsaid. Above all, it gives the appearance of promoting societal efficiency predicated on the concept of satisfaction and enjoyment. However, such 'efficiency' is effectively a satisfaction of vested interests, the wealthy and the talented – those who can inwardly invest financial or human

---

8   Still at time of writing (January 2009).

9   A cynical reader might suggest to us, as authors, that Slavoj Žižek performs as 'one who knows'.

capital (i.e., themselves) – whose needs must be understandably catered for and accommodated, through spatial planning policies such as 'new urbanism' and 'Smart Growth' regardless of the cost to everyone else and to the environment. Those talented in other ways – at performing more manual 'blue-collar' tasks in primary, secondary, or personal service sectors – are thus regarded as the 'less talented', more 'knowledge-challenged' even though they are likely to constitute the majority of any workforce in a city-region. Their needs, compared to those of 'talented' knowledge workers, are rendered less important. This disenfranchised majority, moreover, are also the workers who are likely to be less mobile and less able to move geographically for jobs than the foot-loose talented knowledge workers who the economic development-led planning policies sought to attract in the first place (Bunce 2004; Gunder 2006; Gunder and Searle 2007; McGuirk 2004, 2007; Raco 2005b).

In the economic development axis of spatial planning, social reality is indeed divided! Just as Beauregard (1993) suggested over fifteen years ago, economic development-derived policy continues to partition reality. The only interests continually served by economic development are those capable of the provision of inward capital investment: originally financial capital, but now also human capital.

In response to the dominant 'logic' of global competitiveness, academic technocratic experts and their bureaucratic disciples, including economic development and spatial planning practitioners (perhaps with some public-private governance 'input' or 'leadership') shape, contextualise and implement public policy mainly in the interests of this dominant hegemonic bloc. This occurs in places like Austin, Texas; Sydney, Australia; Toronto, Canada; South East England: in fact, almost anywhere. Further, this is constructed under the logics and knowledges of Lacan's Discourse of the University/Bureaucracy, with an objective to remove existing or potential economic and spatial blight, 'dis-ease' and disfunction detracting from local enjoyment – at least for the talented – and from global competitiveness (Gunder 2005c; McCann 2007; McGuirk 2004; Raco 2005b) – for who can argue against such crucial need!

The hegemonic network, or bloc, initially shapes the debates and draws on appropriate policies of desired success, such as the needs of bohemians, knowledge clusters, or talented knowledge workers, as to what constitutes *their* desired enjoyment (cobblestones, chrome and cappuccinos at sidewalk cafes) and what is therefore lacking in local competitiveness. In turn, this defines what is blighted and dysfunctional and in need of economic, spatial planning, or other, remedy. Such an argument is predicated on a logic, or more accurately a rhetoric, that a lack of a particular defined type of enjoyment, or competitiveness (for surely they are one and the same) is inherently unhealthy for the aggregate social body. Lack and its resolution are generally presented as technical, rather than political issues. Consequently, technocrats in partnership with their 'dominant stakeholders' can ensure the impression of rationally seeking to produce happiness for the many, whilst, of course, achieving their stakeholders' specific interests (Gunder and Hillier 2007a, 469).

The current 'post-democratic' milieu facilitates the above through avoidance of critical policy debate challenging favoured orthodox positions and policy approaches. Consideration of policy deficiencies, or alternative 'solutions', are eradicated from political debate so that while 'token institutions of liberal democracy' are retained, conflicting positions and arguments are negated (Stavrakakis 2003, 59). Consequently, 'the safe names in the field who feed the policy orthodoxy are repeatedly used, or their work drawn upon, by different stakeholders, while more critical voices are silenced by their inability to shape policy debates' (Boland 2007, 1032). The economic development or spatial planning policy analyst thus continues to partition reality ideologically by deploying only the orthodox 'successful' or 'best practice' economic development or spatial planning responses. This further maintains the dominant, or hegemonic, *status quo* while providing 'a cover and shield against critical thought by acting in the manner of a "buffer" isolating the political field from any research that is independent and radical in its conception as in its implications for public policy' (Wacquant 2004, 99). At the same time, adoption of the hegemonic orthodoxy tends to generate similar policy responses for every competing local area or city-region, largely resulting in a zero-sum game (Blair and Kumar 1997).

In the race for global competitiveness, city-region authorities continue to prioritise economic development and supporting spatial planning policies. They maintain the dominant *status quo* by appearing to increase the happiness of material wellbeing for all. The state, its local government and its governance structures, must be seen to be doing something to justify their existence. In addition, and perhaps more importantly, public sector actions, which give the appearance of doing something to improve the local economy and the city-region's amenity, actually address the (primal) desire of most people in society for at least the illusion of a safe and assured happy future of security and prosperity. Even if practitioners can only deliver this as a fantasy-scenario by providing the potential of a limited material increase in happiness for some, even when this may not really be what is actually wanted, this type of response is more acceptable to politicians and the voting public than is the truth that to sate the wants and desires of everyone is an impossibility (Gunder 2003a, 2003b).

## The Beginning Continues ...

Beauregard (1993, 280) concluded his perspective on economic development theory with the statement that his work was 'only a beginning' 'to raise consciousness about the constitutive rules of economic development to facilitate a more critical understanding.' Over 15 years later, we have continued Beauregard's 'beginning' by noting the new emergent narratives of success deployed in contemporary economic development and in wider spatial planning. In particular, we have drawn on the work of Lacan and Žižek to illustrate the important roles that human *jouissance* and desire play in economic development and spatial planning narratives under competitive globalisation, as well as introducing Lacan's discourse theory, particularly the master's and the University/Bureaucracy's Discourses.

Enjoyment underlies human capitalist consumer behaviour. But more fundamentally, the notion of enjoyment – and especially the Lacanian interpretation of it as *jouissance* – explains some of the dimensions as to why local policy decision makers identify with and deploy 'trusted and (perceived) true' dominant narratives of economic development and spatial planning success. They do so even when near-universal application of the same orthodox narratives may result in a 'zero-sum' gain for all concerned, as each local city-region deploys virtually the same economic development or spatial planning policies in order to gain 'unique' competitive advantage over the others.

Fifteen years on from Beauregard's work, economic development practice appears to continue as 'business as usual', perhaps with some newer stories and strategies of success, provided by the 'academic masters who know'. The core practice of seeking inward investment for economic development has perhaps been expanded to include human capital in addition to that of financial capital, with concomitant significant impacts on the practices of spatial planning. However, the partitioning of reality continues. Economic development practitioners and their spatial planning facilitators, policy analysts and their political decision makers largely continue to have regard to only what they desire: successful inward investment. It is their hegemonic choices, driven by their desires for satisfaction and enjoyment, which materialise our local economic development and spatial policy responses, as well as many other dimensions of our social and spatial realities. This, in turn, bestows on those involved with the creation of local economic development-led spatial planning policy and practices, a perceived sense of security and enjoyment that they are doing the 'right' thing. It is what everyone else is doing, so it must be the correct thing to do in our globally competitive world!

# Chapter 7
# *Multiculturalism*:
# The Other Always Steals My Enjoyment

## Introduction

> In order to imagine the ultimately unrepresentable space, life and languages of the city, to make them legible, we translate them into narratives. The way we narrate the city become constitutive of urban reality, affecting the choices we make, the ways we then might act.
>
> Sandercock 2003a, 12

In the Lacanian perspective that we engage in this book, social existence is largely constituted by the identifications that language creates and the interrelationships – and often misrecognitions – that language facilitates. Narratives comprise the knowledges which shape each of our symbolic identifications. These identifications constitute our ego-ideals, our conscious self, which inter-reacts with the other members of society, seeking their acceptance through our speech and actions towards fulfilment of our often unconscious drives and desires (Lacan 1988, 141). For most poststructuralist thinkers, such as Michel Foucault, narratives are 'multiple and competing sets of ideas and concepts which are produced, reproduced and transformed in everyday practices, and through which the material and social world is given meaning'; they 'frame the possibilities of thought, communications and action for practitioners, for participants and non-participants in planning, and for theorists' (Richardson 2002, 354).

Lacan's (2007) discourse theory, however, suggests that narratives and language can profoundly misrepresent, because a central tenet of Lacanian thought, unlike that of many other theorists, is that we are profoundly split subjects, with both a conscious and also an unconscious dimension, central to our comprehension of, and engagement with, the symbolic in language. As Vighi and Feldner (2007) argue, such a distinction has profound implications for ideological critique and comprehension of communities of interest and politics. Most discourse theories, for instance, fail to recognise the Real and the unconscious seeking of *jouissance*, which manifest themselves in the fantasy constructions materialising our shared social realities. In a Lacanian view, signifiers (words) are always slipping from one meaning into another and words alone never capture quite what we are trying to say (Nobus 2004). Language is always incomplete. Further, we interpret what is said by others filtered through our conscious identifications and knowledges, as well as, perhaps more significantly, through our often unconscious memories of past experiences. There is always a void between what is said, what is heard, what is meant (Lacan 2006). We create illusion, dreams and fantasies in our imaginations to paper over what is incomplete or unsatisfactory in our, or others', assertions. The narratives of difference and diversity constituting the 'multicultural city', as exemplified by Sandercock's (1998, 2003c) *Cosmopolis*, comprise one such set of reality shaping stories for spatial planning, which require examination in the spirit of unconscious desire and resultant fantasy construction.

In this chapter, we draw on Lacan and his followers to further illustrate the mechanisms through which persuasive arguments – in this case, those of multiculturalism – develop and gain hegemonic priority within spatial planning practice. We will illustrate how narratives that welcome and promote diversity and difference have emerged as a core belief, or dimension, of spatial planning practice coalescing around the master signifier 'multiculturalism' and, hence, have come to shape public policy substantially. We will suggest that illusion, fantasy and its materialisation – ideology – are essential to this knowledge formation.

In doing so, we explore the human subject's unconscious seeking of *jouissance*. We also further discuss Lacan's (2007) Four Discourses from the perspectives of how and why we acquire knowledge – the 'sociology of knowledge' (according to Berger and Luckmann 1966, and others). In this context we then introduce the discourses of the hysteric and analyst. We agree that difference constitutes the contemporary metropolitan city. Yet, we argue that this is, by necessity, a difference of exclusion and agonism that should be engaged with, not papered over by fantasy constructs of tolerance, that are shown to be mere arguments of, at best, subtle racism (Žižek 1999c, 2008c). Susan Fainstein (2005, 4) suggests that diversity represents a new orthodoxy or guiding principle for spatial planning, because diversity promotes 'the competitive advantage of cities, and [is] thus the most promising approach to attaining economic success'. If so, multiculturalism and diversity demand careful analysis. We evaluate Sandercock's (1998, 2003c) contention for coming to terms with difference by legitimation of alternative voices and knowledges to plan for cities that actively accommodate diversity.

Leonie Sandercock (2003c) proposes seven necessary policy directions for achieving her 'multicultural project'. These range from 'sensitivity training' to the development of appropriate multicultural policies and new conceptualisations of 'citizenship, multiculturalism' and even that of 'urban' (Sandercock 2003b, 322). Her final requirement is a need to understand and work with the emotions that drive ethnic and other forms of urban conflict. We suggest that to begin to resolve the emotional issues of difference requires an understanding of the human subject; an understanding that considers both what the subject can assert in language and what cannot be fully articulated, especially the subject's conscious and unconscious fears and desires.

Whilst for us, the encouragement of diversity and the accommodation of cultural difference are of unquestionable value, we will suggest, however, that Sandercock's proposals for the Cosmopolis city are not without some concern and potential issue in their utopian implementation. Yiftachel (1998, 2000) argues that care must be taken when differentiating Western democratic states (which share a 'thin' good (after Rawls) of tolerance of the Other), from states in internal conflict over matters of deep ethnic or cultural difference. The former states allow and encourage identity politics to arise, and here it is possible for trust between diverse perspectives to develop, e.g., US-American Catholics, Jews, Protestants, Muslims are all, firstly, US-Americans (Stein and Harper 2003; Žižek 1997c, 41-42). In contrast, states comprised of profound ethnic or cultural differences lack this 'thin' good which may result in conflicts, such as those of the Balkans, the Russian/non-Russian fringes of the former USSR, the Levantine, or parts of Africa.

We suggest that this distinction is often blurred in Western multicultural narratives (Allmendinger and Gunder 2005) and that issues of deep cultural conflict and lack of trust also arise in many Western democratic societies. We wish to consider multiculturalism from this thick or 'deep' perspective; a perspective at odds with some of the arguments of identity politics put forward by Sandercock (1998, 2003, 5) for 'radicalised liberal democracies'. For even in supportive cultures, processes of trusting the Other may founder when confronted with deep cultural differences. Further, symptoms of mistrust and misrecognition are found throughout our modern world cities and often in more inclusionary spatial planning processes. Examples are found in communities still partitioned by socio-economic division (Marcuse 1995); when that division is materialised in dysfunctional and unexpected planning outcomes (Watson 2003, 2006); or in inaccurate co-options of cultural identities as a basis for imposition of a planning idea, such as, inappropriate designation of an area as 'China-Town' (Chan 2007); and when represented by fractured narratives of alienation, dissatisfaction and exclusion (Masselos 1995).

The concept of diversity as represented in 'multiculturalism' will be examined as a planning master signifier from this perspective and found to be a desire for tolerance of the Other that may run counter to society's most fundamental desire for security, inclusiveness, and completeness (Žižek 1993). From birth we are 'thrown into the world, we try again and again to reconstitute the sphere of the maternal haven in the guise of family, ethnic community' and wider social order (Žižek 2002a, lxix). Yet, fostering Otherness may negate this search for security. Here Lacan's (1992, 1994) fundamental teaching is that we can, and must, address and then traverse this fantasy of seeking to achieve wholeness. This is yet again the illusion that wider society – the Lacanian 'big Other' – actually cares for us and can be relied on to protect us, and the potentially discriminatory fantasies this desire for 'oneness' constructs. Our desire for completeness results from a 'misrecognition' of our fundamental subjectivity; a subjectivity constituted on an unfulfillable lack – a void or hole – that both creates and *lies* at the core of the human subject.

In the following section, we briefly review notions of identity, knowledge and the Lacanian signifier. Lacan's (2007) theory of the Four Discourses will then be deployed to illustrate how beliefs and knowledge are first acquired by spatial planners and other government experts and then interpellated into the beliefs and narratives of the general public in a manner that obscures conflicting issues and difference as secondary to the major spatial planning issues of the day. The implications of interpellating 'multiculturalism' as a core planning master signifier, at least as its supporting dominant knowledge-sets are currently formulated, will be considered and argued to be at considerable risk of potentially fostering a prejudicial result, if undertaken without due reflection. Such a result may be a consequence of reifying cultural diversity as a mere object(ive) of harmonious urban management, rather than maintaining the ontological integrity of difference in its own right.

## Master Signifiers, Identifications and Difference

To recap briefly, in Lacanian theory, we are constituted as individuals and as members of specific groups in society through our identifications with a range of master signifiers. An aggregate of master signifiers constitutes a person's ego-ideal. In turn, each of our abstract intellectual master signifiers shelters a complex aggregate of ordered signifiers constituting narratives – sets of knowledges, practices and beliefs. Lacan (2006, 681) calls these master signifiers 'button ties' (as found on old-fashioned sofas, mattresses or quilts) that pin related narratives – networks of signifiers – to both the individual subject and wider society. Our identity-bearing master signifiers constitute us as political subjects. All of our 'utterances have as a fundamental aim the reaffirmation of both the importance or dominance of the subject's master signifiers and the subjects of these signifiers, which supports the ego's sense of oneness and wholeness' (Bracher 1999, 45). Master signifiers structure socio-political life, where 'the position of each of us as individual subjects is determined by our place in the system of signifiers; our lives are negotiated in and against a plane of enunciation' (Elliot 2003, 68).

Ethnic conflict – which may relate to fear of the Other – tends to occur between diverse cultural (or other) groups when few of their master signifiers, or their constituting narratives of meaning, overlap. Moreover, each cultural group as a particularity constructs its own definition as to what constitutes social reality. Each group has 'its own notion of the Whole and its part within it. There is no "neutral" universality that would serve as the medium' for discussing each culture's particular position of belief (Žižek in Butler *et al.* 2000, 316). Not only are there few shared identifications to facilitate discussion and interaction between diverse ethnic groups, but specifically, there are few shared modes of delegating their identifications 'to another agent *through whom* they love or hate,' i.e., common religious beliefs or shared foundational mythologies (Žižek 1999c, 267).

Conflicting groups are perceived as simply different to each other, sometimes with few commonalities of norms, for instance, in relation to dress or gender. The 'normal image reflected by the "other" of one's self then features undesirable traits' (Germain and Gagnon 2003, 313). For some, Christian European women bare too much sinful flesh, Moslem women hide their faces, masked as though a criminal, and so on.[1] Without shared master signifiers it is difficult to undertake socio-political discussion in order to overcome difference, as differences may seem too great and even the Others' appearance may offend. Even when speaking the same language, our words, stories and knowledges may have diverse meanings and implications when located under different master-signifiers, or narratives, of context and identity. Take the very word 'knowledge' to illustrate a simplified example. For New Zealand Māori, knowledge ontologically resides in a basket that may be stolen from the gods. For New Zealanders of European ethnicity, knowledge epistemologically resides in books and education. In such an environment of deep difference, it is easy to see how misrecognition and misconception occur.

Much 'new world' and European policy on migration (with, arguably, the exceptions of Canada and Australia (Germain and Gagnon 2003; Sandercock 2003b)) is concerned with the assimilation of diverse migrant groups into the fabric of a wider dominant nationalistic culture and its common practices, though none would openly call it assimilation as such. This 'melting-pot' approach attempts to negate difference and diversity and tends to marginalise those who do not assimilate. You are either one of us, an insider, or not and therefore an outsider, an alien Other. Such processes of assimilation and/or alienation have also inadvertently and progressively created multiple sites of struggle within many of the world's urban environments. These contested spaces constitute what Sandercock (1998, 16) defines as the post-colonial 'landscape of postmodernity, which is a landscape of/marked by difference.' Sandercock continues that positively defining these spaces, 'claiming them, making them safe, imprinting new identities on them, is a central socio-cultural and political dynamic of cities and regions, in which planners have a pivotal role.' For Sandercock (2003a) narratives and stories are central to this process of fostering and protecting difference.

## Planning Signifiers of Difference

Master signifiers of concern to spatial planning constitute the titles of this book's chapters. As outlined in Chapter 1, these signifiers are empty signifiers; they lack a specific object to signify. They have shed succinct meanings in their own right to anchor complex and diverse arguments and narratives under one grouping (Stavrakakis 1999, 80). The master signifier denoting an acceptance of difference and diversity – *multiculturalism* – is an ideal of what ought to be, much like other spatial planning master signifiers, such as achieving *Smart Growth*, or becoming a *globally competitive* city-region. Yet multiculturalism differs in one key dimension. Difference and diversity already exist. They are not transcendental ideals to be achieved, but they are an existing, socially constructed material reality that requires acknowledgement and accommodation, not obscuration via fantasy constructs

---

1    See Charles (2008), Krips (2008) and Ragland (2008) for a detailed discussion of this issue from Lacanian and alternative psychoanalytical perspectives.

purporting that we live in a harmonious consensual polity. As Sandercock (1998) documents, many world cities are multicultural. What is lacking, however, is acceptance of *multiculturalism* as an important master signifier (at least, perhaps, outside of Canada or Australia), where diverse groups and cultures are given truly equal voice and legitimacy to that of some 'dominant majority'. In many environments, difference and cultural diversity, while a demographic fact, are largely negated from the daily perceptions constituting the dominant social reality as to what constitutes the 'harmonious' city, which is still that of the largely male, generally Caucasian (at least in most world cities of the global North) and upper-middle class bohemian. Indeed, Watson (2003, 405) observes that it 'would appear that there is not yet sufficient recognition (in the world of planning theorists at least) of just how deep difference can be, and how often planners find themselves facing situations of fundamental difference and conflicting rationalities.'

Difference is hidden behind the façade and power of dominant cultures, obscured in the borderlands and margins of society because of the hegemonic narratives of the dominant 'majority' (Sandercock 1998). A majority, when examined closely, that is often a very small minority, a minority comprised of actants with disproportional access to financial and intellectual capital, which has the power to construct the dominant vision of social reality and what is desirous and good within it (Gunder and Hillier 2007a). This dominance was clearly apparent in the South Africa of apartheid, or Hussein's Ba'ath Party dominated Iraq, but we argue that it may also occur – though perhaps less overtly and perniciously – in many Western democracies, as well. Traditionally, planning helps to shape and mediate the hegemonic ideological perspective constituting 'our' illusion of a harmonious society. This fantasy tends to exclude the 'disruptive' Other, even when these often multiple Other*s*, in aggregate, constitute the majority of people.

Intentionally accommodating difference in values, tastes and behaviours, the concept of cultural diversity sits at odds with the modernist fantasy of a harmonious society. Moreover, it challenges the fundamental planning fantasy that planning can achieve a utopian state of security and inclusiveness for both 'us' and the Other. To resolve this contradiction, Lacan (1994) would assert that we must traverse this fantasy (Žižek 1997a, 29). The fantasy must be exposed for what it is, 'how the fantasy-formation just masks, fills out a certain void, lack, empty point' of our desire, so that we can move on (Žižek 1989, 74). Of course, a fundamental question raises its ugly head here. Does the dominant 'minority' want to give up their utopian desire for their secure and harmonious world, simply to accommodate the difference of the Other, who, after all, 'is not one of us'? On the other hand, can a new fantasy emerge to 'paper over' this contradiction between harmony and diversity? Any new ideological construct can only emerge, of course, through and within discourse.

### Lacanian Discourses: Including the Hysteric's and Analyst's

Lacan's (2007) Four Discourses were introduced in the previous chapter where the discourses of the master and that of the university/bureaucracy where explored and deployed to investigate the policy dimensions of globalisation. In this section we engage further with these two discourses before surveying the other two discourses; those of the hysteric and the analyst respectively. We then engage all four discourses in a critique of spatial planning's engagement with multiculturalism.

The Lacanian thesis is that all speech acts are composed of four common structural elements. These elements include, first, our identifications or master signifiers $(S_1)$. Second, they include our sets of contested narratives $(S_2)$ constituting meaning or knowledge as to fact, values and how we should act in relationship to our master signifiers. Third, they include our unconscious drives and desires that constitute us as a split subject (\$). The fourth element is that which we constantly seek in the attainment of our *jouissance* (*a*). Speakers deploy all four discourses in their interactions with others, slipping from one discourse to another as the four structural elements slip into four different relationships with each other, though with particular discourse formations tending to dominate in specific roles.

*Agents* driven by some 'inner *truth*' always speak, but never say exactly what they desire to, because words always lack some nuance the speaker is trying to convey. *Other*(s) imperfectly hear the assertion and this produces an *effect* on the listener. This then often generates a further imperfect response back to the initially speaking agent in response to the initiating agent's misperceived 'truth'. Central to Lacan's (2006, 247) theorising about discourse is that speech has a transforming effect on the listening subject where 'the function of language in speech is not to inform but to evoke'.

New spatial planners are largely created through their planning education, under the *University/Bureaucracy's Discourse*. Their teachers, driven by their own planning and other master signifiers, as what they believe is 'truth', instil systemic knowledge and practices into the aspiring student to evoke a transformation of the students' own 'truth'. As Thompson (2003), Fainstein (2005) and Sandercock (1998, 2003c) propose, the master signifier of 'multiculturalism' is one such emerging 'truth'. This 'truth' will become an identification-shaping master signifier, or 'truth', at least, for some students. These students, possibly in a mistaken fashion, will model themselves after their teachers' perceived belief, in what psychoanalysis calls positive transference (Verhaeghe 2001, 44). For such students, the master signifier 'multiculturalism' joins their other identifications and contributes towards defining their ego-ideal, i.e., 'I am a multiculturalist, I believe in supporting cultural difference and diversity'.

Others, who may not fully adopt their lecturer's viewpoint and take on board the concept of 'multiculturalism' as an identifying master signifier, must still internalise this master signifier's knowledge sets of values and practices. This may be simply to pass the course and learn the knowledges necessary to become a spatial planner, or perhaps simply because knowledge is a means to *jouissance* (Lacan 2007, 39). It is their exposure to the master signifier and its supportive knowledges and practices that provides both ideological-explanatory truth about the signifier 'multiculturalism', as well as, the appropriate norms of behaviour as to what is expected of 'good' spatial planners in relationship to this master signifier. This is especially so when planners are confronted with the material manifestations of the 'symptoms' of this 'truth' in undertaking practice within social reality.

Instilling multicultural knowledges, values and practices, such as multicultural literacy, may alienate students from their initial anti-professional behaviours and beliefs, replacing them with the norms, values and beliefs of the professional spatial planner. Fledgling spatial planners position themselves into the system of planning knowledge that constitutes the discipline and by doing so, they then become responsible for further reproducing, applying and reinforcing this knowledge in society via their subsequent professional practices (Gunder 2004). Fundamentally, however, some students may retain their original perspectives, even if inherently racist, as partially repressed values and beliefs. Planning education may have at best trained the student to suppress their continued beliefs so that they will not materialise these non-planning values as a manifestation of professional practice (Gunder and Hillier 2004). Yet, such beliefs reside consciously, or unconsciously, within the planner and may influence their future behaviour outside of the planning office.

The 'truth' of our spatial planning agent is that of a range of planning master signifiers, be they that of the public good, economic growth, sustainability, multiculturalism, and so on (Gunder 2004, 303). These materialise either as an identity-defining truth (where the manifestation of these truths may lead in extreme cases to the practitioner becoming a zealot), or, more likely, as an appearance of believing in such 'truths' (commencing with telling the teacher what the teacher expects to hear). Spatial planners (and other 'products' of education) are socialised/normalised by their education to know that this is what spatial planners are expected to say and do in relationship to each planning master signifier (Gunder and Hillier 2004).

The master signifier guarantees a particular knowledge set. It is the anchor point on which the knowledge set hangs and is contained. This is not just the perceived 'truth' of the ideological identifications of the planning expert, but intrinsically, the hegemonic ideological 'truth' of the dominant paradigms of spatial planning. In professional practice, these 'truths', or, at least the knowledges and accepted practices sustaining them, have previously been interpellated into the expert by their teachers and professional mentors; and, perhaps, updated by continuing professional development and observation of 'best practice'.

However, any signifier may act as a master signifier where knowledge is deployed in its either ideological or epistemological justification (Fink 1995, 132). Flyvbjerg (1998, 6) calls this process of justification: *realrationalität*. The 'black power' of the Nation of Islam, or 'the 'racial purity' and 'white supremacy' of the

Aryan Brotherhood or KKK, are all master signifiers substantiated and re-enforced for their 'true' believers, by 'logics', 'practices' and 'knowledges' deployed via the University/Bureaucratic Discourses of their supporters. Lacan (2007) shows that the University/Bureaucracy's Discourse destabilises objectivity. The essential core of science, that the practitioner must be objective and unbiased, is thus shown to be but a fantasy construct (Verhaeghe 2001, 31). The University/Bureaucracy's Discourse is ultimately the un-reflexive agent of justification shaped by, and for, the beliefs induced by the Master's Discourse.

In the *Master's Discourse*, the master states the new master signifier that reconstitutes an entire new field of knowledge. You *must* be a multiculturalist! It has a transformative capacity to structure the world anew. 'The Master's intervention is momentary, unique, singular, like the magic touch which shifts the perspective and, all of a sudden, transforms chaos into the New Order' (Žižek 2002a, lxxxvii). It is paradigm creating. The Master's Discourse contrasts with the University/Bureaucracy's Discourse which only functions to expand the classification by constructing new stories, knowledges and practices to support the master signifier. The master signifier of the dominant politician or academic guru (such as the 'multiculturalism' of *Cosmopolis*) structures the listener/reader's knowledges and practices in a new way that is supportive of the *author*(ity)'s own truths and values while constraining and repressing the enjoyment of the receiver's illusions and fantasies underlying their own perceived social reality (Bracher 1994, 121). The public, or the academics and their students, make the master. Those are the gurus of economic development illustrated in the last chapter, or the gurus of multiculturalism, discussed in this chapter.

Multiculturalism, competitive globalisation, or Smart Growth, must be good because the *author*(ity) says so and the teaching master confirms this, and both masters are the authorities that know! Frustration, or lack of enjoyment, is alienated from the listeners/readers in obedience to the master's assertion. Hypothetically, perhaps, frustrations might include the pleasure of conspicuous landuse that is lost in obeying the command of Smart Growth, the loss of enjoyment when forced to move out of a gentrifying neighbourhood 'needed' for talented and well paid knowledge workers, or the loss of one's ability to act freely induced by accommodating and respecting the behaviours and beliefs of other ethnic cultures, when supporting multiculturalism.

Spatial planners' authority resides foremost in the dictates of the master's 'truth'. Multiculturalism is intrinsically good because the master says so. The University/Bureaucracy's Discourse produces or imposes the knowledge, evidence, or rationality as to why this is so (Lacan 2007). In late capitalism and the modern state, this Bureaucratic Discourse is dominant. It provides the expert's university-derived knowledge with the authority that requires obedience (Dolar 2006). Consequently, the state, and its supporters in their application of public governance, deploy this relevant knowledge and its related technologies. However, all authority fundamentally resides within the Master's Discourse (which may include the assertion of the political, as well as, intellectual master): that is, that which gives truth to the University/Bureaucracy's Discourse. The expert seldom evokes a new ordering as 'truth'. The expert (and her/his knowledge) is the slave to the master's ideal (Lacan 2007). The expert is both the product and the subsequent agent of the University/Bureaucracy's Discourse.

Planners acquire and internalise the discipline's selected and diffuse sets of values, beliefs, knowledges and traditions. Academics and planners are ever-contesting specific perspectives within the discipline as to which is the most appropriate, or effective, knowledge or practice to deploy under any one master signifier. We always seek more knowledge, because we want to fill the lack, the void, in our understanding. Knowledge gives us *jouissance* by appearing to reduce this lack (Lacan 2007, 39). When one way becomes 'best practice', this particular set of knowledges and practices then tends to be imposed as the only way to shape common issues and limit what is rationally possible as shared solutions for 'viable' spatial planning policies. In this regard, not all may wish to agree and this gives grounds for Lacan's third discourse formation!

*The Hysteric's Discourse*

**Figure 7.1    The Hysteric's Discourse**

In the Hysteric's Discourse (Figure 7.1), the dominant position (top left) is occupied by the split subject, which hails the master signifier to answer the Agent's dissatisfaction. This Agent 'goes at the master and demands that he or she show his or her stuff, prove his or her mettle by producing something serious by way of knowledge' as the 'hysteric gets off on knowledge' (Fink 1995, 133). The Hysteric's Discourse occurs when speakers are dominated by their symptoms of dissatisfaction experienced as *jouissance* (*a*). This may be 'a conflict manifested (in experiences such as shame, meaninglessness, anxiety, and desire) as a failure of the subject (\$) to coincide with, or be satisfied with the *jouissance* underwritten by, the master signifiers (S₁) offered by society and embraced as the subject's ideals' (Bracher 1993, 66). Driven by the *jouissance* of dis-satisfaction in the position of truth for the speaking agent, this discourse is one of disapproval, complaint and often outright resistance (Fink 1995).

Moreover, this is also the discourse of the questioning academic, student, spatial planner, or resident seeking the production and assurance of new knowledge (S₂). It corresponds to the question always arising from students in class: 'But what about ...?' It is also the discourse of populism reacting '*against* an ideological environment' (Hillier 2003b). It is the discourse of the questioning public seeking both the production and then the assurance of new knowledge: 'Justify to me why multiculturalism requires me to put up with *their* smelly and noisy market by my church!'

We suggest that the Hysteric's Discourse is to be taken seriously. It is the discourse from which ethical enquiry, challenge for change, and the potential for creativity may arise. It is a discourse that should be actively encouraged, for it is necessary to develop the passionate, reflective, adaptable, creative and ethical – 'Is this fair?' – practitioner, or citizen. It is also the voice of the ordinary people: '"I don't know what's going on, I just know I've had enough of it! It can't go on! It must stop!"' (Žižek 2008a, 282).

Moreover, despite the hysteric's dissatisfaction with the master signifier, such as multiculturalism, the hysteric 'remains in solidarity with it' (Bracher 1994, 122). The hysteric Agent (\$) hails the receiving master to respond with an answer that contains new knowledge ($S_2$) about the disturbing master signifier ($S_1$). The hysteric specifically seeks knowledge that has 'a secure meaning that will overcome anxiety and give a sense of meaningful, and respectable identity' (Bracher 1993, 67). Further, this quest for promises of certainty can also instigate academic research that continually attacks scientific contradictions and paradoxes until new insights and answers emerge (Fink 1995; 1998). Yet for the questioning actant the answer supplied is inherently not quite the one sought. This is because the new knowledge produced 'is *unable* to produce a particular answer about the particular driving force of [dissatisfaction inducing *jouissance*] at the place of truth' that drives the hysteric agent (Verhaeghe 2001, 29). The void is never filled for the seeking subject and any answer supplied is never that sought. Such is the tyranny of language.

*The Analyst's Discourse*

**Figure 7.2    The Analyst's Discourse**

For Lacan, the Analyst's Discourse (Figure 7.2) is 'the only ultimately effective means for countering the psychological and social tyranny exercised through language' (Bracher 1994, 123). In clinical practice the external factor of the psychoanalyst's desirousness (*a*) is used to draw out the unconscious obstructions and fixations that underlie the analyst's subjective agency ($S_1$). The analyst continually probes the subject at the split between the conscious and unconscious (\$) so that hints and scraps of repressed master signifiers creating dysfunction can slip into speech, for example, literally via a Freudian slip. The task/practice, or 'truth', of the psychoanalyst ($S_2$) is to bring master signifiers induced by forgotten trauma and hidden in the unconscious into relation with conscious signifiers, and in so doing negate them (Fink 1995). A space is thereby created 'in which the subject's desire can be foreground, thus creating the circumstances within which a shift can take place in the subject's relation to' its master signifiers and the ideals that they represent (Glynos 2002, 40).

As Gunder (2003a, 303) has argued, drawing on Bourdieu (2000) and Butler (1997), 'just as the unconscious is not knowable by the conscious, the underlying ideological distortions and norms comprising the spatial planning field, or game, are not always visible, or knowable, to those' immersed within them in spatial planning practice. Similarly, the underlying ideological illusions, values, desires and ideals comprising social reality (including spatial planning processes) are often mis-recognised, not visible, nor even knowable, to those immersed within and/or are affected by this practice. The norms and ends of the spatial planning field produce ideological illusions for the players that can only be exposed by the critical researcher located at a point of observation external to the set of practices under study. To use Sandercock's (1998, 85) exemplar, the theorist's removed position can result in him/her not asking the question as to how best to save the drowning babies, but to ask the better question: why are babies being thrown into the river in the first place? It is suggested that this is perhaps a role for the planning theorist and hence, perhaps, that, along with the continuous questioning of the Hysteric's Discourse, the Analyst's Discourse might also offer a discourse for critical 'academic' research. We suggest, however, that care must be employed here that the analyst does not slip into the position of representing themselves as the pure, value-free *author*(ity), or using the discourse to justify the 'truth' of their particular master signifier.

### Drawing out the Signifiers that Repress: The Value of the Scapegoat

> If identity itself is a slippery, ambiguous and insecure experience, then the political creation and maintenance of the ideological appearance of a true, natural identity can only depend on the production of a scapegoat. (Stavrakakis 2007, 198)

We argue that what allows spatial planning to be accepted is that it reinforces the fantasy-scenario of the fundamental desire of society for a harmonious, secure and certain future, even if it cannot be delivered in actuality. However, 'the fantasy of a utopian harmonious social world can only be sustained if all the persisting disorders can be attributed to an alien intruder ... a certain particularity which cannot be assimilated, but instead must be eliminated' (Stavrakakis 1999, 108).[2]

The alien intruder is the outsider, the Other that is different. It is always the Other that allows the illusion of harmony in our identifications. We must have a gap, or space, to allow a differential relationship to an Other to provide a sense of identification as who we are not. Onto this Other we can blame all the symptoms of disharmony that threaten our fantasy (Žižek 1997a, 5). Difference is necessary to fulfil our fantasy of harmony. Difference provides the victim on which to pin the failure of the fantasy to deliver. In other words, the world would be perfect without the threat of: a) American hegemonic globalisation; b) communism; (or now) c) fundamentalist terrorism [chose one only] (Žižek 2004a, 158-159)!

Our social fantasies need this stranger; the Other that is not us that can act as the 'scapegoat' to be stigmatised as the one to be blamed for our lack: the '*Evil* force that stole our precious *jouissance*' and stopped the fantasy from achieving its utopian vision (Stavrakakis 2003a, 58). Žižek (1998b) highlights two dimensions of such fantasy. The first is the promise of the harmonious covering over of the Thing that is lacking. The second is that this hopeful illusion 'is supported by a disturbing paranoiac fantasy which tells us why things went wrong (why we did not get the girl, why society is antagonistic)' which 'constructs the scene in which the *jouissance* we are deprived of is concentrated in the other who stole it from us' (Žižek 1998b, 209-210). As Stavrakakis (2007, 197-198) observes:

> By focusing on the 'theft of enjoyment', by conveying the idea that someone else ... has stolen our enjoyment, it succeeds on both fronts. It preserves our faith in the existence and the possibility of recapturing our lost enjoyment – a faith enhanced by the partial enjoyment we get from the experience – but projects its full realisation onto the future, when we will manage to get it back from the Other who has stolen it from us.

Of course, the ideological utility, and/or price paid for utilising this scapegoat, is that it diverts attention from the actual problem and its resolution. Rather than acknowledging that there is a problem and identifying what steps can be deployed to resolve it, or at least ameliorate it, we focus not on the flaw, but on the task of removing the ideological 'cause' of the problem: the scapegoat. This seems to be extremely unfair on the Other. Taken to its extreme, it resulted in the worst obscenities and genocides of the 20th century and sadly, it continues to do so in the new century.

In context of the potential for abuse of the scapegoat, let us briefly consider 'multiculturalism' as a planning master signifier. Lacan (2006, 690) asserts that what we really desire is the desire of the Other. Core to the Lacanian thesis is that desire can only be constituted in another person, but because desire (unlike want or need) is always outside of symbolic expression, we can never actually know

---

2  In some instances, this 'other' to be eliminated may be the spatial planners themselves!

what the Other is desiring. This unknowability is compounded further when the Other is a member of a largely not- or mis-understood culture. In this regard, Žižek (1993, 203-207) suggests that one of our greatest fears is that the Other, the member of a different culture, has more enjoyment than us, or, worse, they want to steal our enjoyment and we have no way of knowing this!

> The Lacanian thesis that enjoyment is ultimately always enjoyment of the Other, i.e., enjoyment supposed, imputed to the Other, and that, conversely, the hatred of the other's enjoyment is always the hatred of one's own enjoyment, is perfectly exemplified by this logic of the 'theft of enjoyment' ... Do we not find enjoyment precisely in fantasizing about the Other's enjoyment ... Do we not obtain satisfaction by means of the very supposition that the Other enjoys in a way inaccessible to us? ... *The hatred of the Other is the hatred of our own excess of enjoyment.* (Žižek 1993, 206 – emphasis in original)

This hatred of the Other is constituted in our self-guilt of our own enjoyment derived from this Other. Our failure to succeed in fully achieving our fantasy ambitions must therefore be the fault of this Other that corrupts us. This can only occur because there is a gap in identification between us and them – a rather convenient circular argument and hardly a position from which to foster trust!

### Wearing Scarves is Fine: So is Eating Cows, Whales, Dogs and Pigs, and not to mention, your Vegetables

Shared master signifiers allow us the appearance of *universality*; of identifications in language (at least for those of us who appear to share a common culture), the ability to (partially) communicate who we are, when we disagree in the *particularity* of a meaning or belief, or lack absolute knowledge as to what constitutes some utopian ideal or concept. But, to paraphrase Heidegger: 'Here lies the greatest danger'. We only share common illusions, or fantasies, as misrecognitions of what we individually desire. What we share is our common negation of the undesirable as belonging to, or a consequence of, the 'inferior' corrupting Other that wants to ruin our way of life and steal our very enjoyment (Žižek 1993, 203). This constitutes an illusion of threat from the Other which can only be overcome by asserting our cultural 'superiority' via applying our particular truths as the one possible universal truth. Consider 'multiculturalism' in relationship to narratives of global capitalism and spatial planning in the following quote.

> The ideal form of ideology of this global capitalism is multiculturalism ... it 'respects' the Other's identity, conceiving the Other as a self-enclosed 'authentic' community towards which the multiculturalist maintains a distance made possible by his/her privileged position ... multiculturalist respect of the Other's specificity is the very form of asserting one's own superiority. (Žižek 1999c, 216)

Moreover, Žižek (2008c, 662) observes that liberal 'multiculturalism preaches tolerance between cultures while making it clear that true tolerance is fully possible only in individualistic Western culture' and thus establishes our cultural superiority sufficiently to permit 'even military interventions as an extreme mode of fighting the other's intolerance'.

The Analyst's Discourse suggests, accordingly, that care must be deployed should we employ 'multiculturalism' as an important master signifier of spatial planning education and practice as urged by Thompson (2003) or Sandercock (1998, 2003c). The master signifier of multiculturalism and its supporting narratives are *our* 'neutral universal' definition as to what is good and just for the Other. Yet this is not necessarily a particular 'universal' that is shared by both us and the Other (Žižek in Butler *et al.* 2000, 316). Žižek goes so far as to argue that multiculturalism is a phenomenon of Western 'upper-middle class' identity politics that is only willing to accommodate a 'filtered Other' which conforms to dominant liberal-capitalist standards. For instance, women's headscarves are fine (except in French schools), but unpleasant practices of eating dogs or whales (but not necessarily cows or pigs), burning widows, child marriage, facial tattooing or genital body mutilations are not fine, as they do not pass *our* 'universal' tests of animal and 'human rights, dignity and equality' (Žižek and Daly 2004, 144 and 123-124).

We suggest that, like ourselves, most readers would tend to 'morally' agree with most of the previous sentence, possibly apart from the eating of any animal at all, if a vegetarian. This constitutes Lacan's (1992) Kantian trap of the moral imperative, where to do one's ethical duty we must impose *our* core values on the Other, whether they desire them or not. The question remains as to what justifies and privileges the superiority of *our* values over those of the Other? In response, Lacan suggests that we can only ethically defend 'our' values if we truly believe and agree with them. Specifically, we cannot hide behind the legitimacy of any social order and claim justification for censoring our intrinsic beliefs and values. This applies especially, as discussed in Chapter 3, when we think that society expects this of us as 'good' planners, or 'good' individuals, i.e., political correctly respecting liberal human, or other rights, when our feelings suggest otherwise (Žižek 2007, xxv); particularly, if our assertion is only a pathological response seeking social acceptance for our own benefit.

In contrast, Lacan proposes that we must always be true to our fundamental feelings regardless of the pressures of social conformity and that we should assume responsibility for our own actions, even if this includes transgressing the 'law' of political, or other, correctness; what Foucault (2001, 19) calls a *parrhesian* duty (also see Gunder and Hillier 2004). Phased in a more Lacanian manner: we must not compromise our desire (Žižek 2004a, 163). We suggest that reflection on this injunction implies that it is actually a most difficult ethical and moral ask.

Further, we assert that spatial planning educators have a responsibility to address this perhaps irresolvable moral quandary with their students. We argue that spatial planning academics should ensure that their graduates do not simply employ multiculturalism instrumentally in a bureaucratic institutional context. The self-reflective practitioner should have the necessary awareness to reflect on this issue, and others, in their own right. Multiculturalism has the potential to be a policy formation that may be implicitly racist in its token 'respect' for the Other. Such a policy may be merely supportive of the dominant culture's, and hence the planner's, un-reflexive perceived, or imagined, superiority as to what is universally just – in this case, perhaps, the token regard of facilitating multiculturalism – because that is what 'good' planners are expected to do and believe. Here the Hysteric's Discourse of constant questioning becomes of great importance!

Contrary to Sandercock's (1998, 222) hope, the technical rational planner, constituted in the agency of the unquestioning, but justifying, discourse of the University/Bureaucracy, is still the dominant institutional paradigm (Allmendinger 2002b; Hillier 2002). The public is something to be rationally managed, shepherded and self-directed in a common trajectory towards the future – Foucault's notions of governmentality and bio-politics (Gunder and Mouat 2002). People as subjects are normalised through their schooling and other social systems (including spatial planning) in a manner that constitutes them as self-monitoring/steering actants aiming to contribute to societal economic well-being and aggregate health (Gunder and Hillier 2007a; Pløger 2001b).

Difference and diversity are negated by assimilation, consensual or otherwise – the traditional role of public policy formation (Gunder 2003b; Hillier 2002). Multiculturalism risks reifying the Other simply as an object(ive) requiring secure integration into the holistic fabric of comprehensive urban management. This is a colonising process of negating difference where minor variations of superficial difference may be legitimated in the name of multiculturalism while at the same time important, but perceived aberrant, cultural differences are vanquished. Attempts to instrumentalise ontological difference as an epistemic end are doomed to failure. The important differences of the Other are fundamentally ontological in their nature. Difference is thus irreducible to consensus. Differences must be brought to the fore, as they cannot be negated by reason (Mouffe 2000).

The fledgling spatial planner may well be driven by an ethical 'truth' of the 'goodness' of multiculturalism; but the structure that engages and channels this belief is still founded in the desire for the rational, harmonious city. Indoctrination of spatial planners with multiculturalism (while unquestionably desirable for us as authors) runs the risk of a perverse institutional outcome, one that may constrict difference and diversity to a mere object of urban management (Germain and Gagnon 2003, 298). For instance, implementing 'city policy documents with clear guidelines on the conduct of municipal departments and agencies, institutional changes to ensure inclusive language and outreach to diverse groups, and an examination of assumptions in existing programmes and services' (Pestieau and Wallace 2003, 257) may be a starting point to empower difference and diversity, but we suggest that it is hardly a desirable end-point for accommodating ethnic, or other, difference in the multicultural city of spirit and desire sought by Sandercock (1998, 2003c).

Such actions appear to privilege the spatial planner as condescending expert superficially accommodating difference from a position of cultural superiority. Such an illusion may legitimise and give authority to government in its socio-economic co-ordinating role. In undertaking this role, spatial planners enjoy the legitimacy of the University/Bureaucracy's Discourse; they are the experts that the public desire because they are ones who are supposed to know what must be done, even if this is a mere shallow reflection of a truth expressed by some author(itarian) master.

In their governance role, spatial planners may verbalise a desire for difference and diversity, as this is the politically correct position gained via their planning educations. However, behind their words, they may still harbour a fear or even a hatred of the Other, perhaps to substantiate their own fundamental fantasy (Gunder and Hillier 2004). Yet, while planners might not necessarily materialise this fear in their practices, it may still lurk there, as we believe it is, in wider society. Narratives and practices of multiculturalism may repress our fears of the Other, but are unlikely to negate them. For Lacan (1994), the only resolution to this quandary is to traverse our fantasy constructs. That is, to be profoundly aware of our fundamental seeking to fill the very void that constitutes our subjectivity and the implications this induces in shaping our desires and the resultant illusions these desires produce. One way to begin to traverse the illusions of multiculturalism might therefore be achieved by getting to know the Other better, personally, rather than as an object(ive) of urban management.

## The Exclusion of Inclusion

This chapter has illustrated a Lacanian psychoanalytical perspective from which to understand spatial planning policy formation in relationship to cultural difference. Spatial planning practitioners, in their role as government functionaries, not only supply epistemic knowledge, but also shape public debate by supplying, and often imposing, a range of ideal 'master signifiers' and supporting narratives of how the harmonious city ought to be. Spatial planning master signifiers first provide points of anchor upon which to construct and suture the ego-ideal of the fledgling spatial planners who then manifest these master signifiers as their planning ideals when employed as experts in formulating and regulating public policy. These disciplinary master signifiers, and the university/bureaucracy legitimated knowledge and value sets that support them, generate our urban and strategic visioning plans and narratives. They constitute the issues and content of our urban policies and set the parameters for much of our spatial social reality, even though their foundations may be largely grounded in identification with an ideological belief or 'truth'.

Planning practice concerns more than just passing 'facts' from the planner to the public. The formulation and implementation of urban policy 'gives rise to alienation and transmission of knowledge, resulting in group formation around shared master signifiers, i.e., a "doxa"' (Verhaeghe 2001, 47). A *doxa* is a shared set of beliefs and ideals that initially constitutes the discipline of spatial planning for its members (as do other beliefs for other human disciplines of codified practices). This is then imposed onto the wider public through spatial planning policy narratives for restricting and prescribing potential responses and actions. As discussed in previous chapters, the public desire this imposition of 'good' government through their processes of normalisation as 'good' obedient citizens. The public want and perhaps even perceive that they need the expert functionaries who are supposed to know what must be done. This is because the public largely want their institutions to take responsibility, to do the thinking and formulate their beliefs and dreams of the future for them; they want the 'big Other' to look after them (Dean 2001; Gunder 2003b, 290) and have someone to blame if they do not like what eventuates. In this regard, policy planning involves the shaping of aspects of the public's identity through the adoption of new narratives and master signifiers that produce new modes of urban behaviours – i.e., materialised practices – and regulatory compliance for urban management and city-making.

Spatial planning policy formulations are comprised of ideological ideas that are imposed on the public as the best, and therefore the only, rational choice of action. This is what the public want – the illusion of harmonious direction towards certainty and completeness. This alleviates dis-satisfaction caused by insecurity and induces *jouissance*. Those who know – the spatial planning experts – cannot exist without those who believe in them – the public (Hillier and Gunder 2003, 239). City-making policy formation constitutes new narratives and hence new urban realities desired to obscure the agonistic reality of difference constituting society. Of course, this rather stands at loggerheads with many of the narratives pertaining to difference and diversity. Only by homogenising diversity as the non-Other can harmony be induced and this negates the Other as a colonising object of assimilation. Worse, this privileges spatial planners because the planner 'assumes the position of a judge exempt from what he [*sic*] is passing judgement on (the position of a multiculturalist critic of western cultural imperialism)' (Žižek in Butler *et al.* 2000, 228). As Gunder and Mouat (2002, 131) note, drawing on Lyotard, this constitutes the planner as an agent of victimisation. Hence, we argue for the exclusion of inclusion, at least in an assimilationist guise.

Contrary to the hopes of a paradigm shift away from the 'rationally' managed city, where planners have '*access to other ways of knowing*' (Sandercock 1998, 30), the rationalist model, or at least its façade, still appears dominant in the Australasian city (Gunder 2003a, 2005a; Hillier and Gunder 2005) and we surmise elsewhere, as well (Allmendinger 2002b; Boyer 1983; Brand and Gaffikin 2007; Shmueli *et al.* 2008). As we argue in this, and other, chapters, spatial planning, is not rational. Rather it manufactures a rationalisation (after Flyvbjerg 1998) construed as rational, giving ideological structure to the 'truths' of its master signifiers. For social reality is ultimately a mediated madness constituted on our desire for an impossible wholeness and harmony of being (Žižek 1997b, 10), where 'we're reduced to very fearfully remaining conformist, we are afraid that we'll go a little bit mad as soon as we don't say exactly the same thing as everyone else'

(Lacan 1993, 201). To transgress this position requires spatial planning and wider society to acknowledge this desire for conformity and completeness: to understand that it relates back to our earliest infantile fears and desires of being wanted, first by our mother, and then by wider society, constituted as the big Other.

We suggest that in any effective multiculturalist society of 'Real' inclusion, its members will have traversed this position. In doing so, the process may allow us greater insight into understanding our socially constructed spatial planning and other urban reality-shaping narratives. In particular, it may provide understanding as to how our unconscious desires in seeking *jouissance* produce fantasies to cover over gaps in our symbolic knowledge and serve to assure us that our wants will be fulfilled. Such understanding will inevitably allow new narratives and new fantasies to emerge. Perhaps these new stories and fantasies may be structured within a more equitable and trusting social reality that has regard, or at least awareness of our unconscious dispositions, as well as our conscious articulated wants, and which will have the scope to produce more inclusive cross-cultural identifications. Hopefully, these may be identifications that will allow us to mutually soften and erode the hard edges of deep cultural difference. In the interim, we suggest, the Hysteric's and Analyst's Discourses will remain crucial discursive tools for examining and challenging the often-desirous illusions of harmony induced by many narratives of multiculturalist inclusion.

# Chapter 8
# *Sustainability* of and for the Market?

## Introduction

> *In search of a new 'vision' for planning* ... many commentators believe that there is
> a need for a new vision, one which can 'reach out to society as a whole, addressing
> its wants, needs and insecurities' ... a 'vision to rank with those of Ebenezer Howard
> a century ago' ... There is a consensus that such a vision can now emerge from what
> has come to be called sustainability.
>
> Davoudi 2001, 86

The legitimacy and value of spatial planning as an essential mechanism of
government, deemed to provide rational societal guidance, management and
co-ordination between the economic and social spheres for the common good,
was increasingly challenged during the latter part of the 20th century (Beauregard
1989; Dear 1986; Friedmann 1987). One fundamental reason for this loss of
faith in planning was the decline of the perceived ability of the welfare state to
deliver public goods, including social justice, and the rise of neo-liberal values,
market deregulation and public choice theory as the 'commonsense of the times'
(Allmendinger 2001; Gleeson 2001; Peck and Tickell 2002, 381; Troy 2000;
Sanyal 2005). A loss of belief in spatial planning expertise and the perceived
effectiveness of instrumental rationality to deal with emerging societal concerns
– particularly those pertaining to race, gender and the environment – compounded
that perception (Beauregard 1991; Berke 2002; Gunder 2003a; Marcuse 2000).
These concerns were further complicated by issues of urban decline and fiscal
insolvency in many first-world cities that eventually resulted in the domination of
market-lead values of competitive globalisation as the only 'game in town' (Jessop
2000; McGuirk 2004, 2005, 2007). Levy (1992, 81) writing nearly two decades
ago, attributed the loss of spatial planning's central co-ordinating role to a loss of
the 'guiding principle or central paradigm' of synoptic master planning for the
public good and, as Levy said at the time, 'nothing has come along to replace it.'

Yet, even as Levy was documenting this lament, new guiding principles were
emerging for spatial planning practitioners and academics (Gunder 2004, 303). In
particular, for many, the displacement of planning's traditional purpose and role
has subsequently been recovered via the discipline's response to the increasing
emphasis being focused on the importance of the quality of the natural environment
in many spatial planning related narratives (Cowell and Owens 2006; Davoudi
2000, 2001; Gleeson *et al.* 2004; Healey and Shaw 1994; Jepson 2001; Murdoch
2004; Wheeler 2000). Despite the loss of both its initial expert purpose in the name

of the public good and its traditional role of attempting to provide social justice across classes, spatial planning and its related disciplines sought to develop and adopt new narratives and practices of environmental management. This gave rise to adoption of a new transcendental ideal for spatial planning under the umbrella of the 'master signifier' of sustainability.

> The main 'paradigm' of planning has shifted from rational, synoptic planning ...
> The planning ideal that is forming today is based on a holistic view of the world,
> partly sprung from the well known description of sustainable development as
> a way of meeting our needs without compromising the capacity of the next
> generation to meet *its* need. (Mannberg and Wihlborg 2008, 37 – emphasis in
> original)

In this chapter we explore the rise of sustainability as a diverse set of contestable narratives and practices that has come, we suggest, to occupy a central place within spatial planning as the organising principle of what is probably its most important new discursive field. We focus on how the very word 'sustainability' itself has emerged as a 'catchall' master signifier for many of humanity's diverse environmental concerns and responses, so that it now acts as a point of identification and belief for many in spatial planning and in wider society. We consider the impact that this newly emerged transcendental ideal has played in establishing new spatial planning perspectives and disciplinary practices, as for many, spatial planning is deemed 'to have a key role in the quest for sustainable development' (Cowell and Owens 2006, 403). We subsequently consider a potentially pernicious interpretation of sustainable development as an often dominant, or hegemonic, take on sustainability, and how governments have used this interpretation to justify policies that are not necessarily either environmentally sustainable, or socially just.

We begin by tracing the rise to prominence of sustainability in spatial planning education and its emergence as a dominant spatial planning theme, or master signifier. We then critically argue that the definition of 'sustainability' can be (and often has been) deployed selectively by spatial planners, politicians and others, as a materialisation of dominant institutional ideologies supportive of growth and capital accumulation which serves to maintain the status quo of class inequalities with limited regard to the environment. We suggest that rather than encouraging opportunities for social change that might comprehensively reduce consumer behaviour to those consistent with the earth's carrying capacity, the narrative of sustainable development is often deployed simply to further the interests of an entrepreneurially-supportive state and its institutions. This last is a pro-market interpretation of sustainable development, consistent with Smart Growth and globalisation, that dilutes the concept of sustainability to literally that of 'business as usual', with, at best, an objective to partially reduce urban consumer energy consumption and waste outputs, while still maximising the potential for economic growth with little regard to overall resource depletion. This is of particular concern where diverse socio-economic and environmental issues are constituted under one mantle of a triple (economic, environmental, social), or quadruple (plus creativity and/or cultural) bottom line of accounting which then constitutes an all-embracing 'sustainable development' rubric. Such an approach promises a 'balanced' consideration of the social and environmental good, but gives disproportionately greater consideration to the importance of economic 'sustainability' or profit (Dyllick and Hockerts 2002, 132).

The above interpretation of sustainable development constitutes a new purpose, legitimacy, and, above all, new authority for the discipline of spatial planning and its practitioners. However, it also risks sustaining existing social and environmental injustices, not to mention inducing new forms of social disparity and environmental degradation. These are injuries that stem from society's still dominant cultural imperative of the market place driven by capitalist competition and globalisation, as discussed in Chapters 5 and 6.

The market-orientated reading of sustainable development obscures and subsumes dominant economic objectives under an overtly stated imperative to sustain the environment, against which, in itself, few would argue. Further, this approach largely overlooks injustices that spatial planning traditionally attempted to address as important issues of the urban problematic. Under dominant market interpretations of the narrative of sustainable development, spatial planning risks marginalizing its role of serving the 'public good' in turn for serving the further depletion of the environment.

In this chapter we examine contemporary spatial planning processes that purport to draw on sustainability justifications in South East England; Toronto, Canada; Melbourne and Sydney, Australia. We conclude that, while attention to ecological sustainability is crucial for continued global survival, issues of social justice, human culture and, especially, economic well-being cannot be subsumed as merely a quantified subset of sustainability, for the market imperative of growth and competitive globalisation will continue to illogically dominate all other considerations (Rees 2002, 2003). The merging of market, equity and environment threatens the desire for growth to trump the needs of the environment to sustain. Under sustainable development, the arguments of ecological sustainability are often subsumed as mere justifications, or legitimisations, for policies that are largely market oriented and even justified on grounds of social equity and betterment. Our consumer behaviours, so that they become consistent with the carrying capacities of the planet, are thus largely overlooked, if not negated.

## The Rise of a Master Signifier: Sustainability and Planning Education

Learning about sustainability 'is becoming increasingly important at all levels of the education system including higher education' (Cotton *et al.* 2007, 579). Yet, this educationalist focus on sustainability is a relatively new trend, even in spatial planning education. Gunder and Fookes (1997a, 1997b), reporting a little over a decade ago on the curriculum content of Australasian planning school programmes, did not mention the word 'sustainability'. Their work found that, on average in 1995, accredited planning school curricula focused less than five percent of their total programmes' student contact hours on environmentally related spatial planning issues. Over a quarter of all programmes had no formal environmental orientated courses; at most, one programme had 12 percent of overall course content focused on environmental issues. In contrast, all programmes had components concerned with social and economic issues, averaging 12 percent of programme content, with one programme devoting 31 percent of its content to these concerns.[1]

While ecological and environmental issues were undoubtedly addressed in most, if not all, spatial planning programmes at the time of Gunder and Fookes' study, these issues lacked the focal point of attention necessary to shape them as a specific field of prominent concern within spatial planning education. The concept of sustainability, while beginning to be well articulated in the literature (Jacobs 1991; Healey and Shaw 1994; O'Riodan 1988; Orr 1992; Pearce 1993; Rees 1995), was yet to emerge as a dominant marker that focussed planning education environmental concerns under one categorical master signifier of professional value, interest and identification. As Martin and Beatley (1993, 119 – emphasis in original) reported, a survey of 111 planning schools across North America, planning programmes in the early 1990s demonstrated '*quite strong* emerging interest in environmental ethics', but only '*moderate* emerging interest in sustainability'. At this time, 'sustainability' had yet to emerge as a defining, or anchoring, master signifier for planning concern and focus of environmental issues.

Friedmann (1996, 96) was one of the first to note the emerging importance of sustainability in North American planning education when he reported on the adoption of sustainable development as one of five areas of spatial planning education competences at the University of British Columbia.[2] Friedmann's article, however, did not advocate the adoption of sustainability in his own idealised conceptualisation of a core curriculum for spatial planning. While the teaching of environmental justice as a spatial planning issue was gaining support in educational circles of this period (see: Washington and Strong 1997), sustainability was yet to emerge as a universal concern for spatial planning education. Dalton (2001) noted that both 'new urbanism' and 'sustainability' gave American planning programmes, especially those with a focus on civic design, a boost in the 1990s,

---

1   These findings were consistent with the results of Wendy Sarkissian's (1996) doctoral research on environmental ethics in 14 Australian planning programmes. Even this thesis did not recognise the term 'sustainability' as a core environmental ethics term in the 1990s.

2   Whose School of Community and Regional Planning was then led by Bill Rees, the originator of the ground breaking spatial planning concept 'ecological footprint' (McManus and Haughton 2006).

yet she still considered sustainability to be one strand of many for 21st-century spatial planning education.

The number of North American planning schools offering a dedicated specialism in environmental planning increased more than threefold between 1984 and 2000. At the start of the current decade this specialism was offered by 86 percent of all accredited ACSP[3] schools (Swearingen White and Mayo 2004, 81). In contrast to Martin and Beatley's (1993) survey a decade earlier, Swearingen White and Mayo's survey of environmental planning programmes found that sustainability was now considered as the most important foundational knowledge-set for students.

In the UK, sustainable development emerged as a key spatial planning narrative during the 1990s, especially in relation to tensions created over the demand for housing provision in the countryside (Murdoch and Abram 2002). The Royal Town Planning Institute's (RTPI 2001) report *New Vision for Planning* placed sustainability as a central watchword of the RTPI's new conceptualisation of spatial planning (Batey 2003, 332). Yet recent reforms of British planning education (RTPI 2003), with its shift to 'fast track' one-year Masters courses and focus on life-long learning, leave limited room for in-depth development of key competencies, including those of sustainability (according to Ellis and Weekes 2008).

Leonie Sandercock was one of the first Australasian spatial planning educators to assert the need for ecological literacy as a key constituent of planning education,[4] yet her 1997 article did not use the word 'sustainability'. Richard Cardew (1999, 135) argued for the importance of integrating environmental management into spatial planning education, where 'environmentalism may be regarded more as sustainability, where energy use and transport issues are given more prominence than water quality, water movement, waste management and habitat protection.' Cardew argued that spatial planning students need greater exposure to scientific approaches in environmental management, perhaps best delivered as a consequence of collaboration between spatial planning and environmental departments. It is interesting to note that in his paper, Cardew considered sustainability a socially orientated concept, rather than an ecological one.

In New Zealand, Jenny Dixon (2001, 6) observed that the dominance of neo-liberal values and a regulatory focus on sustainable resource management, was putting pressure on planning education programmes to 'shift from design and social concerns to a more singular focus on scientific', legal and environmental knowledges. She raised the question: was 'sustainable development the new goal of planning?' Indeed, Bruce Glavovic (2003, 25), then head of one of New Zealand's largest planning school programmes, viewed sustainability as the core concern for planning education where 'a good planning education should therefore

---

3   Association of Collegiate Schools of Planning.

4   Acknowledging the importance of Wendy Sarkissian's (1996) research in her appreciation of this need.

provide the quintessential foundation for understanding sustainability issues, and transmogrifying this understanding into workable sustainability solutions.' Similarly, Claire Freeman (2005, 106) reported that at 'the University of Otago [New Zealand], both in the planning programme and in the Geography degree programmes sustainable development is arguably, the most used theoretical paradigm'.

Sustainability has 'come of age'. Internationally, it is now a core master signifier in spatial planning-related literature (see, for example: Agyeman 2005; Davoudi 2001; Næss 2001; Sandercock 2004; Wheeler 2000, 2008). However, sustainability, as a core for spatial planning education, appears to remain a largely undefined ideal. Contemporary educational literature consistently demonstrates difficulty in defining what is actually meant by the concept, and especially how it should be operationalised. For example:

> Sustainability is still being conceived here as a condition or established trend towards the operational realisation of which the whole process – education for sustainability – is susceptible of being directed ... But the issue is, how to frame that ideal – which does not spring in us fully formed – and how to turn it into a political reality, a set of guidelines and constraints for collective and individual decision making. (Foster 2001, 156)

Sustainability, in its rise to becoming a master signifier, yielded any succinct meaning. It had to become an empty signifier. In the following sections we explore the idea of 'sustainability' using Lacanian and Žižekian social critique. As developed in previous chapters, this is a view of the world that considers social reality itself to be an aggregate of shared ideological constructs. Subjects, as participants in society, materialise the symptoms, or artefacts, of their ideological belief sets via their actions and behaviours. In this worldview, sustainability acts as a highly valued identity-shaping concept for its adherents, especially spatial planners, even though they still appear to have great difficulty with defining and operationalising the concept concisely and comprehensively. We argue that it is this very fuzziness that gives sustainability, as for other master signifiers, its ideological power.

## Sustainability as Master Signifier of Diverse Meaning

The word sustainability is used in a manner that Markusen (2003, 702) deems a 'fuzzy concept':

> A fuzzy concept is one which posits an entity, phenomenon or process which possesses two or more alternative meanings and thus cannot be reliably identified or applied by different readers or scholars. In literature framed by fuzzy concepts, researchers may believe they are addressing the same phenomena but may actually be targeting quite different ones.

Sustainability is a concept that everyone purports to understand intuitively but somehow they find it very difficult to represent in concrete terms. Regardless, no spatial planning document can now afford to omit the concept because sustainability, especially in its common use as the term 'sustainable development', 'is declared as the ultimate planning goal although it is not usually specified what it means exactly and how it is to be achieved' (Briassoulis 1999, 889). Sustainability, or sustainable development, 'is something of a political "Trojan horse" – that the very vagueness of the concept leads to general acceptance of, or at least acquiescence with' its often ambiguous principles (Pacione 2007, 263). Consequently, 'the success of the sustainable ideal ... is due especially to its unifying promise, the way it seems to transcend ideological values of the past' (Ratner 2004, 51).

Sustainability is now a master signifier of identification which partially defines the very role spatial planning's.[5] Disciplines, or professions, distinguish themselves from others through the shared use of 'technical' terms, or ideas, whose definitions are often ambiguous, difficult to learn (hence providing barriers to admittance) and often changing and/or evolving. They are a discipline's professional master signifiers of belief. As Gunder (2003b, 286) reported, what ensures a discipline's homogeneity is its specific professional concepts, encapsulated as master signifiers, whose meanings are actually a mystery[6] to all its practitioners – no one knows what they really mean, but everyone assumes that others do. For spatial planning, these concepts include the master signifiers already discussed in this book, as well as the traditional concern of planning for 'social justice' and, more recently, 'sustainability'. Spatial planners regularly use these ambiguous terms; often as justification for their professional actions. For example, we must do this if we want a sustainable city, or, we must do so in the interests of social justice. Yet, what unites spatial planners (and other professions) as a discipline is fundamentally their common, or shared, lack of knowledge.

No one knows, or can succinctly or comprehensively and universally define, what a sustainable city, social justice, or the common good, for that matter, actually is! At best, we can only guess towards some vague notion that lacks a clear focus. But it is this lack of clarity that allows the concept to be a 'real' or 'good Thing' for all those who embrace it, regardless of the particularity of their individual understandings, dreams and desires about this sublime object – which make it profoundly ideological in its very nature (Žižek 2002c, 58). Moreover, this lack of clarity and understanding make ideas, such as sustainability, transcendental objects. They are concepts beyond human knowledge and experience, so that when placed on a pedestal as a desired societal goal they become transcendental ideals (Žižek 1993, 16). A transcendental object or ideal:

---

5   As early as 1996 Geoffrey McDonald proposed *Planning as Sustainable Development.*

6   The archaic name for a guild of crafts-persons or trade was 'mystery' (Concise Oxford Dictionary 1992, 784).

appears mysterious, nonsensical, incomplete, not only to us but even to the Other. For it is just this that appears to open it up to us, allow us to add to it, make it our own. It is just in its lack and unknowability that it calls upon us to realize it, take its place, say what it should be saying. (Butler 2005, 56)

Lacanian theory suggests that the basic functioning of social reality requires ignorance of its subjects, or to phrase it more politely: '*a certain non-knowledge of its participants*' (Žižek 1989, 21). Social reality is constructed symbolically through a set of ideological illusions, or fantasies, which we take on without question to ensure our existence appears complete, while blatantly failing to notice what is missing. The following quote offers an insightful example exposing this 'reality' for spatial planners.

> Does the way that sustainability slides from one meaning into another, as its core challenges, problems and solutions are framed and reframed, leave you uncertain about what it all means or what should be done? Or alternatively do you find that your firm and clear convictions run into the sand time after time as other 'takes' on sustainability seem to hold sway (though it is hard to pin down how or why). (Richardson 2002, 353)

Sustainability is a clear example of an empty signifier, a label without specific meaning, which thereby derives its political and ideological value as an important master signifier of identification. As discussed in the previous two chapters, under the University/Bureaucracy's Discourse spatial planning practitioners and academics teaching planning do not know exactly what sustainability means; they largely just retain a belief that it is a 'good Thing' with which they have to identify and develop more knowledge about (Lacan 2006, 2007).

For some spatial planners, 'sustainability' (or perhaps some other concept, such as 'social justice'), may be a profoundly identity-shaping belief; arguably little different than the faith some people have for spiritual truths. Consequently, this strong belief underlies and consistently guides these spatial planners' professional judgement and actions. Taken to extremes, however, a fanatical belief in a cause, such as sustainability, driven by what Freud or Lacan would call the death drive of negativity, can result in this 'good' becoming 'the primordial form of Evil' when it is imposed on others without consideration of the consequences[7] (Žižek 2008a, 345).

---

7   Examples of sustainability zeal might include: restricting, or banning, car use (or parking) in the name of sustainability without provision of adequate public transit alternatives, or the densification of existing residential zoning in the name of urban containment without equitable consideration of existing occupants adversely impacted by the change (at least for renter occupiers, if not for capital gain benefiting property owners – as documented in Chapter 2 and discussed further in this chapter).

Other spatial planners may personally disagree with the core values, or implications, embedded within these professional beliefs. They may hold neo-conservative perspectives on social justice, or drive a SUV while professionally arguing for more public transport in the name of sustainability. Yet, as discussed in Chapter 3, they know that 'good' planners are supposed to have regard to these dominant concepts, or ideals, such as sustainability, and so, in the planning office, they are likely to act accordingly.

Wider social reality requires ideological master signifiers of belief and identification to be fuzzy and ambiguous in order for our socio-political processes to function. This is particularly so when differing concepts clash together. Looseness and ambiguity allow us to accommodate incompatible beliefs and political positions, as Maarten Hajer (1995, 14) explicitly observed with regard to the unstable mix of both radical and conservative forces supporting sustainable development. Without the linguistic slippage, imprecision and even mis-recognition this ambiguity provides, Žižek (1997a) suggests that society would cease to exist. Further, the conflation of conflicting concepts is often how new ideas emerge, or gain primacy over others. The Bruntdland Commission's (WCED 1987) interpretation of sustainability as 'sustainable development dependent on economic growth' is one such outcome of such political and ideologically shaping process.

## The Value of Sustainability to Spatial Planning

While it is sometimes not easy to defend 'spatial planning' and the value of spatial planning to non-planners, other concepts are particularly easy to defend, for few, if any members of society, would wish to disagree with them. These are literally 'motherhood'[8] statements. Sustainability – protecting the environment for current and future generations – is at present situated readily on this pedestal of unquestionable goodness for most of society, as 'social justice for the collective good' was previously positively situated prior to the demise of the welfare state. As Cotton *et al.* (2007, 592) observe, 'no one is prepared to challenge the fundamental precepts of sustainability (if not sustainable development) because it is an almost universal and self-evident wish for a viable future for the planet and its inhabitants'. Spatial planning reflects wider society's conceptualisation of what is important in constituting 'what is good'. This changes through time. For instance, consider the then positively regarded role of spatial planning in 1950s and 1960s inner-city urban renewal programmes now considered, by many, to constitute one of planning's darker periods (Allmendinger and Gunder 2005, 99).

As Neuman (2005b, 17) observes, sustainability is a fuzzy, but inherently valued, thing for it has now emerged as 'a Platonic idea, a category of the good.'

---

8   In the Lacanian parlance of desire 'mother' is the supreme good, but one that we can never attain (Safouan 2004, 84).

Sustainability currently has great ideological power, particularly when used in conjunction with other concepts, for, by its mere association, it also endorses these other ideas as 'good things' that everyone can identify with. If sustainability is unquestionably good, then sustainable cities must be good, as must sustainable communities, sustainable management, sustainable regeneration, and sustainable development. Who can argue against sustainability and all that is associated with it? Sustainability has become an important political resource, or tactic, capable of co-option 'to legitimate particular policy approaches' (Haughton and Counsell 2004, 141). This provides great value for the current discipline of spatial planning, particularly if sustainability is now the profession's core purpose and goal. Sustainability places justification of spatial planning largely beyond public challenge.

Empty master signifiers, such as sustainability, that can be universally labelled and 'known', even if not clearly understood, convert 'the arbitrary and conventional into the regular and natural' state of the world: 'that by which an implicit order or prescription is made to seem as though it is only the description of a previously existing state of affairs' (Butler 2005, 19). These ideological markers construct social reality and once identified, they appear as ideals, which have always existed, even though they are new concepts and constructions of our aspirations and values. Spatial planning education did address issues of ecological and environmental concern prior to the emergence of the term sustainability (Beatley and Manning 1997). But it was the transcendence of this word into the role of being a 'master signifier' of subject identification and purposeful belief (or, at least, the appearance of belief) that allows this field of diverse issues to coalesce into one unified and constituting ideal of spatial planning mission, even if the story of sustainability remains fuzzy, ambiguous and incomplete.

All this is not without cost, however. In sustainability's looseness is the potential for this ideal to produce unintended pernicious effects. This is especially so when the concept is merged with other conflicting, identity-shaping ideas and values.

## The Pernicious Nature of Sustainability as an Imperative

> To think that their present circumstances and their present societal arrangements
> might be sustained – that is an unsustainable thought for the majority of the
> world's people. (Marcuse 1998, 103)

The sustainability imperative has been interpreted, at least for the Australian city, to imply 'a profound reconfiguration of urban morphology that would reduce the ecological footprint (resource demands and waste outputs) of cities and their hinterland[s]' through urban intensification (Gleeson *et al.* 2004, 351). This is a reconfiguration of settlements that may have little regard to the costs imposed on those who currently live in, or will live, in these environments. Further, such a view has been predicated on a simplistic assumption that the mere physical design of a community can affect human behaviours sufficiently to lead to the creation of a sustainable community, when, in actuality, any potential achievement of sustainable settlements will be dependent on a multiplicity of co-evolutionary processes (Neuman 2005b). As Bauriedl and Wissen (2002, 109) observe, sustainability tends to be perceived as 'a broadly accepted norm' that is considered 'to be in everybody's interest'. Consequently, planning regulation often 'neglects that what is sustainable for the one can threaten the living conditions of the other'. In addition, state regulation justified in the name of sustainability effectively controls aspects of both the environment, and implicitly, but often obscurely, the very 'social contradictions of capitalist societalization' (Bauriedl and Wissen 2002, 109). As Markusen (2003, 704) comments:

> Political organizers often look for umbrella concepts that can pull strange bedfellows together – 'sustainability' might be an example. Or, someone wishing to obscure a hegemonic or power relationship might choose to use a rhetoric of inclusion.

Similarly, Marcuse (1998, 104) notes, with regard to the deployment of 'sustainability' as a mechanism of ideological inclusion in relation to housing policy and urban development:

> Sustainability is both an honourable goal for carefully defined purposes and a camouflaged trap for the well-intentioned unwary. As a concept and a slogan, it has an honourable pedigree in the environmental movement which has, by and large, succeeded in its fight to have the standards of sustainability generally accepted by all sides ... The acceptance of sustainability, at least in principle, in the environment arena by virtually all actors has led to the desire to use such a universally acceptable goal as a slogan also in campaigns that have nothing to do with the environment but where the lure of universal acceptance is a powerful attraction ... 'sustainability' [here becomes] a trap.

Sustainability is often utilised simply as an ideological tool to anchor or quilt the narrative to us as an unassailable object of desire and importance (Žižek 1989, 88). It implies that everyone has a common stake in 'sustainable transport', 'sustainable housing', 'sustainable development' or 'sustainable cities'; such that 'if we all simply recognized our common interests everything would be fine, we would end poverty, exploitation, segregation, inadequate housing, congestion, ugliness, abandonment and homelessness' (Marcuse 1998, 105).

Marcuse (1998, 105) continues, however, that this is a ruse, because the very 'idea of universal acceptance of meaningful goals is a chimera.' The urban problematic is constructed from conflicting positions and desires, where one's gain is another's loss (Gunder 2005b). The land developer's gain (profit) is the home purchaser's loss; a new 'sustainable' rail corridor means noise, vibration and loss of amenities for residents adjacent to the new line, little different to the adverse effects of a new 'unsustainable' motorway. Similarly, high density residential development without careful design and construction may mean low residential amenity at a local scale, even though it fits the desirable ability to sustain public transit at the regional level (Dixon and Dupuis 2003). This list could be long!

## The 'Sustainable Development' Imposition of Social Injustice and even Environmental Ambivalence

> Urban policy is both socially produced and helps to make the urban problem seem natural, taken for granted. Dominant understandings of urban policy both reflect and influence the ways in which people experience urban living; urban policies help to define the urban 'problem' or even the urban 'crisis'. They are not just responses to those problems but help to constitute them. (Cochrane 2000, 540)

Spatial planning, driven and/or justified by dominant institutional interpretations of 'sustainability', is often no longer concerned about the traditional ideal of 'social justice' or 'balancing' market and social interests in the 'public good'. Spatial planning is now seemingly primarily concerned with 'sustainable cities that balance environmental concerns, the needs of future populations, and economic growth' (Beauregard 2005, 204). For many people, the new urban crisis appears to be that our cities are simply not sustainable. So what has happened to traditional concerns about fairness, equity and social justice? Under the hegemonic crisis of 'unsustainability', issues such as homelessness, racism or inequality appear not to be 'burning' urban issues. Yet, they have not gone away.[9] Exploitation still occurs, but is seldom considered as an urban problem of major institutional concern, especially compared with the importance of reducing our ecological footprint! Is this obscuring of injustice by some who claim to act in the name of sustainability not ideology at its most insidious?

In stark contrast to the radical position of ecological sustainability that economic activity and resource use must decline to be consistent with the earth's carrying capacity (McManus and Haughton 2006, 114); the dominant spatial planning readings of sustainability appear to be derived from the politically palatable view of the Brundtland Commission, i.e., 'sustainable development' (WCED 1987). Central to this position is that 'economic development is essential to meet social goals of sustainable development' (Haughton 1999, 234), or of 'environmental improvements' (Davoudi 2000, 128); a position referred to as

---

9 Narratives of environmental justice specifically address these issues. The difficulty, of course, is that these critical narratives are seldom accounts of interest to the major institutions which shape the dominant debate. Indeed, they may even sit in conflict with these institutions, e.g., eco-violence or 'just sustainability' (see: Agyeman 2005; Agyeman and Evans 2003, 2004; de Soysa 2002; Haughton 1999).

ecological modernisation by those authors and others, such as Maarten Hajer (1995) or David Harvey (1995, 1999). Brundtland offers the highly desirable and seductive possibility that we can have both economic prosperity and environmental protection at the same time (Jordon 2008, 17). This is a narrative largely framed by 'Northern elites', even if purporting to have consideration of the issues of the South. It is directly constrained, if not indeed constructed, by institutional and market imperatives of competition, growth and globalisation, the very causative factors of capital generating inequality, exploitation and degradation of both the Northern and Southern worlds' peoples and environments (Barry and Paterson 2004; Bryne and Glover 2002; Doyle 1998; Keil 2007; Rees 2003, 31)! Yet this sustainable development narrative has repeatedly and 'powerfully reaffirmed' itself 'as *the* overarching objective of human development internationally, regionally, and more locally' (Jordan 2008, 18 – emphasis in original). 'Instead of throwing a wrench into the capitalist machine, sustainability subsequently gets redefined as one of the possible route for a neoliberal renewal of the capitalist accumulation process' so the sustainable development becomes 'the new governmentality of a neoliberalized global capitalism' (Keil 2007, 46).

*Sustainability*, in itself, thus acts as an empty signifier or label of an ideal that many can believe and identify with, as do the master signifiers of economic *growth* and *development* discussed in Chapters 5 and 6. 'Sustainable development' combines these largely contradictory concepts into an even more potent single master signifier with a particularly powerful signification that combines both the potential for economic growth and environmental salvation. This dual master signifier of belief and identification is particularly attractive for our existing institutions of state and governance because it continues to engage and even privilege the capital imperative of growth, or at least to give the economic equal value to that of the social and the environmental. We can have our capitalist 'cake' and at least maintain the global myth, or fantasy, that we can continue to consume it for future generations (Rees 2002). Consequently, for those spatial planners and others who give primacy to the ideals of progress, growth and continuous wealth accumulation; and, perhaps more importantly, for the institutions that provide legitimisation for acceptance of the highly utilitarian market imperative of this development, sustainable development becomes the only acceptable – hence hegemonic – articulation of sustainability. Sustainable development has thus become the international orthodoxy for government-led spatial planning (Cowell and Haughton 2006; De Roo and Miller 2000; Jordon 2008). Unfortunately, this often results in policy responses that are, at best, 'only marginal reforms when the problem demands fundamental change' (Rees 2003, 30).

Furthermore, from the Lacanian position of the University/Bureaucracy's Discourse, sustainable development is the public policy position constituted by some symbolic authority that sets up a limit of acceptable behaviour that can both guarantee stability for a polity and also provide enjoyment for those that transgress this norm or prohibition (for *jouissance* is produced in transgression) (Žižek 1997a, 39). When entwined with sustainable development, late capitalism's limitless injunction to consume and enjoy gains extra value. The true function of the master signifier of 'sustainable development' is to demonstrate '*the absence of explicit limitation*' so that the term '*confronts us with the Limit as such, the inherent obstacle to satisfaction*; the true function of the explicit limitation is thus to sustain the illusion that, through transgressing it, we can attain the limitless' (Žižek 2006c, 282 – emphasis in original). Like 'Smart Growth' (see Chapter 5), sustainable development promotes and supports the fantasy and illusion of 'sustainable economic development' – capitalist growth and resource depletion – without end!

Indeed, while the Bruntdland Commission's work is 'translated usually into the simultaneous satisfaction of three objectives: economic efficiency; environmental protection; and social justice' – often referred to as 'the triple bottom line' (Briassoulis 1999, 890) – the main focus appears to be the needs of the market, which generally trumps those of the environment, with social equity being, at best, a distant third (Marcuse 1998). Davoudi (2001, 91) reports that within Britain, at least, notwithstanding 'the rhetoric of sustainable development, the planning system has remained deeply preoccupied with short-term economic priorities against the interests of long term environmental concerns'. Davoudi's comment is confirmed by Cowell and Owens (2006) with regard to recent British statutory spatial planning guidance; as well by Bulkeley (2006, 1036) regarding performance-orientated spatial planning processes for the promotion of sustainable and compact, or high density, urban development.

Britain's current focus on spatial planning is heavily premised, at least rhetorically, 'on a wide (socioeconomic) interpretation of sustainable development' where local authorities have a duty to prepare community strategies that seek 'the economic, social and environmental well-being of their areas and contribute to the achievement of sustainable development in the UK' (Doak and Parker 2005, 24). Accordingly, it has been suggested in UK Government policy documents, that development growth should be encouraged away from environmentally sensitive and already densely populated areas in South East England (Turok 2004, 1075). Yet, the Government has consciously intervened to back the continued pro-development case for this region (Haughton and Counsell 2004, 142). As the Strategic Policy Advisor for the UK Environment Agency wrote: rather than making 'choices between economic growth and the environment' the crucial issue is how far 'Smart Growth' can be deployed to 'achieve high outputs and productivity with a minimum of consequential physical development' (Howes 2004, 45-46). The 'political rationality' that dominated UK planning policy, at least for the provision of housing to address labour market shortfalls in the South East:

> effectively involved the rather selective appropriation of elements within the sustainability discourse by CPRE [Council for the Protection of Rural England] and central government. Sustainability was now interpreted not in its usual sense as a *balancing* of economic, social and environmental criteria within the

development process but rather as the *re*-development [and intensification] of already-developed land. (Murdoch 2004, 53 – emphasis in original)

The label 'sustainable communities' is deployed in a hybrid manner to describe the region's overly-optimistic strategic goal of settlement creation on what are largely brownfield sites in order to overcome shortfalls in housing provision for 'key workers' needed for the region's continuing economic growth (Pacione 2007; Raco 2005a, 2005b, 2006, 2008). As discussed in Chapters 5 and 6, 'key workers' is a concept based 'on particular interpretations about what it is that makes a place "competitive", whose "presence" is necessary for the socio-economic sustainability of a region' (Raco 2008, 738).

In a neo-liberal institutional agenda, the emphasis is on quantitative physical infrastructure improvements for economic growth, while issues of social equity are covered in 'simultaneous references to qualitative notions of sustainability, such as the creation of a sense of "place" and the benefits of community diversity and vibrancy' (Raco 2005b, 333-334). In addition, the environment is somewhat superficially addressed through intensification and reuse of existing sites, regardless of the accumulative effect of population increase on the surrounding environment.

In many narratives of sustainable development, the concern for the third criterion of social equity is inherently political and marginalised outside the techno-rational scientific approach central to market efficiency and environmental protection (Briassoulis 1999). While it is consistently argued that social equity is intrinsic to sustainable development, one or more dimension, be it social inclusion, inter-generational, intra-generational, geographical procedural human equity, or even that of inter-species equity; is generally overlooked in many instances of sustainability's practice-led spatial planning implementation (Haughton 1999). Absence may stem from tensions between social equity and dominant neo-liberal market values. Social equity also may be too difficult to quantify from a rational perspective. For example, how could local spatial planners determine the net present value of the needs of future generations in local development plans, or the impacts of global warming on residents of oceanic atolls on the other side of the planet?

Fundamentally, the market does not favour the disadvantaged. As Rees (2002, 255) states: the 'market model eschews moral and ethical considerations, ignores distributional equity, abolishes "the common good," and undermines intangible values such as loyalty to person and place, community, self-reliance, and local cultural mores.' These are all positions that spatial planning has traditionally sought to espouse! Moreover, 'linking sustainability with social justice is not necessarily a straightforward endeavor, as social equity means redistributing resources and burdens that are unevenly shared' (Leuenberger and Wakin 2007, 403). Yet, as Rees (2002) observes, the market ensures that wealth accumulation from economic growth tends to accrue to those who are already affluent. In contrast to the Brundtland proposition of the need for sustainable development to have economic growth to alleviate local and global poverty, increased wealth creation at the local, regional, national, or international level is seldom, if ever, equitably distributed in our global capitalist system. While some trickle down of economic development may occur, it is not without uneven geographical distribution and substantial and disproportional social and environmental cost (Harvey 2005; Kapstein 2006).

Furthermore, 'programmes and policies can be sustainable and socially just, but unfortunately, they can be sustainable and unjust' for sustainability 'and social justice do not necessarily go hand in hand' (Marcuse 1998, 103). As outlined in the previous section, a dominant approach to sustainability as adopted by spatial planners is urban (re)design geared towards more sustainable urban forms. This approach often has, at best, implicit, rather than explicit regard towards equity issues (Haughton 1999, 238). Indeed, as Pat Troy (2000, 552) observed:

> The search for sustainable urban development under which cities develop and operate imposing minimum stress on the environment has led, in its first phase, to the acceptance of well-intentioned but empirically unsupported policies of containment. They have been buttressed by notions of 'the urban' which are at variation with the aspirations and behaviours of the great majority of the population.

In some cases, the arguments of urban intensification in the name of sustainable development are literally ideological foils for actions specifically directed at promoting the economic competitiveness of 'entrepreneurial' city-regions. As documented in Chapter 2, arguments of sustainable development in Toronto, Canada, were used as a mechanism to justify gentrification in aid of the city-region's global competitiveness (Bunce 2004; Keil and Boudreau 2005). Urban containment and intensification may be justified as minimising the environmental footprint, but may result in the promotion of techniques of social regulation and imposed settlement patterns that are often contrary to the majority's perception as to what constitutes a higher quality of life (Neuman 2005b; Troy 1996). While globally foot-loose talented knowledge workers may well desire a high density urbanised lifestyle of 'vibrancy and liveability in the central city' (Bunce 2004, 181), they usually have the necessary incomes to afford (and demand) this petit-bourgeois and potentially 'culturally exciting' standard of living. However, most other city residents lack the affluence necessary to access this 'good life', or even the ability to re-locate regionally, yet alone globally. Gilbert (2004, 248) documents how Toronto's urban intensification has 'generated new socio-spatial disparities leaving many marginalised residents without any benefit' to offset the cost of their loss of original community. This is consistent with what Wheeler (2008, 3) reports in the United States at the city-region level where 'equity concerns often take a backseat within' spatial planning, which tends to focus 'on regional economic competiveness that benefits elites while not necessarily improving the welfare of lower income groups'.

The same intensification and nodal development promoted in the name of Smart Growth and vibrancy and sustainability – especially when facilitating the viability of public transit infrastructure – tends to ghettoise the working poor into high-density environments of poor built form, amenity and service. Further, these often non-knowledge, non-bourgeois workers are distanced from the 'liveable' and 'culturally interesting' central city due to high land prices and resultant high inner-city rents (Dixon and Dupuis 2003; Troy 1996). Burton (2000, 1987) found in an empirical study of 25 English cities that urban compactness lead to the socially disadvantaged experiencing social injustices with regard to 'less domestic living space; lack of affordable housing; increased crime levels; and [surprisingly] lower levels of walking and cycling.' Moreover, British policy responses to tackle issues of urban disadvantage have largely 'failed to recognise the important environmental concerns of deprived communities' (Lucas and Fuller 2005, 462). Other arguments against urban intensification also have a significant environmental dimension, including reduced per capita open and green space, increased segregation and congestion, as well as less effective local decision-making (Frey 1999, 25), and the loss of access to natural environments (van den Berg *et al.* 2007).

The affluent, talented knowledge workers of Florida's (2002c) creative city (explored in Chapter 6) may well benefit and be attracted to cities with policies, similar to those of Toronto, that promote loft conversions, café society and active vibrant city centres. Nevertheless, this may well occur with the price being paid by the less globally mobile, less 'knowledge'-talented, less affluent members of the community who actually constitute the majority off the city's population. Further, the quest for economic competitiveness, under the imperative of globalisation may have substantial environmental costs that are only moderately mitigated by policies of urban intensification. The ideological power of the two master signifiers 'sustainable' and 'development', when combined, is indeed powerful! We would argue, however, that they negate each other, creating language without possibility.

## In the Name of Competitiveness: Sustainability Deployed as an Authoritarian Illusion

Sustainability purports to be a scientific narrative, grounded on facts, even if it is an undefinable concept. Yet as Cardew (1999) reported, sustainability is actually a social construct largely concerned with human endeavours such as energy consumption and transport issues and not at all directly concerned with environmental quality. Nor is 'sustainability' an object of direct study by environmental, or other formal, physical sciences. Sustainability and the narratives that unsuccessfully attempt to articulate it are ideological social constructs fabricated by the University/ Bureaucracy's Discourse driven and legitimised by the sublime 'truth' of an unknowable transcendental ideal. Sustainability and its contestable knowledge sets are seldom based directly on irrefutable scientific principles, such as the laws of thermodynamics. Yet, spatial planners deploy their interpretation of sustainability – or perhaps that of their political masters' belief – through the Discourse of the University/Bureaucracy as though it were an incontestable scientific edict – the one and only truth. The master signifier of 'sustainability' may have many contested meanings, but the Brundtland definition of 'sustainable development' dominates. Here the position of 'sustainable development' resides as the new master signifier, that of power, itself (Žižek 2006a, 307).

We recognise that there is a scientific basis to the environmental problematic underlying the broad sustainability context. Issues of bio-diversity, global warming, ecological footprint and related meta-issues are emphatically valid areas of scientific inquiry and concern. However, we worry about the extrapolation of these meta-issues as the logic and justification underlying site-specific local planning regulation. Newman and Kenworthy's (1989) broad-brush analysis of energy usage and urban density is often cited as the justification for policies of urban containment and intensification. However, numerous authors have demonstrated that the broad assumptions used in Newman and Kenworthy's calculations do not withstand challenge across a range of site-specific empirical studies and methodological challenges (e.g., Breheny 1995; Buxton and Scheurer 2007; Hall 2001; O'Connor 2003; Neuman 2005b). As Troy (1996; 2000) has repeatedly pointed out, there is little or no empirical research underlying many of the policy and regulatory prescriptions for compact cities made in the name of sustainability.

Paul Mees (2003) questions the nature of the scientific reason and justification (i.e., the empirical scientific research) supporting the policy objective in the *Melbourne 2030 Plan* that 20 percent of all motorised Melbourne trips should be on public transit by 2020 (Department of Sustainability and Environment 2005). Mees (2003, 292) claims that this 'ambitious-sounding patronage target [was] introduced without justification or analysis' while the same plan proposed freeway developments costing '$3 billion, or some 15 times the cost of the proposed rail extensions.' Can the two perspectives be reconciled? Mees suggests that Melbourne's plan for urban intensification was largely a continuation of the region's existing market-led growth plan, albeit, addressing the 'risks and opportunities posed by globalisation' (Gleeson *et al.* 2004, 356). Perhaps the plan was more concerned with creating an attractive environment to attract and retain knowledge workers to enhance global competitiveness (Yigitcanlar *et al.* 2008) than with environmental and social sustainability?

Similarly, Sydney's current Metropolitan Strategy is predicated on promoting a competitive, or entrepreneurial, city and provides little evidence of provision to address issues of social equity (Gunder and Searle 2007). Sydney's Strategy is also based in part explicitly on the seeking of talented and creative workers to infuse 'new human capital as [a] central ingredient in economic growth' (Blakely *et al.* 2007, 456). While the Strategy purports to follow a sustainable development 'triple-bottom-line approach', issues of affordable housing or transportation infrastructure are only addressed to 'ensure that "key [service] worker" are not excluded from those neighbourhoods inhabited by their better renumerated counterparts, the "knowledge workers"' (McGuirk 2005, 64).

So, is the 'rhetoric of sustainable development, public transport and diversity … merely a smokescreen to cover the fact that the substantive proposals involve no significant change' as Mees (2003, 293) claims? Are the 'real issues of multiculturalism and sustainability … reduced to forms of "political correctness" that can be satisfied by the inclusion of appropriate slogans and pretty pictures' (Mees 2003, 298)? Meanwhile, are highway engineers and the market continuing to dominate development in Melbourne, or Sydney, in the interest of competitive globalisation 'untroubled by post-modern angst about the nature of the task' (Mees 2003, 298)?

Sadly, we see some validity in these arguments. As Lefebvre (2003, 166) suggested, spatial planning policy is often constructed by drawing on a strategy that mixes ideological values and beliefs with rationality as though it is all technological science. This makes the rationality of spatial planning a rather arbitrary ideological construct of the planners' beliefs and values. Planners do what they think 'good' spatial planners are supposed to do.

As some commentators argue: 'sustainable development requires not just altering behaviour patterns in relation to the environment, but about changing the broader systems that shape human behaviour' (Haughton 1999, 235). In this regard, some spatial planners take the position that the ends justify the means and that they should thus have the right to impose their vision and the necessary behavioural changes in the name of 'sustainability'. In the case of Melbourne:

> A need for sharing the vision for a sustainable future and bringing the community along with the [spatial planning] profession in pursuit of this vision is long overdue and can be achieved through an *appropriate framework for education and behaviour change* utilising existing structures and authorities to deliver such a message. (Donnison 2005, 18 – emphasis added)

Is such an approach justifiable, where experts induce behaviour change on the public through their self-decreed authority to know best? Can a point be reached where the 'good' of sustainability begins to verge on the point of 'evil' in its draconian and fanatical implementation (Žižek 2008a, 345)? Where might this point be? On the other hand, are planners' beliefs and their motivations for a better, more sustainable world, being channelled by other interests of capital accumulation resulting in 'business as usual' – especially when economic recession bites, businesses close, jobs are lost and any economic investment is seen as 'good'?

Just as sustainable development has largely gained hegemonic domination of the wider sustainability narrative for government-led agency in the interests of competitive globalisation and economic growth, the economic imperative embedded within sustainable development also has hegemonic primacy. The other dimensions which constitute the sustainable development narrative – creativity/culture, social justice, and the environment – appear to be deployed often in a manner that facilitates this dominant market imperative. The assumption is implicit that we must first have economic growth and wealth creation in order that we can address these other issues.

The spatial planning discipline has heartily adopted the term sustainability. But, due to the strength of the market imperative that constitutes the dominant global worldview – at least for the corporations and institutions of state and governance – the only politically palatable interpretation of sustainability appears to be that of sustainable development, where the market imperative dominates. Spatial planning's saving grace may well be sustainability, as it may be for the rest of society, yet, so far, the dominant articulation of this ideal has been captured to maintain 'business as usual.'

### Saving the Baby, but Throwing out the Pernicious Bath-Water

> The exemplary figures of evil today are not ordinary consumers who pollute the environment and live in a violent world of disintegrating social links, but those who, while fully engaged in creating conditions for such universal devastation and pollution, buy their way out of their activity, living in gated communities, eating organic food, taking holidays in wildlife preserves, and so on. (Žižek 2008d, 27)

Bill Rees (2003, 31) sadly suggests that the failure of our dominant worldview to accept that the global carrying capacity is finite and, consequently, that indefinite growth is an impossibility 'raises the unsettling possibility that much of even our present cultural worldview may consist largely of shared illusions!' We would strongly agree with this, highly Lacanian, insight. Many of us seek the appearance of security and certainty in our institutions' actions, reflective of our dreams and desires for a better, more secure, future. Our dominant worldviews are still largely predicated on a hope for a better future based in materialistic terms of growth and economic progress. Consequently, the underlying premise of 'sustainability poses a far more serious challenge to many of society's most basic beliefs and analytic concepts than most mainstream planners and policy makers have so far been prepared to contemplate' (Rees 2003, 31).

This and other chapters have illustrated how such mechanisms of illusion may occur and how the domination of the sustainability response has been so often captured by the dominant cultural imperative of economic growth. We suggest that the sustainability narrative, as often implemented, is one such illusion the tends to provide 'renewed institutional legitimacy that "greenwashes" an unsustainable economic status quo in the refreshing, but not cleaning, waters of sustainable development' (Luke 2008, 1811). The question is, how do we re-articulate sustainability's core concern, not as a mechanism for justification for more pro-market behaviours, but as a means to displace the economic imperative from its throne of supremacy over that of social equity, cultural appreciation and the environment? How do we change this dominant worldview, especially at a time of economic crisis? We all know 'the real state of affairs very well, but we do not believe it' because 'the big Other [in its multifarious but illusory demands of material fidelity, consumption and growth] prevents us from believing in it, from assuming this knowledge and responsibility' (Žižek 2008a, 454).

Sustainability as an ideal societal goal, as captured and embodied by sustainable development, may well serve to protect the status quo of competitive globalisation and facilitate the maintenance of the interests of already-advantaged groups or individuals, such as talented knowledge workers. It does not substantively address the maintenance of the biosphere, the issues of natural resource depletion, or loss of bio-diversity. Nor does it often address the needs of the socially or economically disadvantaged. In dealing with issues of social justice, such as the problem of poor housing provision, or the location of toxic waste dumps in the global South, we suggest that meeting existing needs of the disadvantaged may be just as, if not more important than, providing the wants of present or future generations of talented knowledge workers.

Sustainability has emerged as a dominant concept of spatial planning education and 'good' practice. Ecological sustainability for us is indeed, a profoundly important principle, but it should not be used as a blunt ideological instrument perpetrating social injustice and the neo-liberal values of globalisation, particularly as deployed under the rubric of sustainable development. Triple/quadruple bottom line based 'sustainable development' is not the same as single bottom line 'ecological sustainability'. To combine them is to risk both the environment and the social in the name of sustainable wealth creation for the dominant minority who profit from competitive globalisation. Mainstream spatial planning's apparent acceptance of this materialist view of sustainability precludes, for us, a more socially and environmentally just and responsible articulation. If the (illusionary) big Other precludes belief in a responsible articulation of sustainability, how might we change social reality in order that we can responsibly articulate this position? We suggest, in the final chapters, that one approach to the question of responsibility resides in the ethics of the Real.

# Chapter 9
## *Responsibility* to Whom?

### To Be Responsible

A word with which to escape responsibility.

Watson 2004, 321

In this penultimate chapter, we consider the signifier 'responsibility' as it is deployed in contemporary spatial planning practice. We then broaden this concept of responsibility, drawing from the philosophical thought of Emmanuel Lévinas, Jacques Derrida, Iris Marion Young and, from Lacanian-derived literature what is often called the *Ethics of the Real* (Zupančič 2000). We argue for a new ethics of globally conscious spatial planning. We suggest that this could possibly be accomplished by practising an understanding of responsibility that is predicated on a premise of 'avoidance of avoidance', especially when actors are aware of the global implications of their actions.

*Responsible Planning: A Vignette*

In 1996, a planner working for the Auckland Regional Council (ARC) in New Zealand was under pressure to make the 'right' decision. The 'right' action would pave the way for approval of unchallengeable development consents for an Auckland City Council (ACC) initiated project that required the excavation of a 3.2 hectare waterfront site to the depth of a five storey building in Auckland's CBD. All that was necessary was the ARC planner's decision that the excavation would have only minor environmental and/or structural effects on the area and its surrounding buildings. Resource (development) consent could then be given in-house without public notification.

The excavation site was to contain a 2,900 place underground car park, a public transit station and underpinning support for the site's above ground development, all of which was to be located under a ground level capping concrete slab. The slab would in turn provide the foundation for construction of a high density, multi-storey, multi-building development that would provide nearly a half million square metres of additional CBD floor space (ACC 1996), which would, we suggest, have had a profound impact on Auckland CBD's future development.

Under New Zealand's Resource Management Act, if the ARC planner decided that the effects of sediment control, water take and damming on the excavation of the site were minor (i.e., readily manageable with little potential risk to the built or natural environment), this would avoid the need for public hearings. The latter would likely open the application to contentious litigation in the Environment and High Courts.

Compounding the pressure on the ARC planner was that the development was being driven by the majority political will of the ACC; a Council controlled by the same political affiliation that then largely dominated the ARC. Yet this political will sat at odds with a strong public interest opposed to the development, largely on grounds of appropriateness, cost, lack of consultation and heritage preservation. Further, the ACC was in charge of the above ground development control of the site. Once the ARC gave consent on the excavation there would be little check on the ACC's Property Department initiative. This was a Department, which, with the support of the Council's dominant politicians, had excluded not only the public, but its own Planning Department's consideration of the project by covertly using off-shore consultants to develop the scheme (Gunder 1998, 2000b).

Regardless of pressure, the ARC planner notified that the application required a public hearing, because of likely significant environmental effects of the excavation. On this 'responsible' decision rode a different future for Auckland's CBD. The following year the independent ARC commissioners 'declined the consents because the principle applicant had not established that the preposed dewatering associated with the construction of the Britomart project [would] not result in damage to buildings neighbouring the site' (ARC 1997, np).

In 1999, following further expert and legal examination via the court system, the planner's initial convictions were found to be sound. This eventually resulted in an amended project. The development of the site, as first proposed, was eventually terminated due to a change of Council political control in late 1998 and the original City Council contracted development consortium being unable, on its own, to meet the cost of posting the necessary bonds to cover potential structural damage of the excavation (*New Zealand Herald*, 3/11/1999, A15). A much smaller scale project was eventually agreed. This was an amended proposal, developed via public consultation and a publicly contested architectural competition that made significant provision for heritage preservation and public transit, was of lower density and was without inclusion of the 2,900 place car park.

## *The Meaning of Responsibility*

We would suggest that the ARC planner acted responsibly in the face of significant pressure. To most readers that person would be a planning hero. Yet, does such responsibility always occur in spatial planning practice? At what point does the advice of the planner's superiors and political leaders, or even public sentiment, transcend the planner's own judgement? Where does the planner's responsibility ultimately lie? How do planners know that their judgements and actions are responsible? What does the act of responsibility mean?

In this chapter we seek to engage with the diverse meanings of 'responsibility', which, we suggest, is another empty signifier. The word 'responsibility' has a prominent position in the conventional rhetoric of spatial planning. The profession has traditionally laboured under an implicit expectation that it acts with responsibility with regard to the public interest and/or good (Campbell and Fainstein 2003, 13; Forester 1989). Recently, planners are also expected to be responsible to the environment and to act in ways that create sustainable futures (Næss 2001; Wheeler 2000).

With advice and exhortation to responsibility, how is it that although spatial planners set out to create sustainable communities and regions responsibly, they often end up creating outcomes that materialise dominant institutional ideologies supportive of growth and capital accumulation? How is it that plans often water down the concept of sustainability, or the public good, to no more than that of 'business as usual'? Do spatial planners act responsibly when they appear to hide in illusions that the planet's environment is indestructible; that the public good is best achieved by increasing consumer consumption; or that a toxic pollutant is less important if spilt in another part of the globe away from our territory (Hillier 2009)? What are the mechanisms at work, ideological or other, which permit this to occur?

After contextualising the question of responsibility in the rest of this section, we examine two traditional theoretical perspectives: responsibility as deontic duty and responsibility as delineation of the good. Deontic duty is a concept largely derived from the work of Immanuel Kant (1959), in which he prescribes that we must only act in respect to duty and not for personal self-interest. Responsibility to the good is derived from classical philosophy and is concerned about the attainment of good ends (Arendt 2003), yet as previous chapters have illustrated, both doing one's duty and seeking to be 'good' are open to Lacanian-inspired critique.

We then examine two alternative perspectives of responsibility. The first derives from the phenomenology-trained philosopher Emmanuel Lévinas (1969, 1985, 1993) who argued that we have an inherent responsibility to the Other. Such a position develops from the inherent face-to-face empathy that Lévinas suggests exists in all 'normal' human relationships. This empathic relationship demands a caring response to the Other. Such response, Lévinas argues, constitutes us ontologically (i.e., it defines our very being-ness) as human subjects. The second perspective is that of the deconstructionist philosopher Jacques Derrida (1978, 1997a, 1997b, 2000b) who was influenced by Lévinas. For Derrida responsibility is the ability to respond – to act – in-the-face of undecidability and ambiguity whilst retaining an ability to respect and accommodate future radical change, and accepting the consequences of one's actions.

We suggest that 'responsibility is like a string we can only see the middle of. Both ends are out of sight', (William McFee 1916, 90). However, spatial planners must continue to act in the world, so we conclude, after Derrida, that responsibility actually relates to an ability to act and accept the consequences of those actions even in the face of aporia (a state of puzzlement and paradox) and uncertainty. We then suggest some implications from this stance for spatial planning practice.

*The Context of Responsibility*

In this section we problematise issues of what responsibility is. We also ask the question how are we to be responsible if there is no particular end to be achieved – i.e., there no end point, but only a continuing middle to be sustained? As Louis Albrechts (2005, 263) asserts, 'the implicit responsibility of planners can no longer simply be to "be efficient" or to function smoothly as a neutral means of obtaining given ... ends'. We begin by arguing that planning decisions are inherently moral decisions. Local land-use decisions, either individually or collectively, may have enormous ethical, social and environmental impacts (Hillier 2004). Such decisions generally require thought-processes that involve the exercise of judgement rather than the 'mere application of rules' (Campbell and Marshall 2005, 199).

We argue that 'responsibility' is an empty signifier, containing a range of contested meanings, each of which is inadequately problematised. We believe that responsibility encompasses more than 'where the buck stops', 'normative blameworthiness' (Haji and Cuypers 2005): responsibility *for.* We propose this to be a too-simplistic approach to responsibility. This includes Kaufman's (1980) work on 'right and wrong in land planning' and Tong (1987) on excuses and justifications for moral failings, both of which propose an approach that often attempts to *avoid* taking responsibility for difficult issues such as environmental pollution (Beck 1992), or homelessness (Waldron 1991), or the differing other (Derrida 2000b; Sandercock 2003c) and justifies merely being a 'bystander' (Arendt 1994, 4-5).

We also argue that responsibility is more than its overly-used meaning of accountability; responsibility *to.* Traditionally, the responsibility of public servants was understood as both 'an inward sense of moral obligation' (Finer 1941, 338) and a responsibility to external political direction (Weber 2004, 54). This dutiful, or duty-based, responsibility is often derived from religious or secular tradition, from historical contingency and/or institutional mandate. It is often grounded in the 'way things have always been done' which, Derrida (1997a, 167) suggests we should openly challenge and question. Currently, there is still an ethos of accountability to 'a boss, a State, a constituency or a God', that is an audience presumed to 'have some moral authority to pass judgment' (Deetz and White 1999, 113). In contemporary bureaucratic processes, this is often reified into readily measurable targets of process accountability predicated on quantitative indicators of timeliness and performance, such as the Audit Commission's Best Value Performance Indicators in England and Wales (ODPM 2005a). Yet, targets often bear little regard to the actual quality and value of the spatial planning outcomes achieved.

Consequently, we argue that responsibility is more than duty or the fulfilment of obligations: *practical* responsibility. Ezrahi (1990, cited in Deetz and White 1999, 113) refers to practical responsibility as 'technicalisation' of action; action purified of personal ends. This is the form of micro-level responsibility with which much of the early spatial planning-related research was concerned, including Howe and

Kaufman's (1979, 1981) and Howe's (1992, 1994) surveys of American practising planners, through Taylor's (1992), Hendler's (1996, 2005; Bickenbach and Hendler 1994) and Esnard's (1996) concern with professional codes of practice as 'moral mandates' of the profession. These works of practical responsibility also include Bolan's (1985) three-dimensional matrix of ethical choice in planning (moral communities of obligation, culturally received ideologies and norms, diversity of contexts of choice in practice). All of these publications are well worked-through moral cartographies of a 'professional' ethos of individual practitioner behaviours. We claim, however, that responsibility requires more than just meeting a prescribed moral check-list.

Finally, we suggest that responsibility has a spatial dimension that has changed over time with our increasingly wider understanding of the inter-connectedness of the planet. The 'responsible' citizen of classical Athens had a responsibility to family and fellow citizens in the democratic management of the city-state of a few tens of thousand people (Arendt 1961). With the rise of the modern state, one had, at most, a responsibility to one's nation-state and perhaps its empire. Concepts of democratic ethically responsible action were, and largely still are, bounded within the institutional structures of the nation-state. For example, John Rawls' conceptualisation of thin good ('those primary goods that any rational individual will require to pursue whatever plan of life they might have') and thick good ('the particular ends and life plans individuals may pursue') together constitutes the ability to have shared and contested pluralistic positions within a single nation-state of mutual responsibility (O'Neil 2005, 483; Rawls 1971, 1993b). This is a pluralism that does not readily transcend borders, however (Nussbaum 2001b; Rawls 1993a).

We live in a world of global flows and connectivities. An action on one side of the world can have profound impact on the other. Responsibility has taken on a global dimension, identified over twenty years ago by Jonas (1984) and given an ethical prescription of responsibility via the concept of 'future-care' towards nature. Yet this prescription has subsequently invoked, at best, only limited responses towards global responsibility. We argue that most spatial planning action is still focused on consideration of particular local outcomes, or contained within a framework of national policy intentions such as the UK SMART targets (ODPM 2005b, 23). Correspondingly, traditional understandings of responsibility, which are generally predicated on concepts of duty, or the achievement of the better 'good', reflect local or national perspectives and are geographically bounded. We suggest that it is time for spatial planners to consider responsibility more globally.

Hillier (2009) documents a British case study of local planning process regarding the dismantling of End-of-Life, or so-called 'toxic-ships' in Hartlepool. Regardless of the local particularity of the necessary consents and permits to dismantle these ships, the vessels and their toxic environmental contents originate in the US and are an artefact of US policy in World War II and after, to help protect Western Europe against the threat of military incursion. The consequences of the British local authority planning outcome to refuse the environmental risk of ship disassembly under rigorously controlled UK, European Community and International Maritime Organisation standards for environmental protection and the health and safety of workers, could have potentially resulted in their manual disassembly on an Asian beach. In a globalised world where does responsibility reside? Are traditional understandings of the concept of planning responsibility still relevant in our contemporary world: a world of interconnected environmental, economic and social flows, where the consequences of our individual energy and material consumption impact even more on a Pacific tropical atoll and its inhabitants than in our own backyards?

In this context, what premises should underlie any social construction of the concept of responsibility to engage with others in a globalised world? Further, while we recognise that the Earth's carrying capacity is finite, yet why is it that we so often in our 'responsible' planning policy prescriptions, behaviours and attitudes carry on giving this, at best, token regard?

The premise in this chapter is to engage with responsibility primarily in its role as a relational social construct. Indeed, humans generally act in respect to how we think others expect and want us to act in our various personal and professional roles. Žižek (1989, 2005a) would argue that we materialise what we think are the expectations of the Other in our actions and this constitutes the ideology underlying and driving our very social reality. Consequently, our interrelations with other actors are integral to the development of senses of responsibility to the self and towards others. The actions that constitute our 'responsibility' are a materialisation of this ideology. Responsibility is a social construct, 'negotiated' in stylised mythical contractual manner, in what we consider to be our deep and 'open moral communities' (Mandelbaum 2000).

While the Auckland spatial planner, mentioned in the vignette above, engaged in an act of responsibility, this was with regard to a planning judgement about the environmental consequences of a ground excavation contained in a particular locale with little overt geographical externalities. However, a secondary consequence of the planner's action was that it eventually resulted in 2,900 fewer CBD car parking spaces and the potential reduction of daily car usage and greenhouse gases that this might induce. Where then does the horizon of responsibility reside in an age of globalisation and climate change?

## Modernist Responsibility: Duty and the Delineated Good

In this section we are concerned with two traditional interpretations of responsibility: responsibility as duty and responsibility to an ideal transcendental 'good'. We critique the weaknesses of contemporary extrapolations of Kant's categorical imperative, which lies as a central foundation of the deontic interpretation of responsibility, especially as constituted in US-American liberal concepts of rights and reciprocal obligations. The latter part of the section considers how spatial planning is largely premised on a responsibility to create a 'better' world. The key concern in this mission is 'how' and 'for whom', and particularly, 'in whose interest is this betterment framed'? Central to both areas of critique is the concept of power, an area conventionally overlooked in much spatial planning theory that seeks a view of the world predicated on normative idealism (Flyvbjerg and Richardson 2002, 60).

## Responsibility as Duty

In modernity, arguably the strongest and most common interpretation of 'responsibility' is as a duty. Deontological, or duty-based conceptualisations, as to what constitute 'good' or responsible action are largely constituted in and derived from the late 18th-century philosophy of Kant (1959). Central to Kant's ethical logic is his categorical imperative to 'only act in such a way that I could not also will that my maxim should be a universal law' (Kant 1959, 18). In Kant's ethics there 'is only one moral good, defined as an act accomplished in conformity with duty and strictly for the sake of duty' (Zupančič 2000, 53). Often this is presented as a dutiful obligation presented in relationship to a set of reciprocal rights.

The idea of responsibility as duty may be criticised on several fronts. Firstly, following procedural rules to the letter ignores the potential consequences of actions. Kant's stress on the importance of universal rules as leading to impartial decisions and protecting human rights is reflected in Rawls' (1971) prioritisation of the 'right' over the 'good'. All these views disregard that rules, themselves, are social constructs produced at a particular time by a particular society. Somewhere along the way Kant's categorical imperative to 'only act in such a way that I could not also will that my maxim should be a universal law' became reified, especially under the US-American interpretation of liberalism, with the replacement of 'my maxim *should be* a universal law' with 'my rules *are* a universal law'! Yet, rules are fraught with politics and exclusions and are far from impartial. As Upton (2002, 260) states, 'we choose, ultimately, the rules we use; but we choose them to fix the values that we seek to enact'. Often these rules are little different from common sense beliefs, the antithesis of Kant's (1990) foundation of reason predicated on daring to know truth for oneself. As Zupančič (2000, 93) observes; 'every ideology works hard to make certain things "obvious", and the more we find these things obvious, self-evident and unquestionable, the more successfully the ideology has done its job'. Here resides Gramsci's (1971) 'common sense of the day' that, at least in the neo-liberal worldview of globalisation, constitutes rights and duties in relationship to obligations of justice, as universal truths of unquestionable, hence metaphysical, foundations.

This is compounded further by Kant's call to duty where 'the dutiful agent takes no responsibility for the consequence of his [*sic*] acts' even when one's reflection-less duty is perverted into perpetrating evil (Kohn 2003, xxii). The work of Harper and Stein (1983, 1995, 2006) demonstrates this perspective in the planning literature from a Rawlsian neo-pragmatic perspective. Their work draws heavily on Kant via Rawls' (1971, 1993b, 2001) use of the categorical imperative as a principle of justice, where 'the notion of morality is based in rational choice among free and equal persons' (Grcic 1983, 237). The latter is perhaps a reading of Kant open to ideological critique as it replaces the universalism of the categorical imperative as a necessity with that of contingency predicated on consensus (Grcic 1983, 239-240). Indeed, with regard to universality, 'Rawls assumes that the scope of those who have obligations of justice to one another is a single relatively closed society' (Young 2006, 103). As discussed in Chapter 7, Rawls' approach cannot, therefore, be universalised, or globalised. We reside in a world of diverse nation-states, cultures and faiths, which in their diversity collectively fail to share a minimal 'thin' good necessary (in Rawls' argument) to partake in pluralistic debate.

We also question the Rawlsian conceptualisation of the 'social division of responsibility'. This is where 'society, citizens as a collective body, accepts responsibility for maintaining the equal basic liberties and fair equality of opportunity, and for providing a fair share of the primary goods for all within this framework; while citizens as individuals and associations accept responsibility for revising and adjusting their ends and aspirations in view of the all-purpose means they can expect, given their present and foreseeable situation' (Rawls 1993b, 189). Such an allocation of responsibility depends on the ability of people to assume responsibility for their own ends and, accordingly, to curb the demands they make on their society's finite 'goods' and resources. How are these wants and desires of primary goods set? Moreover, how are these limits of provision and responsibility set and regulated and, fundamentally, in whose interest (after Flyvbjerg 1998) and to whose accountability?

Responsibility as duty brackets the important issue of power. As Michel Foucault (1982, 1988) has demonstrated, power is always present in human relations, 'whether it be a question of communicating verbally ... or a question of a love relationship, an institutional or economic relationship' (Foucault 1987, 6 cited in Smart 1998, 81). Such power relations may potentially be resisted, challenged and/or transgressed (Foucault 1982). Smart (1998) suggests that there is a need to relate the exercise of power to the concept of responsibility, something which he identifies as lacking in Foucault's work. He proposes that 'universal rule-dictated *duties*' (1998, 83) have usurped actors' individual moral responsibility for their behaviour in a progressive governmentalisation of power relations. Similarly, Williams (2006, 210) observes that normative liberal theory also tends to underplay and neglect 'the structuring power of social and economic, as well as political, institutions – a structuring that is essential if individual autonomy is to be meaningful and responsibly realised.'

Nikolas Rose's (1999, 2001) analysis of this issue demonstrates how governmental utilisation of personal ethics as a technology for shaping conduct 'works through the values, beliefs and sentiments thought to underpin techniques of responsible self-government and the management of obligations to others' (Flint 2003, 613). Such techniques involve an explicit moral rationality working through the invocation of 'responsible' conduct, both by agents of governance in their obligations to communities and by those communities members' obligations to themselves and to the agencies of governance. As Flint (2003, 613) comments, 'such reflexive government seeks to act upon the performance of governmental institutions and techniques, through a range of technologies that engender forms of responsible autonomy and rational choice for both service "consumers" and providers'.

For providers, such as spatial planning authorities, their 'responsible autonomy' is earned through duty-full managerialism manifest in 'good' performance in governmental audits. We argue that regarding responsibility as duty in this way, such as achieving set performance targets, is blind to the pernicious operation of power in structuring the form of that duty. Responsibility 'without the conception of power ... is a poisoned gift: it does not allow a critical stance towards responsibility, but responsibility can be used to suppress the Other by doing more [or less] than the Other wants to be done' (Junge 2001, 114). Alternatively, responsibility as duty may codify the good into a reified performance target, or contract, of procedures whose successful dutiful achievement may have no actual regard to the attainment of good or bad resultant outcomes as a consequence of the process itself (Gunder 2003a, 266-267).

Further, conceptualisation of responsibility as a duty facilitates what Buchanan and Decamp (2006, 96) refer to as 'duty dumping'. Here to '"dump" a duty ... means to ascribe obligations to individuals or institutions, holding them accountable for the adverse ... effects of their policies, without offering adequate justification for why particular obligations should be imposed' (96). For example, for agencies of government to assert that home-owners have a duty to ensure that their homes are built and maintained in a sustainable manner, without having the necessary policies, building and development controls in place to ensure that developers actually build sustainable structures, would be duty dumping. While duty dumping may, in the short term, be a useful political strategy, even if unprincipled, it is also a 'powerful mechanism for the evasion of responsibility' (97) on the part of institutions of governance.

Viewing responsibility as duty codifies, standardises and/or normalises responsibility. It makes responsibility insensitive to the particulars of relationships and events. We prefer, in contrast, Carol Gilligan's (1982) approach, which frames the notion of responsibility as caring and a concern for others within the specific context. Gilligan stresses application of care and connectedness rather than rules and justice (Gergen 1999); arguing the complementarity of ethics of care and justice (Schwickert 2005). As Cloke (2002, 598) explains, whilst individuals may comply strictly with the rules, they lack thought about the 'unanticipated/ invisible/distant' consequences of their actions on other human and non-human actors. Further, these individuals may have little or no say as to the values or 'goods' sought by these rules in the first place. This is particularly the case when imposed externally on a culture through imperialistic actions of a nation-state such as the '*Pax Americana*', or the wider commercial imperatives of economic globalisation. We argue, therefore, that in duty-full responsibility, systemic power relations are being sustained, and even enhanced, by the normalised behaviour of the collectivity of individuals.

*Responsibility as Delineation of the Good*

The search to define and create the 'good' has been a central quest at least since Plato and Aristotle. However, as Arendt (1961, 113) observed, by the mid-20th century, the decline in the western world of the previous state of near-universal religious faith and traditional values of paternalistic authority had resulted in a decline in the power of any one call to a 'responsibility to the good' to dictate unquestioned universal action. The unquestionable authority of the secular state or dominant religious dogma gradually paled in an increasingly diverse world of contestable facts, norms and truths. Moreover, the loss of such a call to a universal tradition, especially of a religious nature, and its relatively fixed definition of any good (derived and legitimised from past belief and authority) has laid the grounds for the contemporary political 'good' to be open to contestation and hegemonic articulation. As discussed in previous chapters, the secular 'good' has become an empty and/or floating signifier to be captured by competing hegemonic projects. In contrast to a call of traditional authority of the Book or Leader 'that Knows' (with a capital 'K'), the deployment of hegemonic power by resource-full interest groups through multiple means, including the promotion of selected 'knowledge' via the media, has become a central dimension defining the 'good' in a secular world.

Nevertheless, a responsibility to the creation of a better world still underlies 'the development of planning thought and the emergence of the planning profession: planning should, first and foremost, act to improve people's (mainly physical) living conditions' (Yiftachel 1994, 217). However, while spatial planning's broad enlightenment consensus to build a 'better' world is widely agreed by the profession, planning practice does not always produce results that are judged as being 'good' (Allmendinger and Gunder 2005). Yiftachel (1995, 2000, 434-435) and others document how planning can also be deployed explicitly or implicitly to produce outcomes that result in 'a stratified and segregated … space which reinforced and reproduced social inequalities and polarization'.

As we have indicated throughout this book, multiculturalism, sustainability, Smart Growth, and global competitiveness, are all examples of prescriptive, but empty, and therefore contestable, signifiers, which spatial planners invoke in pursuit of a 'good' or better world. These ideological 'solutions' are an unobtainable transcendental ideal which influences planning practice, whilst at the same time seducing practitioners into believing that they are somehow achieving this 'good'. Yet, as Žižek (2008a, 344-355) argues 'the subject never rises [fully] to the level of its responsibility towards the Call of the Good' because a fanatical commitment to any all encompassing 'good' would actually becomes a 'bad', or even evil, as it 'introduces into the flow of (social life) a violent cut that throws it out of joint'.

It is only an ideal's partial failure to achieve an absolute 'good' that allows its successful acceptance. The previous chapter's exploration of the importance of the transcendental ideal, or 'good', of sustainability in spatial planning practice suggests that while the quest for sustainability gives new vitality to planning's perceived worth and societal value, it does so largely by the adoption of a particular slant on sustainability which contradicts its original aim of ecological global protection and limitations to growth by maintaining the status quo of economic development. At best, sustainability is used as a foil to ensure an appropriately bourgeois cosmopolitan environment defined as 'good' by urban 'gurus' such as Richard Florida (2000, 2002c) in the quest for success in 'the global age of talent'. Behind these visions of the good city lies the unquestioned driving force of the 'good' of economic growth and the assumption that places with high amenity for the 'worthy' professional classes will be more successful than their competitor cities under the imperatives of globalisation.

This section has considered responsibility in the light of Kantian predicated duty and found it wanting. The universality of Kant's categorical imperative in actual, if not in ideal, practice is bounded. 'Universality' seldom extends beyond single cultures, or nation-states that can form a degree of, at best, consensus or, more likely, hegemony for sets of accepted value rules that shape and reify duty. Further, such accountability of duty is dependant on the authority and power of institutions, few of which extend beyond the confines of the nation-state. Moreover, those broader institutions, such as the United Nations, are relatively powerless under the vetoes, checks and 'balances' of the dominant state powers, or alternatively act non-democratically as one arm of state imperialist will, such as the IMF or World Bank, in the name of global capitalism. Similarly, with contestable and multiple 'goods', a responsibility to the good – while still a driving force underlying the modern spatial planning project – remains open to the influences of power and further hegemonic domination.

## Alternative Abilities that Respond

In this section, we explore the thinking of Lévinas and Derrida on responsibility. Both positions are grounded in a relationship between the subject and the other. It is a relation premised on empathy and a reflection of one's own potential for suffering. It is a conceptualisation of responsibility, which transcends Kant's deontic turn; and, we suggest, one that can be extended beyond our local communities to have effect in a complex globalised world. Derrida's conceptualisation of responsibility is also explored in the context of aporia or paradox and undecidability. We suggest that his position – where responsibility means to act in the face of uncertainty and to accept the consequences of one's actions – is a particularly important ethical position for spatial planning in our contemporary world. However, Lévinas and Derrida's positions are not without their own concerns. We accordingly conclude with a Žižekian critique that suggests a possible way forward.

*Lévinas: Responsibility to the Other*

Lévinas (1985, 95) states that 'responsibility is the essential, primary and fundamental structure of subjectivity' which appears as a relationship of responsibility to and for the other (Popke 2004, 303). Responsibility for the other 'is precisely what goes beyond the legal and obliges beyond contracts' (Lévinas 1989, 180). It is ethically impossible to transfer one's responsibility to a third party (Lévinas 1993, 44). Responsibility, for Lévinas, is the essence of subjectivity, not a mere philosophical or moral commitment to some other. Consequently, ethics comprises a condition of being hostage to an unconditional responsibility towards the other, 'not as a code or rule to be followed, but as a fundamental feature of our subjectivity, our collective humanity' (Popke 2004, 303). Lévinas defines responsibility in three interrelated parameters, summarised as:

1. 'responsibility' as responding *to* the other in an indeclinable fashion;
2. 'responsibility' as responding *for oneself* to the other person and its demands; and
3. 'responsibility' as responding *for the other* in the sense of substituting oneself for the other person in its responsibilities'. (Hutchens 2004, 19 – emphasis in original)

Lévinas called for a responsibility that transcends the economic and the political realms. His call is for us never to lose sight of the other; 'to pay attention to the other and take account of him [*sic*] and the strange world he inhabits' (Metselaar 2005, 63). 'The face before me summons me ... The Other becomes my neighbour precisely through the way the face summons me, calls for me, begs for me, and in so doing recalls my responsibility' (Lévinas 1989, 83, cited in Smart 1995, 106).

Our TV screens beam images of suffering into our homes from around the world. Faces ravaged by famine, tsunamis, war, appeal to our responsibility as wealthy Westerners to donate charitably: 'naked and destitute, the face commands: "Do not leave me in solitude"' (Lindahl 2002, np). While circumstances which are reported by the media using harrowing, pity-full images tend to catch the public's attention and charity, there are far more equally serious circumstances in the world that are not reported. Out of sight becomes out of mind.

Can we extend such a face-to-face relation of responsibility to unknown, unseen, face-less actors? For Lévinas (1993, 124), responsibility towards the other is universalised. It is an ontological dimension of our very humanity – it is what makes us human – without regard to spatial and temporal proximity. As such, our 'responsibility is unconditional, and holds equally to those who are "distant" as those who are near' (Popke 2003, 304). Responsibility for the suffering of this other, in the spatio-temporal immediacy of the face-to-face, entails responsibility for all others (Irvine 2005). Ethical proximity, therefore, transgresses spatial, ideological and temporal barriers. Llewelyn (1991), for instance, has drawn on Lévinas to extend this responsibility to the wider environment including all living beings and the non-living on earth. To act sustainably is to act responsibly to all, not just to the market imperative dominating sustainable development. We find ourselves responsible for those whose faces we cannot face; an infinite responsibility (Lévinas 1989, 206), for with the other our accounts are never settled (Lévinas 1993, 125).

Lévinas' concept of responsibility is not without its critics. Both Derrida (1978, 160) and Ricoeur (1992, 355) question the individual's ability to have an asymmetrical relationship of responsibility to the other. Although Derrida concedes the impossibility of unbounded responsibility, he nonetheless indicates how its aporias/paradoxes are actually the condition of its possibility as we indicate below.

## *Derridean Responsibility for Decisions*

> If the whole political project would be ... [a] consequence of assured knowledge (euphoric, without paradox, without aporia, free of contradiction, without undecidabilities to decide), that would be a machine that runs without us, without responsibility, without decision, at bottom without ethics, nor law, nor politics. There is no decision nor responsibility without the test of aporia or undecidability. (Derrida 2000a, np)

Emmanuel Lévinas' work exerted a 'powerful and continuous influence' (Critchley 2004, 127) on that of Jacques Derrida. Derrida adapts Lévinas' relation to the other, adding a much greater understanding of context and otherness. His relation to the other thus not only concerns the other person, but also other non-human actors, other ways of being and of seeing, 'other races, other genders, another time ... other languages, other traditions' (Roffe 2004, 44).

Derrida addresses the relationship between the responsibility to act and the responsibility to otherness. He refers to the tensions in responsibility for architects (and spatial planners), whose responsibility encompasses irreconcilable obligations both to the singularity of each citizen and to the universality of the law (Derrida 1997b, 22). Derrida also identifies irreconcilable tensions between responsibilities to others generally (including all humans and non-humans) and to a singular other (such as a partner, client, employer, God, etc.) (Derrida 1995, 57-70). Of course, absolute responsibility to everyone and everything is an impossibility in practice. Responsibility is always conditional, advanced to certain determinate others.

Derrida emphasises that such tensions tend to be ignored by the 'knights of responsibility' (1995, 85) who 'presume that accountability and responsibility ... is [*sic*] quite easily established' (Reynolds 2004, 49) and who insist on the provision of concrete ethical guidelines. These 'knights' and their Codes of Practice completely ignore the deep complexities of responsibility, 'which demands something importantly different from merely behaving dutifully' (Reynolds 2004, 49).

Derrida suggests that behaving dutifully, automatically following rules or guidelines, is actually *ir*responsible and *un*ethical. 'When the path is clear and given, when a certain knowledge opens up the way in advance, the decision is already made, it might as well be said there is none to make: irresponsibly, and in good conscience, one simply applies or implements a program' (Derrida 1992a, 41). A clear course of action merely makes ethics and politics a 'technology' and not a decision as such (Derrida 1992a, 43). Although contrary to strict rule-following, as Lucy (2004, 107) explains, a fully personal decision – one not taking into account any social, ethical, political or other pressures to be responsible – would not be a decision either, but merely a self-gratifying whim.

Derridean responsibility, therefore, involves struggling with the undecidability of differences within and between prescribed (rule-following), experimental, and personal decisions; for, whatever is decided, one could have always decided differently. It is 'excessive' (Derrida 1991, 118), an 'experience and experiment of the possibility of the impossible' (Derrida 1992a, 41 cited in Lucy 2004, 107). It is a responsibility without limits; excessive, incalculable and 'before memory' (Derrida 1990, 953), a responsibility in the face of a heritage of a 'whole network of connected concepts (property, intentionality, will, conscience, self-consciousness, subject, self, person, community, decision, and so forth)' (1990, 955).

Responsible decisions are undecidable as they could always be otherwise. Undecidability is thus a 'necessary condition' of decidability (Derrida 1988, 116). Responsible decisions have to risk being wrong. No wonder that Derrida claimed responsibility to be 'anxiety-ridden' (1990, 955) and decisions 'trials' (1988, 116) and 'ordeals' (1990, 957). We argue that spatial planning decisions exemplify undecidability because at the time of the decision eventual outcomes cannot be known.[1]

As observed in Chapter 4, responsible decision-making for Derrida, combines an imperative to act with the patience of respecting the 'radical alterity [alternative or otherness] of the future' by 'prising open' the gap between knowledge and action (Barnett 2004, 517). There is always uncertainty when making a decision, regardless of how well one has attained and reflected upon the available knowledge about an issue (Derrida and Roudinesco 2001, 92 cited in Egéa-Kuehne 2003, 278). There is never complete or perfect knowledge or information from which to decide.

Responsibility for actions is thus assumed in the absence of perfect knowledge and certainty. For Trifonas (2003, 112) it is an 'instant of madness'. One can never completely justify any responsible decision (Derrida 1995, 70) and we can never really know whether the decision taken was the 'best' or the 'right' one (Derrida 2002, 232). This deciding action of responsibility relates to Lacan's (2007) Master's Discourse. Decision-makers partake in this discourse because it empowers them to slash through the complicated issues, analyses and material considerations of a wicked problem to assert 'a simple "Yes" or "No"' making a 'gesture that can

---

1    For more detailed discussion of undecidability see Lucy (2004, 147-151).

never be fully grounded in reasons,' because it is the assertion of the master who must be obeyed (Žižek 1998a, 76, 2008d, 34)!

Derrida's concern with responsibility is predicated on the complexity of the actual world, not some idealised modernist construct of truth, morality or justice that is dependent on stark binaries of assumed and all-knowable singular presence that provide simplified rules and limits. Even when a decision seems straightforward, to be responsible implies that 'it is not enough to act only in accordance with categorical knowledge, calculative judgement and pre-given laws', but one must constantly challenge the dominant presence on which these knowledges, judgements and laws claim legitimacy (Derrida 1995, 27; Shildrick 2003, 188).

It is in Derrida's notion of responsibility as hospitality where we find the major differences between his work and that of Lévinas. Derrida extends Lévinas' face-to-face conceptualisation of responsibility to that of unconditional hospitality: hospitality to the other, the distant and unfamiliar, with strangers (Savić 2005). Derrida (1994, xix) reminds us that 'without this responsibility and this respect for justice concerning those who are not here, of those who are no longer or who are not yet present and living, what sense would there be to ask the question "where?"'; of our responsibility to examine other geographies and other temporalities.

Those who are absent ('not here') not only include geographically and temporally distant human actors, such as women workers in Asian clothing factories, or workers dismantling toxic-ships on Bangladeshi beaches, but also non-human actors (air, water, soils, flora, fauna, etc.) which should be inserted into responsibility (see Llewelyn 1991). Responsibility, for Derrida, is composed of 'response' plus 'ability', that is, the ability to respond, to hear, whereby it is a play of listening and speaking as Hardy (2002, 472) observes:

> The face-to-face is an individual ordeal. The responsibility (which is not the same as blame) is individual. But with the dissolution of the face-to-face the responsibility of the I becomes response ability in the world. This dissolution marks the movement from ethics to politics.

Derrida argues that such an unconditional, impossibly limitless form of responsibility is necessary to impact politics or to bring about change (Patton 2004) by attempting to include currently excluded others. He recognises the role of power in the exercise of boundary-drawing, limiting or conditioning responsibility. Decision makers engage in 'choosing, electing, filtering, selecting' (Derrida 2000b, 55) those to whom they will extend hospitality (e.g., through granting asylum or planning consent) and thereby exclude and do violence to those others not included.

Derrida's conception of responsibility aspires to be consequential, to 'engage with events and transformations already underway in a manner that contributes to making the future different from and in some sense "better" than the past' (Patton 2003, 159). This is a transformative future in which law and politics are recast

(Derrida 1990, 971). But it is also an unpresentable future; a future that is not identified with 'any future present but rather with something that remains in the future, a ... future which will never be actualised in any present even though it remains capable of acting in or upon the present' (Patton 2003, 166-167). All responsible decisions thus inherently contain a component of undecidability as to what the future will become.

> However careful one is in the theoretical preparation of a decision, the instant of the decision, if there is to be a decision, must be heterogeneous to the accumulation of knowledge. Otherwise, there is no responsibility. In this sense not only must the person taking the decision not know everything ... the decision ... must advance towards the future which is not known, which cannot be anticipated. (Derrida 2002, 231)

Derrida (1990, 971) suggests that while the unpresentable exceeds the knowable, this should not serve as an excuse to avoid ethical and political engagement. Rather it should act as a reason for experimentation, for innovation and reinvention, for going beyond the place we find ourselves 'so that the coming be that of the other' (Derrida 1993, 216). For Derrida, responsibility demands that we give up dreams of total knowledge, fantasies of mastery and duty-full rationalism. He offers us a different way of thinking responsibility and responsibly with potential to be far more receptive and responsive to the dissonant multiplicity of voices across space-time. There is no end to Derridean responsibility. We are 'never responsible enough' (Derrida 1995, 51).

*What Žižek Says ...*

The Žižekian position has considerable regard for both Lévinas' and Derrida's stances on responsibility. Žižek observes that rather than 'preaching an easy grounding of politics in the ethics of the respect and responsibility for the Other, Lévinas instead insists on their absolute incompatibility, on the gap separating the two dimensions: ethics involves an asymmetric relationship in which I am always-already responsible for the Other, while politics is the domain of symmetrical equality and distributional justice' (Žižek 2005c, 149). In this regard, ethics 'hardens its skin' as soon as one moves into the political world of 'the impersonal "third" – the world of government, institutions, tribunals, schools, committees, and so on' – the political (Lévinas and Kearney 1986, 30). Accordingly, Žižek (2005a, 343-344) suggests that, influenced by Lévinas, Derrida positions responsibility in a gap located between ethics and politics where ethics is grounded in undecidability and the political performs resolution.

As developed in previous chapters, the Lacanian and Žižekian position of the subject must always exist in relationship to the Other – we fundamentally want to be wanted by others, hence we strive to give the Other what we think, rightly or wrongly, the Other wants. However, of course, we do not even know what we want ourselves – an understanding of our own desire and underlying unconscious 'truths' is always lacking – so guessing the Other's secret desires and repressed 'truths' is an even greater impossibility. These 'truths' reside in the Real. Žižek (1997b, 50-51) observes that the subject relates to, has sympathy and even shared understanding with the Other: when

> I become aware of how the very problem that was bothering me (the nature of the Other's secret) is already bothering the Other itself. The dimension of the Universal thus emerges when the two lacks – mine and that of the Other – overlap … What we and the inaccessible Other share is the empty signifier that stands for the X which eludes both positions.

This is an ethical relationship with regard to what is inherently a political issue. The attempted determination of X, the lacking knowledge about our desires, by its very nature, is a political act (Laclau 2005). However, this is an act grounded in an inherently ethical relationship without the need for any external 'big Other' to guarantee it. It is therefore in this response that the traditional separation between ethics and politics disintegrates. Both become one and the same to open up a space of action without the need for any 'big Other'.

Žižek suggests that this provides a point of transition from the position of justice, as Duty, to one of caring, where care is 'a fundamental feature of being human' (Popke 2006, 507). Consequently, 'the ultimate horizon for ethics is *not* the infinite debt towards an abyssal Otherness … [it is] the suspension of the "big *Other*"' (Žižek 2005a, 345 – emphasis in original). It is to take responsibility for our actions as there is no 'ultimate guarantee of Meaning' (Žižek 2008, 442). This is an ethics predicated on the Real.

In the following concluding section, we suggest that spatial planners are particularly well placed to engage in such an ethics of care and responsible action via the political world of planning processes. Moreover, we will articulate why, in our interconnected world, we believe that spatial planners have an especially important responsibility to do so.

## Towards Responsible Spatial Planning

This section seeks to provide a synthesis of the Lévinasian and Derridian positions in relationship to an ethics of the Real. This is an ethics predicated on our shared lack of knowledge about that which is currently unknown or is potentially unknowable; that which resides in the Real, as developed in Chapter 4. It is the Real that fundamentally constitutes aporia, undeciderability and antagonism, for it is 'the disavowed X on account of which our vision of reality is anamorphically distorted' (Žižek 2008a, 287-288). This includes our own desire, and that of the Other, because desire is repressed in the unconscious and consequently resides outside of the very abilities of symbolic articulation (Lacan 2006). At best, the symptoms of the affects of the Real haunt us from the periphery of our perceptions through our wants, dissatisfactions and insecurities.

We also draw on the work of Iris Marion Young (2004, 2006) on connected responsibility. If there is no 'big Other' providing the illusion of authority, legitimation and adjudication for our actions – no final or last judgement to give legitimacy and meaning – this provides a new engagement with the concept of responsibility (Žižek 2008, 224). This is an engagement that is consistent with the Derridian position, but one that moves critical understandings of responsibility into a more implementable light. It is a position that is not necessarily bounded and given authority by the norms and values of an individual's culture, society, state, or their fantasy construct of the 'big Other', which is always seemingly watching and judging.

*Responsible Theory: Towards Responsible Planning in a Globalised World*

Max Weber (2004, 54) observed in 1919 that it is the bureaucrats' task explicitly to follow the orders of their political leaders on whom the responsibility for the eventual outcomes of these acts lies. Unfortunately, history has shown this to be a rather dubious injunction. Hannah Arendt (2003) also addressed political responsibility. In direct contrast to Weber, she observed 'that political responsibility … is a responsibility for what we have *not done*' (Young 2004, 377 – emphasis in original). The wider social structures of nation-states have *allowed* ethnic cleansing or other perverse inhuman or non-human actions to occur on numerous occasions, not through the collective action of the many, but often through their very inaction.

Samuel Scheffler (2004) argues that allowing harm to occur, or failing to prevent harm occurring, should be attributed less responsibility than if one actually perpetrates the harm directly. This contentious argument would suggest that a spatial planner who fails to impose conditions on a potentially polluting development cannot be held directly responsible for any pollution which results. Many disagree with Scheffler. Bradley and Stocker (2005) and Thompson (2006), for instance, argue that 'allowing' is 'doing' if one knows about the potential harm. In this light, we suggest that, especially for spatial planners processing development approvals, allowing *is* doing.

Such is the reasoning behind Iris Marion Young's (2003, 2004) model of political responsibility, later, and more appropriately we believe, reworked as the social connection model (2006). Young suggests that individuals bear responsibility because they contribute by their actions ('doing'), or their inactions as actions ('allowing'), to processes producing unjust or uncaring outcomes: 'our responsibility derives from belonging together with others in a system of interdependent processes of co-operation and competition through which we seek benefits and aim to realise projects' (2006, 119).

If everyone on the planet is really separated by only six degrees of separation (Watts 1999, 2003), then responsibilities are complex, multiple and interlocking.

The local spatial planner in the toxic-ship example, by following the accepted procedures and rules of spatial planning legislation, inevitably contributes to a greater or lesser degree to the re/production of some form of injustice in some spatial location, whether in England or Asia. The social relations that connect actors are not restricted to local authority or national borders. As such, O'Neill (1985, 1996) argues that we (including spatial planning practitioners) have practical moral commitments to distant others by virtue of our actions. We also have relations of responsibility to processes themselves (Young 2004, 372).

Socially connected responsibility is both backward- and forward-looking, though it tends to emphasise forward-looking issues (Young 2006, 121). It is also shared responsibility, as each actor is only responsible for an outcome in a partial manner. A complex web of actors is involved. However, as Young (2006, 125) indicates, the degree of power to influence the processes that produce unjust outcomes is important in distinguishing degrees of responsibility.

Young (2004, 2006) follows Feinberg (1980), as well as Derrida (1992a), in distinguishing between duty and responsibility. Whereas duty specifies an obligatory rule of action, responsibility consists in seeking to bring about a specified outcome. Additionally, as Young (2006, 126) suggests, part of what it means to be responsible is 'to be accountable to others with whom one shares responsibility'. Within a network which materially connects spatial planning practitioners in the UK with residents and workers internationally, for example, in Asian ship-breaking yards or scrap recycling factories, Young would argue that spatial planners have responsibilities to be concerned with the wellbeing of those overseas.

Should spatial planners be morally responsible for consequences that they cannot prevent? As Sparti (2000, 90) points out, an initial reaction to such questions tends to be avoidance or denial: 'I shut my eyes on you, removing you from my world' (Cavell 1979, 430). Our view is that as humans, we should avoid avoidance and acknowledge the Other (human and non-human), and, when it is at all possible, actually act in regard to their interests (Sparti 2000). We believe that spatial planners, as agents of governance, have a moral responsibility as they have 'guidance control' and 'regulative control' over events (Fischer and Ravizza 1998). It is an issue of taking responsibility for what one says (Kitching 2003, 214). This is a response to social and environmental justice that raises the questions of what is the spatial extent of a socially or environmentally just 'community' (e.g., the planet, the region, the local authority administrative area?), and who and what might constitute 'community' (from all entities to local ratepayers only) and 'justice' (equal treatment, affirmative action, etc.).

So, who can and who should take responsibility? As authors such as Amin (2004a, 2004b) and Massey (2004, 2005) ask, should 'local' people take decisions which have international implications; should elected politicians in the Houses of Parliament; should bureaucrats in Whitehall, or Canberra, or Washington? And what about non-human 'decisions'; the dynamic multiplicity of the ocean, its flora and fauna; the dynamics of End-of-Life ships as multiplicities of active chemicals, metals, plastics and living beings (barnacles, rats, spiders and so on)?

We propose a much broader consideration of responsibility for spatial planning, derived from Lévinasian and Derridean ideas of responsibility to the unconditional other. This would imply a radically different, relational form of political and spatial planning responsibility in practice; 'one that accepts responsibility for its participation in and performances of the world' (Law 2003, 9). The boundaries of such responsibility would not be coterminous with territorial boundaries, but rather caringly 'unite human beings as moral persons beyond borders' (Benhabib 2005, 18). Responsibility would transgress borders of the human/non-human, of space and time.

Derridean responsibility is impossible, as is the attainment of perfect knowledge, having certainty towards the future, or even a basic means to articulate the Real. There is, unfortunately, no 'getting it right'. Certainty eradicates responsibility. Nevertheless, we agree with Paul Cloke (2002, 596-597) that 'a gloomy acceptance of an inability to change things represents an abrogation of the responsibility to recognise the extent of [a] capacity for action, as well as a fear that the engagement of this capacity may demand significant and unacceptable changes in the (self-centred) ways in which we live our lives'.

Responsibility is a social construct. As such, the values and assumptions underlying conceptualisations of responsibility and their implications across human and non-human actors, across space and time, should be more openly and transparently discussed. Yet whatever wonderfully 'responsible' principles we may invoke and agree upon in theory must be practicable, and that is where the 'real world' of politics and practice is likely to intervene.

It is all too easy to suggest creating some new modalities of political agency, such as international institutions and norms of law for dealing with asylum seekers, shipments of toxic waste and so on, whereby a third party takes on the responsibility of individuals. We suggest that such impersonalisation risks the dangers of Foucauldian governmentality, reducing humans and non-humans to normalised case numbers and statistics, removing the very 'face-to-face'ness of Lévinasian responsibility, thereby avoiding it. It is at best simply another form of institutional 'duty dumping'.

We believe that responsibility lies in avoiding avoidance. We may excuse genuine ignorance (not knowing about others) but not avoidance (ignoring others). Once we are aware of a potentially violent, unsafe or negative outcome from a particular decision, if we choose to avoid that knowledge and recommend that decision, we become involved and implicated in that avoidance. If we regard a decision as a 'future-oriented action governed by the anticipation of being held to account, expected to give reasons, and asked to make justifications' (Barnett 2004, 519), then deliberate ignorance and avoidance become inexcusable.

Lévinas (1985, 28) states that his philosophical thinking was motivated by 'a fear of being in the world without novel possibilities, without a future of hope, a world where everything is regulated in advance.' Derrida extensively describes and discusses 'how the dilemmas ... [of d]ouble injunctions, contradictions, aporias ... are inherent in the concept of responsibility, are in fact *the very condition* of its possibility' (Egéa-Kuehne 2003, 278). Consequently, it is this point of *acting* that Žižek (in Žižek and Daly, 2004, 106) fully endorses in 'a heroic decisionism in which there is a strong emphasis on risking outcomes and taking responsibility for them in real terms.' However, central to any action is the following observation:

> My very status as a subject depends on its links to the substantial Other: not only the regulative-symbolic [big] Other of the tradition in which I am embedded, but also ... the fact that, in the core of my being, I am irreducibly vulnerable, exposed to the Other(s). And far from limiting my ethical status (autonomy), this primordial vulnerability due to my constitutive exposure to the Other *grounds* it: what makes an individual *human* and thus something for which we are responsible, towards whom we have a duty to help, is his/her very finitude and vulnerability. (Žižek 2005c, 138 – emphasis in original)

For Žižek (2005c, 138-139), full recognition of the Other is not a realisation of the Other in a particularly defined daily capacity of the accepted lifeworld; rather it is an acknowledgement and appreciation of an abstract 'you in the abyss of your very impenetrability and opacity'. The reciprocated constraint or misrecognition between any two subjects thus opens up a shared area of sociality that is constituted by the shared solidarity of each subjects' vulnerability. While this is an ethical task, in itself, for Žižek this is but a starting point.

> [T]he true ethical step is the one *beyond* the face of the other, the one of *suspending* the hold of the face, the one of choosing *against* the face, for the *third* ... It is only such a shift of focus onto the Third that effectively *uproots* justice, liberating it from the contingent umbilical link that renders it 'embedded in a particular situation'. (Žižek 2005c, 183-184 – emphasis in original)

It is only a focus on the abstract, unseen, 'third face' that allows responsibility to be globalised; that is, to be universalised towards all individual Others. Derrida (1978, 110) quotes Lévinas as stating that: '[i]t is ... towards a pluralism which does not fuse into unity that we wish to make our way'! This is not a Lévinasian nor a Derridian 'neutral plurality of equal citizens [the citizens of John Rawls' veil of ignorance], but a radical incommensurability between the other who exists before the self, and a self that is broken open, demanded of, or called by the other, before it can hole itself up in the ivory tower of self-sufficiency, self-consciousness and mastery' (Roffe 2004, 40). It is the unrestricted call of all Others.

Moreover, this is not justice or a law of the 'big Other' or nation-state. Rather, this is a responsibility that addresses 'the gap between the reality of everyday material social life (people interacting among themselves and with nature, suffering, consuming, and so on) and the Real[2] of the speculative dance of capital, its self-propelling movement which seems to be disconnected from ordinary reality' (Žižek 2006a, 383). Of course, this is an impossible responsibility. Yet, it is an impossibility that might perhaps be ameliorated by an analysis of responsibility as a Law in a manner that may strive towards some greater global awareness of our actions on the Other. Law, not as a law imposed by an institution of state, rather a Law – or moral principle – of universal, or global, responsibility. It is this capitalised Law, once we have an awareness of its consequences, which calls forth an impossible responsibility to the global Other. This Law[3] gives inherent motivation to responsible action even in the face of undecidability. This is not responsibility induced by the gaze of an illusionary 'big Other', but via an autonomous responsibility of care for a material 'all Other' which constitutes our finite planet.

As we suggested earlier, 'real' decisions are inherently undecidable. Yet undecidability never prevents the demand to decide: 'the world continues to issue its demands, and we must still respond, still take responsibility, make that decision in the face of undecidability' (O'Byrne 2005, 402). We argue, therefore, that Gilles Deleuze and Félix Guattari's approach to responsibility is of value here. Importantly, Deleuze and Guattari's (1987) consideration of responsibility is similar to that of Derrida in its unbounded relational emphasis. As Holloway (2002, 78) observes, a Deleuzian conceptualisation of distanced responsibility and care to the other, is inherent in 'the networks of relations between the heterogeneous assemblages in which they are constituted'; they are relational ethics arising from associations and encounter between distanced things. However, there is a major difference between Derridian and Deleuze/Guattari's positions. Derrida's (after Lévinas) is inherently a transcendent philosophy. He postulates an absolute responsibility for the other that transcends human knowledge and experience. Deleuze and Guattari's philosophy is emergent and pragmatist. For Deleuze and Guattari the fundamental question is not a Derridean moral 'what *must* I do?', but rather 'what *can* I do?' As Smith (2003, 62) explains, 'an absolute responsibility for the other that I can never assume, or an infinite call to justice that I can never satisfy – are ... imperatives whose effect is to separate me from my capacity to act'. For Derrida and Lévinas then, ethics is derived from transcendence, external to the world we know, while for Deleuze and Guattari, transcendence prevents ethics from taking place. Pragmatic global responsibility derived from an understanding of a Lacanian ethics of the Real, might, perhaps, begin to shift social reality with regard to the care of all the Others of our world.

---

2    This is an articulation of the Real that manifests itself in the 'inexorable "abstract," spectral logic of capital' – the invisible hand of the market – that inexplicitly 'determines what goes on in social reality' (Žižek 2008d, 13).

3    The concept of the Law is perhaps similar, if deployed as a guiding moral principle to that of Kant's mis-directed Categorical Imperative.

What does all this imply for a spatial planning that seeks to be globally responsible? We do not advocate any specific prescription, although we list some suggestions for globally responsible practice, which might aid the reader's self-reflection:

- An acceptance of uncertainty and aporia/paradox;
- A willingness to act under uncertainty and aporia/paradox;
- A willingness to have regard to feelings of 'dis-ease' and dissatisfaction about expected courses of action, and to explore why these feelings arise;
- A willingness to take responsibility for the outcomes of our actions;
- A willingness of care for the other;
- A willingness to consider our actions in a global context, not just within our territorial and institutional boundaries;
- A willingness to support global justice towards the Other, human or otherwise;
- A willingness to critically reflect on our personal consumption behaviours and those of our wider society, in light of ecological sustainability;
- A willingness to advise political decision-makers, accordingly; and
- Above all, the avoidance of avoidance.

The list confirms that we advocate a teleological or consequential practice ethics of responsibility, justified by the eventual outcome/end/purpose served, rather than a deontological, Kantian-based ethics of responsibility as duty and obligation to a set of rules. We believe that responsibility should be embedded in a set of spatial planning practices of 'acceptance' and 'willingness' responding to the presence of the other rather than codified in a set of normative principles from which claims of 'rightness' and 'justice' are derived (Sparti 2000, 100). As Sparti argues, if we regard ourselves as responsive to an other/another, although moral inclinations may be apparent, no strong normative public ethics can be derived (2000, 100).

Sparti (2000, 85) regards such a 'craving' for absolute criteria as an impulse or demand to overcome the human condition. Yet, from Žižek's (1997b, 51) perspective, there can never be closure because justice or '"human rights" always functions also as an "empty signifier": one can never enumerate them; that is, it is part of the very notion of human rights that they are never "complete," that there are always new (positive) rights to be added to the list – and the awareness of this "openness" is what enables us and individuals belonging to another culture to engage in communication and, perhaps, arrive at a common point by acknowledging the limitations of one's own position'.

We agree that spatial planning practitioners can never fully know the Other. However, we would argue, like Sparti (2000), that we do not need to know them in detail. What is important is that we acknowledge the Other and show such acknowledgement in our actions. In this context we do not argue for a concept based on a 'duty' to some abstract 'big Other', rather an acknowledgement that all others sharing the planet with us and that we accordingly have to act, wherever and whenever possible, with responsibility.

# Chapter 10
# Beyond the Mere *Rationality* of Planning

## Introduction

A kind of code that we must at least appear to understand.

Watson 2004, 2

In this concluding chapter we consider the idea of rationality in spatial planning and revisit the question as to whether spatial planning is art, science or ideology. We suggest that once Lacanian conceptualisations of discourse, culture, *jouissance* and the Real are considered with regard to human subjectification, the ideological dimensions of spatial planning become central. We then reflect on spatial planners, in this context, as Lacanian subjects. We conclude the text by considering what type of theoretical understanding Lacan and his followers bring to spatial planning. We have suggested throughout this book that Lacan provides a critical awareness of, or insight into, the role of identification, fantasy and belief in spatial planning and how this is often synonymous, or at least covariant, with the deployment of power in shaping our communities of aspiration. Consequently, we propose that Lacanian theorising offers an alternative and compelling illumination of spatial planning practice with regard to responsible action.

We caution, however, that Lacanian thought does not provide a prescriptive theory as to how to go about effectively practising spatial planning without its inherent ideological dimensions. It does not suggest how planning might traverse its role of filling an identified lack so as to create the illusion of 'wholeness' for a community or a city-region. Nor does Lacanian-derived thinking suggest a means to overcome a reliance on the ideological consequences of spatial planning's need for master signifiers. If the discipline wishes to engage with and address its current reliance on illusion and desire, we argue that there is a need to look beyond the dominance of its hegemonic master signifiers. We conclude by referring to an alternative theoretical approach to spatial planning that may begin to displace spatial planning's need for reliance on empty signifiers and the ideological constructs that they induce for the achievement of transcendental ideals.

## The Problems of Rationality

the planning of time became the modern equivalent of the magical practices of archaic societies: it seemed to be a reasonable antidote to the uncertainties generated by the future. (Leccardi 2008, 123)

Rationality from the Latin *ratio* traditionally means the balancing of facts, so as to act with reason (see Alexander 2000). In the case of spatial planning, rationality is traditionally deployed as instrumental, or purposive, rationality: a process of practical reasoning by which 'subjects' choose the best means to achieve their pre-given ends (Raz 2005). Instrumental rationality does not question the ends, but only how to achieve those ends. Such a planning process is predicated on balancing 'facts' of public good, frequently reduced to an economic nature, or pertaining to economic efficiency. This is an approach predicated on an economic model of utility, where each additionally acquired 'good' adds to marginally-increasing aggregate satisfaction, from which is derived happiness. Actors theoretically seek to maximise their utility within households and firms, with, in the latter case, this being measured as capital accumulation and profits (Duncan 2007; Schroeder 2000).

We suggest that spatial planning in practice often attempts to give an illusion of optimisation of means for individualistic, community or national utility maximisation via the deployment of rational planning tools, such as cost-benefit analysis. However, and importantly, we suggest that such use of planning tools selectively performs rhetorical 'window dressing' and that rationality in spatial planning is actually often not the balancing of facts to maximise predicable and 'measurable' utility, but rather the balancing of desires, values and aspirations, strongly influenced by the power inequalities of the actants involved (see, for example: Dabinett and Richardson 1999; Flyvbjerg 1998; Flyvbjerg *et al.* 2003; Mandelbaum 1996; Throgmorton 1993). Moreover, from a Lacanian perspective, this is a never-ending process, as desire can never be sated. As such, we agree with Alexander's (2000, 242) assertion that if spatial planning is highly rational then it is probably 'associated with misplaced scientism, overweening technocracy, and self-serving professionalism'.

The utilitarian assumptions of traditional economics, as deployed in 'rational planning', assume that one can totalise and balance aggregate happiness (Harvey 2005). This is the measurable happiness of contemporary neo-classical economics 'revealed' by the 'preferences of consumer choice' and reified into totalisable and calculatable aggregates of prices paid and volumes of goods consumed (Duncan 2007, 89). It culminates in the neo-liberal state's most critical scorecard of competitive market success: its per capita GDP.[1] But, we suggest that this 'reason' of rationality fails – if it was ever viable as an intellectual construct in the first place[2] – if we replace the simple concept of utilitarian happiness with a wider and deeper understanding of human 'enjoyment' based on, and driven by, Lacanian *jouissance*. We cannot totalise or even measure the perverse pleasure/pain of *jouissance*, for it resides not in the epistemological realm of the symbolic, but,

---

1   Gross Domestic Product.

2   As Paul Ormerod observed in Urry *et al.* (2007, 114), 'rational choice theory is exhausted within economics, but other social science disciplines might seem easy prey for those wanting to use it.'

rather, in the realm of the Real. Indeed, *jouissance*, in contrast to the supposed happiness-seeking of economically rational 'man', explains 'why we so often act in ways that are calculated to decrease, rather than increase, our happiness' (Schroeder 2000, 158). Further, this understanding helps explain why we continue in an aberrant search for growth when such behaviour is unsustainable and destructive of both the human spirit and the environment.

> Production and consumption under advanced capitalism are premised upon the ceaseless and unbalanced search for growth, innovation and ever-new objects of desire that serve to incite Desire *per se* ... Capitalism, rather than providing for happiness and satisfaction, manufactures an ever-widening field of desire, and innovative ways in which commodities create invidious distinctions, and hence ever-widening gulfs of resentment, dissatisfaction and anxiety. While happiness blandly evokes the pleasure principle, the 'organisation of enjoyment' (Jouissance) underlying the injunction 'consume!' (or 'desire more!') cannot be equated with unalloyed pleasure. (Duncan 2007, 95)

Such behaviour also risks inducing human loneliness (Declercq 2006), as desire for consumption channels human interests towards things: objects, not social relationships. Further, the Lacanian split subject is constituted in its subjectivity by lack and misrecognition in language, so that a consumer, 'from a Lacanian perspective, is condemned to living life as a series of errors' (Shankar *et al.* 2006, 498). In the light of *jouissance*, how can any consumer act be a rational and predictable action in terms of market preference? Alternatively, if the choice of market preferences is rational, how can inherently 'irrational' characteristics of consumerism be explained, such as constant changes of fashion or style? Schroeder (2000, 227) argues that Lacanian theory is well placed to explain consumerism as it 'is precisely a theory as to both how the taste for intersubjective recognition (a category that includes 'style') arise and remains constant as well as why the tastes for individual commodities within this general taste are in a constant state of flux.' Our desired objects, whether new clothes, new car or new house, fail to satisfy once obtained and so our 'objects of desire are constantly changing – as soon as we achieve one object of desire, we necessarily seek out a new one because our true desire is not met' (Schroeder 2000, 228).

Objects can never provide our primordially desired, yet always lacking, impossible wholeness. Nevertheless, we continue to seek completeness or the illusion that we have achieved it, via both our material consumption and in our intellectual identifications and beliefs. The latter is why some spatial planners, economic development specialists and economists tend to cling to certain theories and beliefs despite empirical facts to the contrary, such as dismissal of the empirical reality of global warming or continued belief in the purely 'rational subject'. These actors 'try to satisfy the universal desire for wholeness by suppressing the dynamic – and, therefore, necessarily incomplete – nature of the symbolic orders of law and markets' (Schroeder 2000, 229).

This impossibility of completeness and wholeness similarly applies to the impossibility of communicative planning's ideal of distortion-free and non-agonistic speech, allowing unforced consensual agreement, as predicated by Jürgen Habermas' theory of communicative rationality (Gunder 2003a). Habermas (1979) contrasted instrumental rationality with other forms of rationality concerned with promoting understanding and with improving the human condition. His notion of communicative rationality, was predicated on the logic of argument to reach consensus based on agreed norms and values associated with communication (Habermas 1984, 1987). Here the 'counterpart to classic rationality's ideal model of the rational self-interested *homo economicus* is *homo communitarius*, motivated solely by the search for mutual consensus' (Alexander 2000, 250). The object of the communicatively rational planner's desire is the creation of an 'ideal speech situation' where 'complete' and 'whole' distortion-free communication and reciprocal understanding would occur. Lacan's (2007) discourse theory illustrates why undistorted communication is impossible (Hillier 2003a). The object of a communicative rational planner's desire is ultimately no different than of any other human subject in seeking ideal 'wholeness'.

Similarly, economists' desires of 'achieving the efficiency of the perfect market', requires complete or 'whole' information, which is again impossible in Lacanian conceptualisation. Achievement of these desires can only reside in the impossible Real (Schroeder 1998, 513). Communicative action-based planning theory fails in its very rationality, as does the invisible hand of the market. Spatial planning's deployment of economic or communicative rational arguments and their resulting tools and processes, are based on a presumed rationality of the actors involved, when in reality participants in the market, or in a polity engaged in a collaborative participation, are human actors actually driven by irrational *jouissance*.

In addition, neo-classical economics is premised on the allocation of finite resources based on unlimited growth and resource substitution, or even on infinite resources. But, we live on a finite planet whose natural limits have already been reached, if not already exceeded. As Žižek (2008a, 346) observes, the irony of utilitarian ethics is not that it cannot properly account for 'the true Good', but that it cannot account for 'Evil itself', which is ultimately against my long-term interests'. Moreover, the authority of tradition or of the master who knows has changed. We do not really need Beck (1992, 2006a) to tell us that there is something fundamentally wrong in the traditional scientific-technological attitude of rational reason and positivistic prediction, for we must realise for ourselves that we cannot know what is yet to occur, or emerge as new knowledge.

Scientific facts are largely used as rhetoric in spatial planning and tend to give an almost priestly legitimacy to planning narratives of both '"hope" and censorship', which were traditionally provided by the Church (Žižek 2008a, 446). 'Science functions as a social force, as an ideological institution, its function', just like that of spatial planning 'is to provide certainty, to be a point of reference on which one can rely and to provide hope'[3] via technological innovation, 'science provides the security that was once provided by religion' (446). If economic 'man' is actually irrational, and if science functions as theology, is it not logical, therefore, that spatial planning, functions as an ideology? This is an ideology of materialised belief predicated on providing an illusion of certainty in the fulfilment of desires and dreams for a better city. Consistent with Žižek's argument of consumerist post-democracy under the imperative of enjoyment (developed in Chapters 5 and 6), have not key dimensions of traditional placed-based politics been transformed 'into apolitical administration', or, at best, unaccountable governance (see McGuirk 2004), where 'individuals pursue their consumerist fantasies in the space regulated by expert social administration' (Žižek 2008a, 325). We have argued in this book that spatial planning plays a central role in such a process of 'administration of social and ecological matters' (Swyngedouw 2007, 24), as an art or craft structured by ideological belief that often deploys a rhetoric of scientism in its legitimisation.

In this regard, a core mission of spatial planning could be argued as being the control of space to reduce the uncertainty of the 'persistent sense of the unknown' that pervades and haunts reality to prevent space becoming threatening. We suggest that spatial planning is inherently risk adverse, and/or mitigating, at least at two levels. First, spatial planning appears to eliminate risk for those it plans. Planning alleviates the fear of the unknown for those 'planned' by creating the illusion of 'certainty' towards the use and control of space in both the present and in the future. Second, spatial planning provides predictability and comfort for those 'planned' by framing planning issues in a known context and by then applying universally recognised, hence hegemonic, ideas and established solutions to planning goal setting and problem solving. Accordingly, planning is generally risk-adverse in not creating and framing new issues for consideration, nor in seeking new ways of thinking. We have suggested, in this book, that planning seeks to deploy a largely universal orthodoxy of practice predicated on a range of dominant ideas or master signifiers, such as those of 'sustainability', 'globally competitive cities', 'Smart Growth' or 'liveable cities' and the like. For how can you go wrong if you are doing the same thing as everyone else? Surely, it must be 'best practice'?

We do not condemn spatial planning, however. Through co-ordinating hope and aspirations for our city-making and wider built environments, not to mention in co-ordinating collective and individual property rights, spatial planning plays a necessary and sought-after function of governance and societal guidance via policy development, the regulation of property markets, and in the implementation of the law (Murdoch and Abram 2002; Needham 2006). Yet the question remains: are there alternative ways for spatial planners to undertake these important functions, without a reliance on master signifiers, the illusion of scientism and the

---

3   Anderson and Holden (2008, 144 – emphasis in original) define hope as 'a state of suspension' or 'as a *blank* around which multiple ambivalent hopes accumulate'.

deployment of false-rationality? Or stated more bluntly: are there better ways to practice spatial planning? Let us begin to explore this question by first reviewing what we have written about spatial planners as Lacanian subjects.

## Spatial Planners as Lacanian Subjects

As we have developed throughout this text, in Lacanian theory social reality is composed of sets of shared ideological beliefs that are anchored, or sutured, in and between us and others, via master signifiers. The Lacanian subject's recognition of itself as a conscious actant is predicated on 'the illusions of autonomy in which it puts its faith to the ego's constitutive misrecognitions' (Lacan 2006, 80). To belong and be 'whole', to have the illusion of being a full person, requires us to believe, or give the appearance of believing by acting correctly, as determined by dominant narratives and practices of 'good' behaviour prescribed within our master signifiers; ie, the dominant rules of our knowledge sets and techniques, conduct and law. This allows us, our groups and wider society to function (Žižek 2001a, 88). If we lack some dimension of belief; (ie, there is a gap between ourselves and our group), the pressures of our self-imposed social conformity require us to give the appearance of belief if we want to fulfil our desire to belong. For a planner this might include 'mandatory' or 'professionally correct' beliefs in such things as social equity, gender and race equality, support for public transit, energy conservation, and, above all, a belief in the validity of the dominant master signifiers of spatial planning identified and discussed in this book and their deployment in plans and planning processes. For most spatial planners, what is imperative is to give society – constituted unreflectively as the big Other – and specifically the groups that we particularly desire to belong to within that society, what (we think) these others want from our belief and resultant actions and behaviours (Sharpe 2001).

As Žižek (1997a, 6) observes: 'if you do not believe, kneel down, act as if you believe, and belief will come by itself.' Or phrased in a more secular manner: 'Fake it until you make it' (Žižek 2006a, 353). '[I]deological identification exerts a true hold on us precisely when we maintain an awareness that we are not fully identical to' what we are supposed to believe and how we are supposed to act (Žižek 1997a, 21). Importantly, the true logic of ideology is to displace belief onto another, so that by kneeling down, or faking it even when you do not believe, 'you will thereby *make someone else believe!*' (Žižek 2006a, 353). Žižek argues that for an ideology to function, it must hold that 'every individual believes that *someone else* knows and/ or "truly believes"' (Sharpe 2006, 111 – emphasis in original). From a Žižekian perspective, 'ideology actually operates *through* objective truth – what it conceals is not the essential interests of the subject, but rather a particular position of power from which it is articulated' (Newman 2004, 162). This is the power of the master signifier (Žižek 2006a, 373): the power to induce 'action without belief' and to sustain 'structures and relationships of domination' (Newman 2004, 164).[4]

We want to consider ourselves unique and special, morally decent human beings, above the sometimes adverse actions required and demanded of us – the law – by the big Other and our place within it. For example, a spatial planner might want to recommend approval of a development application out of compassion, because the applicant is a nice person or because the application is supporting a good cause, even though the proposal is contrary to the Plan rules (which we may even consider ill-founded). The planner may then go out of their way to seek exceptions or special circumstances that might apply (see Tewdwr-Jones 2002). Even when they fail and have to recommend 'no', they can then go home in the evening feeling morally good in the rationalisation that at least they tried.

Yet this rationalisation – that we tried but ultimately failed – is itself an instance of 'the very form of ideology, of its "practical efficiency"' (Žižek 1997a, 21). Many of us may only give lip service to specific aspects of social reality and its many norms and accepted behaviours. Nevertheless, we do give regard to them in order that we are allowed to adopt or retain desired characteristics and identifications (including our jobs) – our master signifiers. Performing these 'token' material practices and utterances actually defines them to wider society as our apparent symbolic identifications and beliefs, even if they only occur in our outward practices and not in our hearts. Moreover, and profoundly, the aggregate of our individual material utterances and practices actually forms the ideological structures creating social reality, even though they may be given to this abstract 'big Other' without belief, because that is what we think it wants and hence what we have to do. Of course, what we materially do is what is observable and measurable by others. Whether our consumer behaviours or our planning practices, our aggregate actions constitute the materially measurable social reality of the world. 'Cynics may have a distance from social reality, but their actions still accord with it … because ideology comes into play not just at the level of knowing (uncovering truth) but at the level of doing (materialising belief)' (Dean 2001, 649).

*Desire and Power*

Traditional power was thought to act epistemologically in the symbolic through texts, utterances and narratives, but Lacan and his followers show that it actually acts ontologically in the Real, via *jouissance* and desire (Lash 2007). What

---

4   Although, as Žižek (1999c, 184) observes, any 'ruling ideology, in order to be operative, has to incorporate a series of features in which the exploited/dominated majority will be able to recognize its authentic longings'. Žižek in the same text further contends that in 'order to capture subjects, power must give something back to subjects in exchange for their allegiance … there is always a series of "you may, *provided that you continue to obey*"' (Sharpe 2006, 113-114 – emphasis in original). The attainment of *jouissance* is central to this ideological process.

empowers 'power' is this desire to be wanted, to belong within our groups. We conform to the knowledges and values of our master signifiers because we are vulnerable beings who fundamentally desire to be wanted by the Other and have the illusion of a sense of security that this perceived belonging provides (Žižek 2002e, 61). Similarly, extending this desire, we conform to the wider general norms and laws of society – the symbolic order – as well as to the group identifications that constitute us in our social reality; whether we truly believe in all the specific values associated with an identification, or whether we simply conform to a specific identification because we desire the 'badge' of that identity.

Foucault (1977) documents how modern institutions, such as schools, universities, the military and, if necessary, prisons, discipline populations into becoming productive members of society. Even if this conformity, or normalisation, is at odds with our dominant beliefs as a consequence of our most fundamental identifications, most people still want to conform to belong (or avoid sanction), and so give at least an outward appearance of doing so (Žižek 1989, 1997a).

Foucault's (1977, 1980, 1982) conceptualisations, both of power as capillary (power as a process constitutes relationships), and also of resistance to particular identifications and/or the actions they sanction and legitimate, are also relevant. According to Lacanian thinking, there is a separation (or lack, or gap) between the oppressed and the processes of power that cause the oppression (Newman 2001, 2004). This is the space in which resistance can occur. Lacanian understanding of politics is constituted by the very lack or gap in the process of power. Laws and societal values exist to proscribe actions in Lacanian theory. 'Laws' and 'rules' can only function through the action of their transgression – being broken or bent (Žižek 1997a, 39). Only a breach of custom, a violated norm or a transgression of regulation can induce the application of constraints, social penalties and their enforcement. Yet most members of society conform within the accepted boundaries and norms of their identifications and within society's formal laws. The overwhelming majority of people govern themselves and behave as though they are under an authoritarian gaze. For them the 'big Other' is always watching. This docile self-moderation to conform is the very causative agent that propagates and thereby perpetuates power (Badiou 2001, 74; Žižek 1989, 36). Phrased alternatively, in the search for harmony and security, society craves rules and authority (Caudill 1997). Where there is a void of norms, rules and regulation we create our own, because we generally desire to be 'good' and hence be desired by others who in abstract aggregate constitute the illusionary 'big Other'.

*Expectations, Norms and Values*

As developed in Chapter 3, the desire to be and do 'good' affects the behaviours of spatial planners. Let us consider another example, of a recommendation on a development application where the applicant is seeking an outcome that the planner believes to constitute a public good. However, the application is contrary to the rules of the plan, or perhaps it is an activity that will generate significant public opposition – such as the controlled, environmentally safe dismantling of a ship containing toxic chemicals (a 'toxic-ship') in contrast to the alternative of its being broken up on an Asian mud-flat (see Hillier 2009). As Žižek (2001a, 141) indicates, the Lacanian big Other of the symbolically constructed social reality does not designate just the explicit, symbolic rules of law, but also 'the intricate cobweb of *unwritten* "implicit" rules' (emphasis in original), the particular interpretation of a policy or what the elected politicians and the community might support. There are therefore two levels of decision for the spatial planner, as Žižek (2001a, 162) points out. There is a gap, not only between the applicant's request and the planner's '(ultimately always inadequate, pragmatic, calculated, contingent, unfounded) decision how to translate this' request 'into a concrete intervention'; but the decision itself is split into 'the [big] Other's decision in oneself' (an identification with the letter of the law) and a decision to accommodate some acceptable and implementable pragmatic political intervention as the answer to the big Other's decision in oneself.

The first level of decision is thus a decision on what to do statutorily. The second level is the spatial planner's responsibility to translate that decision into a concrete intervention that obeys specific 'pragmatic/strategic/political considerations' of what is possible in that particular situation. In these decisions lies the scope for a spatial planner to either implement the letter of the law as precisely and stringently as possible, or to demonstrate some degree of flexibility in their interpretation of a policy, perhaps in the light of special circumstances. The latter, in extreme, would represent an intervention in social reality itself, which changes what is perceived as 'possible.' 'It redefines what counts as good' and creates a new social reality (Žižek 2001a, 167). So, when might it be ethically acceptable to transgress the law? When might it be acceptable, for example, to act responsibly in light of global concerns raised in the previous chapter?

A Lacanian-inspired 'ethics of the Real' suggests a reversal of the traditional hierarchy of the forms of evil. From a Lacanian ethical perspective, the worst behaviour would be planners' compliance with the law for the wrong pathological reasons. For example, to satisfy vanity, to be racist against a minority, or to impress their peers or boss with their rigour, a spatial planner might recommend refusal of a development application by invoking the letter of the law regarding a seldom-enforced plan rule; one known to always be overturned under appeal, but only at considerable cost to the applicant. The planner might say to the applicant something such as: 'I know this can be painful, but what can I do; this is my duty'; or 'it's not my responsibility; it's my duty towards planning', 'these are the rules'.

Next worst would be a straightforward disregard for the law. The planner might give approval to a non-complying development, for a friend, in return for a bribe, or just out of malice. Finally, the least worst in the Lacanian ethical hierarchy is doing the wrong thing for the right reason. The planner, motivated by concern for environmental justice, publicly notifies the proposal for 'toxic-ship' dismantling over the summer holiday period in an obscure publication to minimise public objection. This last form of transgression, which Kant termed 'diabolical evil' and considered the highest evil is, as Žižek (2001a) and Zupančič (2000) propose, formally indistinguishable from the highest good.

'Irrational obedience' to, or rationalisation of the law is an action for those, according to Žižek (1997a, 223) 'who need the illusion that there are good and proper reasons for the orders they must obey.' They remain unaware that the law is grounded only in its own act of enunciation, ie, in itself. The 'law is no longer regarded as dependent on the Good, but on the contrary, the Good is made to depend on the law' (Deleuze 1991, 82).

'Doing the wrong thing for the right reason' invokes the sort of ethics espoused by Connolly (1991, 1998, 2005), as we indicated in Chapter 9. This type of approach to others is one of responsibility; a responsibility neither conditioned nor measured by any acts of which it would be the consequence. Perhaps the next time spatial planners are confronted with making a recommendation they believe is ultimately wrong, either locally or globally, but which is the only technically 'correct' recommendation for a 'planner' to make, we suggest that they pause and reflect. 'The heart of all ethics' is encountering 'something that happens to us, surprises us, throws us out of joint', something that causes a 'rupture, a break or interruption' – this is the Lacanian Real (Zupančič 2000, 235). It is the examination of this dissonance, such as an expectation that we 'must' do something even though we may think that it is not right or good, and the subsequent adaptation of our actions to ignore, accommodate, or overturn this 'dis-ease', that constitutes the ethical and responsible act.

## To be an Ethical Spatial Planner

To be a spatial planner, at least in an Anglo-influenced legislative context, is to have a set of specific identifications of belief – master signifiers and their supporting knowledge sets of facts, values and practices – acquired primarily through tertiary education, that are subsequently re-enforced by having a position in society labelled 'spatial planner'. Yet symbolic interactions with others – between spatial planners and those they 'plan' – are always incomplete. There is always something beyond the signifier, something somehow distorting reality (Žižek 2008a, 287). This unsymbolisable registry, the Lacanian Real, provides new insight for spatial planning and planning theory as to why the profession is often less successful than hoped; why plans never quite work out. Discussion of the inevitable incompleteness of the symbolic and the impossible completeness of the Real and consequently the illusionary concreteness and absoluteness of planning law (and policy) as always constituting and producing 'good' poses questions concerning the legitimacy of spatial planning activities. If the fundamental structure, on which spatial planning as a practice is predicated, is full of gaps, then what remains?

Lacanian thinking could be argues as being poststructuralist in that it claims a radical indeterminacy in the constituting structures of social reality, which are limited by the dimension of the Real. In other words, there must be something beyond our perceived understanding of social reality that symbolic theories of structure – scientific, or otherwise – cannot entirely grasp. Symbolic structure cannot include everything. There must be a lack, a conceptual limit or 'outside' to symbolisation itself.

It is here that the Lacanian conceptualisation of fantasy is relevant. The role of fantasy is to conceal the lack: 'fantasy emerges to cover the antagonisms and inconsistencies that pervade the social field' (Dean 2001, 627). Fantasy is the dimension that sustains reality. It outlines the ideological character of reality, where ideology in the Lacanian sense operates through objective truth – what is observable and measurable in our 'doing'. It thus serves to legitimise spatial planning practice, sustaining the fantasy of its wholeness: 'we indulge in the notion of society [spatial planning practice] as an organic whole kept together by forces of solidarity and co-operation' (Žižek 1999b, 91).

Similarly, Lacanian validation of Kantian 'diabolical evil', or doing the wrong thing for the right reason, raises ethical issues. Yet it is that very lack beyond the structure which allows the possibility of such responsible resistance, an effective subversion or undermining of that structure; a form of insurgent practice. For Lacan 'ethics belongs to the Real' where in 'the Lacanian notion of ... an act, I precisely redefine the very co-ordinates of what I cannot and must do' (Žižek 2006a, 49). As Moulaert and Cabaret (2006, 67) extol, drawing on Žižek (2002d), spatial planners must '"look into the mouth of power"', they 'must become ... active in arenas that may affect the transformation of the deep structures of society'. '[T]he genuine ethical act, is always subversive; it is never simply the result of an "improvement" or a "reform"' (Zupančič 2000, 11).

Perhaps practitioners can implement effective change by shifting the grounds of social reality, including that of spatial planning processes by changing accepted norms and values of what is possible. Of course, the critical consideration is what moral imperative, if any, provides structure and direction for actions in this context. Lacan (1992) exhorts us to be true to our desires, to confront our fantasies and understand what creates and motivates them. These may be our fundamental but unachievable desires – for example for social harmony and unity and for global sustainability – that may, in turn, constitute a personal desire for fairness, justice, market individualism, or alternatively collectivism, in the world. These are all utopian desires for a better world (Friedmann 2002). Yet these are personal fantasies, or at best, idealised shared dreams of a potential fuzzy reality, perhaps shaped, prodded and sutured via our continued infatuation with (and also misrecognition of) our common master signifiers of shared identification. But these are individual desires that we can never fully articulate or even fully share with others in our materialised and actualised social reality. Dreams ultimately reside beyond the material realms of symbolisation, just as ultimately do ethics. Both belong to the Real (Žižek 2006a, 49). The realisation that these desires are merely idealised dreams and fantasies, not futures likely to materialise as our built environments, no matter how hard we strive, is an important self-awareness. That this unconscious 'truth' should also guide us in our reflective actions is perhaps Lacan's most important teaching for spatial planners striving to create a 'better' world.

### If Lacan Makes Sense: What Then?

Lacan and his disciples provide us with a theory of understanding the overarching ideological societal framework in which contemporary spatial planning resides. It is a theory 'of' planning in wider society: it is about spatial planning. It is not a theory 'in' spatial planning: how to do it. Lacanian-derived understandings of human subjectivity and how ideology is materialised by the human subject in the creation of social reality give significant insight into spatial planning, and other human endeavours, especially those concerned with the future, human betterment and the search for 'certainty'. However, apart from providing new ethical perspectives and giving new grounds for reflective critique about the potentially pernicious nature of our planning master signifiers and the illusions they induce, Lacanian thought does not really provide new tools, or approaches, with which to plan more effectively, in whatever manner we might wish to measure effectiveness. Nor does Lacanian theory supply the means to replace, or overcome, the flaws that Lacanian thought exposes in the human seeking of wholeness and in spatial planning's pursuit of its sublime transcendental ideals: its seductive master signifiers, whose resolution and understanding only reside as states of being beyond existing human knowledge and experience.

As McGowan (2008, 49) observes, the problem with applying Lacanian psychoanalytical perspectives prescriptively to social-technical processes, such as those of spatial planning, is the very propensity of psychoanalysis to respect and sustain the status of lack and human incompleteness. It regards the individual subject as a patient requiring 'cure' through their own development of self-understanding. Psychoanalysis fails to appreciate the wider political implications of the lacking subject 'and the pervasive desire to fill it' (49). It fails to consider a socio-economic interest in hegemonically exploiting this human characteristic to manipulate populations in a manner that may facilitate pernicious, inequitable, or unfair outcomes. As Verhaeghe (1997, 247) similarly remarks, the curative aim of Lacanian psychoanalysis is that of self-enlightenment and acceptance; accordingly, 'it ought not to deteriorate into a system which presents itself as an answer to the lack'.

The Lacanian psychoanalytical process is concerned with traversing the subject's individual fantasies, or perhaps those shared by a group, community or nation. It is concerned with exposing the underlying traumatic master signifiers, which induce fantasy constructs, and with negating their ability to cause 'dis-ease' and disfunction. Implicitly, while the patient's (or polity's) understanding of how to engage with the world may improve with this understanding, new master signifiers will inevitably come along to replace those that have been traversed. To offer a spatial planning example: just as 'individual mobility' and 'freeways' were the resolution to public transport congestion on city streets some 50 years or more ago, this orthodox resolution of one spatial planning problem raised new problems needing new master signifiers, such as 'transit oriented design' and 'mass-transit', in their place (Gunder 2002a).

A key question that remains for spatial planning is whether planning theory and practice can provide new goal-setting mechanisms that do not rely on the transcendental nature of master signifiers, and if so, what might they be? Phrased alternatively: can spatial planning theoretically and practically mediate space effectively without setting fuzzy, undefined goals, which can facilitate identification with, and support from, a community, polity, or society only via their very ambiguity of signification? Can spatial planning be undertaken without the deployment of empty signifiers?

Traditional spatial planning predicated on master signifiers always leaves a remainder that is not addressed, an issue that is not tackled, a side effect that will in turn induce further problems. But this has not been traditionally recognised, or if it has, it has rarely been overtly accepted and stated. In order to encompass such issues, we suggest that spatial planning theory and practice has the potential to move beyond the orthodox form of thinking and planning that our Lacanian analyses have exposed. Spatial planning, we suggest, requires theories that seek to directly engage with the world, as it is, not what it ought to be. These are theories that engage with the particularity and differences of the world, with transformation or immanence, rather than theories that impose what 'must be' in the name of rationality, economic efficiency, globalisation, Smart Growth, or whatever.

Deleuze's process-based philosophy may be one source of such a theory (Hillier 2005, 2007, 2008a, 2008b, 2009). Deleuzian-inspired thinking offers a process-based theory and practice of spatial planning as becoming that does not seek to achieve the mastery of singular transcendent end-states. Rather than conceptualising the world as composed of separate structures and objects, each individually comprised of logically necessary components that constitute some totality (such as, the components of a society, country, city, car, computer, person, or environment), a Deleuzian-inspired approach would constitute the world very differently. This is a worldview predicated on the relationalities and connectivities of components that constantly create networks or assemblages where elements can be detached and plugged into different assemblages. Moreover, assemblages constantly emerge and disappear; such as the flows of people, goods, ideas, capital, etc., constantly flowing through and constituting a public market, a government, an organisation, or a community (Delanda 2006). In contrast to reinforcing the illusion of certainty – appearing to overcome lack to create wholeness – this approach permits a planning for multiplicity and diverse potentials that seek to act as 'modes of expansion, propagation, occupation, contagion [and] peopling' to make new connections and promote new and creative opportunities for our spatial and other communities of interest (Deleuze and Guattari 1987, 239). But, this, of course, is a different story which requires a different book!

**Conclusion**

In this book, we have suggested that practitioners tend to predetermine the issues
that they consider important in the context of popular ideas and resolutions: based
on their spatial planning master signifiers. If we commence planning, with goal-
setting towards some desired end state, rather than learning about our situation
(tracing how it came to be, Hillier 2008b) and how we might want to address it
(mapping what it might become, Hillier 2008b); do we not risk implementing
pre-determined, often universal, goals derived from outside of our specific and
particular communities of interest and place? Do we not thereby implement a
'copy-paste' or 'cookie-cutter' template (e.g., waterside regeneration replete with
shops and pavement cafes: cobbles, chrome and cappuccinos), as a means to a pre-
defined end-state of urban competitiveness regardless of local issues, problems,
needs and wants? Each idea (such as consumer-oriented regeneration or the urban
nodal intensification of Smart Growth) is a known 'solution', which in itself, tends
to mechanistically define and pre-shape the very urban issues and problems that it
seeks to address.

In this context we ask:

- Should strategic spatial planning practice be about challenging the
  appropriateness of pre-determined and often universally-defined goals?
  and
- Should strategic spatial planning also be about the learning of where we
  are, where we may wish to go and what we might wish to become as a
  particular set of communities?

We consider both questions to be important: 'Politicians and planners ... favor
the idea of rationality and functionalism as the design key to "engineering a space
of certainty", a space of order and self-regulatory neighborhoods (see: Amin and
Thrift (2002) "machinic city")'. Urban spaces or communities 'cannot, however, be
seen as static but should be understood as always in process, always connected on
one hand to flows of simultaneity and assemblies (lines of structural dependency)
and on the other hand to unpredictable events, situations or mobility' (Pløger 2006,
393-394).

We have demonstrated throughout this book that mechanistic pre-shaping
of planning issues – through application of universal spatial planning master
signifiers (or those of economic development) and their dominant supporting
knowledge sets to shape the frame of discussion – allows solutions to define
problems. This precludes what may be far more pressing issues from consideration
and often results in opting for a particular version of both problem and solution
that is already constrained by an over-determined structure that planners have
themselves imposed. In *Difference and Repetition* (1994), Deleuze defines a
problem as something that does not have a single, simple solution. A problem is
something which involves a complex array of different and conflicting challenges,

where a 'solution' to one aspect or challenge merely transforms the 'problem' and reveals new tensions and conflicts which demand attention.

But when spatial planners think about 'problems', they tend to think in terms of 'solutions'. 'It is though a problem were merely a particular lack or fault that a solution will fill or rectify' (May 2005, 83). A solution makes problems disappear! Or it causes other problems. To continue with another freeway or motorway example, construction of a toll-motorway may divert traffic onto a rat-run through residential streets. 'Far from disappearing in this overlay, however, [the problem] insists and persists in these solutions' (Deleuze 1994, 163). Perhaps instead of regarding problems as something to be definitively 'solved', planners could regard them as opening up areas for discussion and negotiation of different possibilities, recognising that every possibility will capture something, but not everything, of the problem and that there is a need to think through what any one possible solution renders present and absent. It is also important to recognise the implications, advantages and disadvantages of each possibility for different socio-economic groups, for non-humans and so on. The toll-motorway example, above, offers a 'correct' solution to those who travel by car or express bus and may cut several minutes from their journey, but to those living adjacent, or along a resultant rat-run, who may suffer noise, fumes, reduction in property value and dissection of their community, the solution is far from satisfactory.

We must be careful not to allow the solution to define the problem (e.g., what we think that politicians or the public want, what there is lottery funding for, what 'best practice' tells us to do). Solutions are actual – real, stable identities, whereas problems are virtual – inexhaustible 'open fields' (May 2005). We thus tend to see solutions in terms of their actuality rather than their virtuality. In other words, we let the solution determine how we see or frame the problem. We may, therefore, ignore many virtual issues requiring address, opting for a particular version of a known solution that is already constrained by an over-determined structure that we desire to impose. This is because it is considered 'good practice' as an orthodox spatial planning response, or suturing master signifier of resolution, to contemporary metropolitan issues, whether or not it directly addresses the particularity of the specific urban problematic in question. At least its deployment gives the 'illusion' that something is being done to resolve the problem.

In this regard, Lacan has illustrated that our spatial planning responses are predicated on an ideological response of desire, identification and belief that we suggest that spatial planning practitioners could move beyond. Perhaps Deleuze and his adherents provide one alternative way to engage with the world as a mechanism of change, flow, connectivity and becoming. Undoubtedly, there are other ways to do this, as well. We suggest that for spatial planning to be innovative and world improving, and not just world maintaining or even degrading (in supporting continued belief in growth and consumption), 'responsible' theorists and practitioners need to engage with these challenges and alternative ways of doing and thinking.

We have argued that spatial planning today is largely ideological, what ought to be, residing in the realm of our dreams, fantasies and desires. Alternative engagements with the ideology deployed in shaping social reality may give us innovative ways to engage with the new, the different and even the unknown when 'we do not know what it is we do not know', and allow us to seek alternative paths on which to travel. Lacan and his followers illuminate how and why we obscure the issues and problems requiring address in our globalised world. Once we are aware of these issues, we suggest, it is up to all of us to begin to act responsibly (but only if we believe!) and find the means to engage with and traverse these conditions in our finite globe of interlocking connection, value and potential. To conclude:

> our painful progress of knowledge, our confusions, our search for solutions, that is to say, precisely that which seems to *separate* us from the way reality is out there, is already the innermost constituent of reality itself. The fact that we cannot ever 'fully know' reality is thus not a sign of our limitation of knowledge but the sign that reality itself is 'incomplete,' open, an actualization of the underlying virtual process of Becoming. (Žižek 2004a, 56 – emphasis in original)

# Bibliography

Abbott, J. (2005) 'Understanding and Managing the Unknown: The Nature of Uncertainty in Planning', *Journal of Planning Education and Research* 24:2, 237-251.

Adams, M. (2006) 'Hybridizing Habitus and Reflexivity: Towards an Understanding of Contemporary Identity?', *Sociology* 40:3, 511-528.

Agamben, G. (1998) *Homo Sacer: Sovereign Power and Bare Life* (Stanford, Stanford University Press).

Agyeman, J. (2005) *Sustainable Communities and the Challenge of Environmental Justice* (New York, New York University Press).

Agyeman, J., Evans, B. (2003) 'Towards Just Sustainability in Urban Communities: Building Equity Rights with Sustainable Solutions', *Annals of the American Academy of Political and Social Science* 590:1, 35-53.

Agyeman, J., Evans, B. (2004) '"Just sustainability": the emerging discourse of environmental justice in Britain?' *The Geographical Journal* 170:2, 155-164.

Albrechts, L. (2005) 'Creativity as a drive for change', *Planning Theory* 4:3, 247-269.

Albrechts, L. (2006) 'Shifts in strategic spatial planning? Some evidence from Europe and Australia', *Environment and Planning A* 38:6, 1149-1170.

Alcorn, M. (1994) 'The Subject of Discourse: Reading Lacan through (and beyond) Poststructuralist Contexts', in Bracher, M., *et al.* (eds) *Lacanian Theory of Discourse* (New York, New York University Press).

Alexander, E. (2000) 'Rationality Revisited: Planning Paradigms in a Post-Postmodern Perspective', *Journal of Planning Education and Research* 19:3, 242-256.

Allmendinger, P. (2001) *Planning in Postmodern Times* (London, Routledge).

Allmendinger, P. (2002a) 'Towards a Post-Positivistic Typology of Planning Theory', *Planning Theory* 1:1, 77-99.

Allmendinger, P. (2002b) *Planning Theory* (New York, Palgrave).

Allmendinger, P. (2003) 'Rescaling, Integration and Competition: Future Challenges for Development Planning', *International Planning Studies* 8:4, 323-328.

Allmendinger, P., Gunder, M. (2005) 'Applying Lacanian Insight and a Dash of Derridean Deconstruction to Planning's "Dark Side"', *Planning Theory* 4:1, 87-112.

Althusser, L. (1996) *Writings on Psychoanalysis* (New York, Columbia University Press).

Amin, A. (1999) 'An Institutional Perspective on Regional Economic Development', *International Journal of Urban and Regional Research* 23:2, 365-378.

Amin, A. (2002) 'Spatialities of Globalisation', *Environment and Planning: A* 24:3, 385-399.

Amin A. (2004a) 'Regions unbound: towards a new politics of place', *Geografiska Annaler* 86B, 33-44.

Amin A. (2004b) 'Regulating economic globalisation', *Transactions of the Institute of British Geographers NS* 29, 217-233.

Amin, A. (2006) 'The Good City', *Urban Studies* 43:5/6, 1009-1023.

Amin, A., Thrift, N. (2002) *Cities: Reimagining the Urban* (Cambridge, Polity).

Amis, M. (2002) 'The books interview', *Observer,* 8 August, 18.

Anthony, J. (2006) 'State Growth Management and Housing Prices', *Social Science Quarterly* 87:1, 122-141.

APA (2002) *Planning for Smart Growth* (Chicago, American Planning Association).

Apollon. W. (1994) 'The discourse of gangs in the stake of male repression and narcissism', in Bracher M., *et al.* (eds) *Lacanian Theory of Discourse*, 201-219 (New York, New York University Press).

Apollon. W. (1996) 'A lasting heresy, the failure of political desire', in Apollon W., Feldstein R. (eds) *Lacan, Politics, Aesthetics*, 31-44 (Albany, SUNY).

ARC (1997) Auckland Regional Council News Media Release, 19 May 1997.

Arendt, H. (1961) 'What is Authority?' in *Between Past and Future*, 91-142 (London, Faber and Faber).

Arendt, H. (1994) *Essays in Understanding 1930-1954* (New York, Harcourt Brace).

Arendt, H. (2003) 'Collective Responsibility', in Kohn J. (ed.) *Responsibility and Judgement*, 147-158 (New York, Schocken Books).

Armstrong, H., Wells, P. (2006) 'Structural Funds and the Evaluation of Community Economic Development Initiatives in the UK: A Critical Perspective', *Regional Studies* 40:2, 259-272.

Arnstein, S. (1969) 'A ladder of citizen participation', *Journal of the American Institute of Planners* 35:4, 216-224.

Ashworth, W. (1954) *The Genesis of Modern British Town Planning* (London, Routledge).

Atkinson, W. (2007) 'Beck, individualization and the death of class: a critique', *The British Journal of Sociology* 58:3, 349-366.

Auckland City Council [ACC] (1996) *Auckland City Council Britomart Transport Centre*, Report to Harbour Edge and Central Area Planning Committee, 30 October.

Auckland Regional Council [ARC] (2003) *Auckland Regional Transport Strategy 2003* (Auckland, ARC).

Auckland Regional Council [ARC] (2004) *Regional Growth Forum: horizons*, 17 September.

Auckland Regional Council [ARC] (2005) *The ARC Environment Awards* <http://www.arc.govt.nz/arc/environment/e-awards/>, accessed 1 June 2005.

Auckland Regional Growth Forum (1999) *Auckland Regional Growth Strategy 2050,* Auckland Regional Council.

Badiou, A. (2001) 'The political as a procedure of truth', *Lacanian Ink* 19, 70-81.

Badiou, A. (2005) *Being and Event* (London, Continuum).

Badiou, A. (2008) *Number and Numbers* (Cambridge, Polity).

Baeten, G. (2002a) 'The spaces of utopia and dystopia', *Geografiska Annaler* special issue, 84B, 3-4.

Baeten, G (2002b) 'Hypochondriac geographies of the city and the new urban dystopia: coming to terms with the "other" city', *City* 6:1, 103-115.

Bannerjee, T. (1993) 'Antiplanning undercurrents in US planning education: antithesis or ideology?' *Environment and Planning B* 20:5, 519-536.

Barnett, C. (2004) 'Deconstructing radical democracy: articulation, representation, and being-with-others', *Political Geography* 23:5, 503-528.

Barry, J., Paterson, M. (2004) 'Globalisation, Ecological Modernisation and New Labour', *Political Studies* 52:4, 767-784.

Batey, P. (2003) 'Introductory Note: The Planning Education Commission Report', *Town Planning Review* 74:3, 331-332.

Baum, H. (1989) 'Organisational politics against organisational culture: a psychoanalytic perspective', *Human Resource Management* 28:2, 191-206.

Baum, H. (1991a) 'How bureaucracy discourages responsibility', in Kets de Vries M. *et al.* (eds) *Organisations on the Couch*, 264-285 (San Francisco, Jossey-Bass).

Baum, H. (1991b) 'Creating a family in the workplace', *Human Relations* 44, 1137-1159.

Baum, H. (1994) 'Community and consensus: reality and fantasy in planning', *Journal of Planning Education and Research* 13, 251-262.

Baum, H. (1995) 'Practising Planning Theory in a Political World, in Mandelbaum, S., *et al.* (eds) *Explorations in Planning Theory*, 365-382 (New Brunswick, Rutgers).

Baum, H. (1997) 'Teaching Practice', *Journal of Planning Education and Research* 17:1, 21-29.

Baum, H. (2000) 'Fantasies and Realities in University-Community Partnerships', *Journal of Planning Education and Research* 20:3, 234-246.

Bauman, Z. (2003) 'Utopia with no topos', *History of the Human Sciences* 16:1, 11-25.

Bauriedl, S., Wissen, M. (2002) 'Post-Fordist Transformation, the Sustainability Concept and Social Relations with Nature: A Case Study of the Hamburg Region', *Journal of Environmental Policy Planning* 4:2, 107-121.

Beatley, T., Manning, K. (1997) *The Ecology of Place* (Washington, Island Press).

Beauregard, R. (1989) 'Between modernity and postmodernity: the ambiguous position of US planning', *Environment and Planning D* 7:3, 381-395.

Beauregard, R. (1991) 'Without a net: Modernist planning and the postmodern abyss', *Journal of Planning Education and Research* 10:3, 189-194.

Beauregard, R. (1993) 'Constituting Economic Development: A Theoretical Perspective', in Bingham, R., Mier, R. (eds) *Theories of Local Economic Development: Perspectives From Across the Disciplines*, 267-283 (London, Sage).

Beauregard, R. (2001) 'The Multiplicities of Planning', *Journal of Planning Education and Research* 20:4, 437-439.

Beauregard, R. (2005) 'Introduction: Institutional Transformations', *Planning Theory* 4:3, 203-207.

Beaverstock, J., Taylor, P., Smith, R. (1999) 'A roster of world cities', *Cities* 16:6, 445-458.

Beck, U. (1992) *Risk Society* (London, Sage).

Beck, U. (1995) *Ecological Enlightenment* (New Jersey: Humanities Press).

Beck, U. (1998) *Democracy Without Enemies* (Cambridge, Polity Press).

Beck, U. (1999) *World Risk Society* (Cambridge, Polity Press).

Beck, U. (2002) 'The Terrorist Threat: World Risk Society Revisited', *Theory, Culture and Society* 19:4, 39-55.

Beck, U. (2003) 'The Silence of Words: On Terror and War', *Security Dialogue* 34:3, 255-267.

Beck, U. (2004) 'Cosmopolitical realism: on the distinction between cosmopolitanism in philosophy and the social sciences', *Global Networks* 4:2, 131-156.

Beck, U. (2005a) 'War is Peace: On Post-National War', *Security Dialogue* 36:1, 5-26.

Beck, U. (2005b) 'The Cosmopolitan State: Redefining Power in the Global Age', *International Journal of Politics, Culture, and Society* 18:3/4, 143-159.

Beck, U. (2006a) 'Living in the world risk society', *Economy and Society* 35:3, 329-345.

Beck, U. (2006b) *The Cosmopolitan Vision* (Cambridge, Polity).

Beck, U. (2008) 'Reframing Power in the Globilized World', *Organisational Studies* 29:5, 793-804.

Bentham, J. (1969) A Bentham Reader (New York, Pegasus).

Berger, P., Luckmann, T. (1966) *The Social Construction of Reality: A Treatise in the Sociology of Knowledge* (Garden City, New York, Anchor Books).

Berke, P. (2002) 'Does Sustainable Development Offer a New Direction for Planning? Challenges for the Twenty-First Century', *Journal of Planning Literature* 17:1, 21-36.

Bernstein, R. (2006) 'Derrida: The Aporia of Forgiveness?', *Constellations* 13:3, 394-406.

Bickenbach, J., Hendler, S. (1994) 'The moral mandate of the "profession" of planning', in Thomas, H. (ed.) *Values and Planning*, 162-177 (Aldershot, Avebury).

Bickerstaff, K., Walker, G. (2002) 'Risk, responsibility, and blame: analysing vocabularies of motive in air pollution(ing) discourses', *Environment and Planning A* 34:12, 2175-2192.

Bickerstaff, K., Simmons, P., Pidgeon, N. (2006) 'Situating local experience of risk: Peripherality, marginality and place identity in the UK foot and mouth disease crisis', *Geoforum* 37:5, 844-858.

Bickerstaff, K., Simmons, P., Pidgeon, N. (2008) 'Constructing responsibilities for risk: negotiating citizen – state relationships', *Environment and Planning: A* 40:6, 1312-1330.

Birch, E. (2001) 'Practitioners and the Art of Planning', *Journal of Planning Education and Research* 20:4, 407-422.

Blair, J., Kumar, R. (1997) 'Is local economic development a zero-sum game?', in Bingham R., Mier, R. (eds) *Dilemmas of Urban Economic Development: Issues in Theory and Practice*, 1-20 (Thousand Oaks, Sage).

Blakeley, E., Bista, S., Khan, A. (2007) 'Flee Sydney: A Prospectus on Human Capital Competition between New South Wales and Queensland', *Urban Policy and Research* 25:4, 455-471.

Bloch, E. (2000) *The Spirit of Utopia* (Stanford, Stanford University Press).

Blum, V., Nast, H. (1996) 'Where's the difference? The hetrosexualization of alternity in Henri Lefebvre and Jacques Lacan', *Environment and Planning D* 14:4, 559-580.

Blum, V., Nast, H. (2000) 'Jacques Lacan's two-dimensional subjectivity', in Crang, M., Thrift, N. (eds), *Thinking Space*, 183-204 (Routledge, London).

Bolan, R. (1985) 'The structure of ethical choice in planning practice', in Wachs, M. (ed.) *Ethics in Planning*, 70-89 (New Brunswick, Centre for Urban Policy Research).

Boland, P. (1999) 'Contested Multi-level Governance: Merseyside and the European Structural Funds', *European Planning Studies* 7:5, 647-664.

Boland, P. (2007) 'Unpacking the Theory-Policy Interface of Local Economic Development: An Analysis of Cardiff and Liverpool', *Urban Studies* 44(5/6), 1019-1039.

Boothby, R. (2001) *Freud as Philosopher: Metapsychology After Lacan* (London, Routledge).

Boucher, G. (2006) 'Bureaucratic Speech Acts and the University Discourse: Lacan's Theory of Modernity', in Clemens, J., Grigg, R. (eds) *Jacques Lacan and the Other Side of Psychoanalysis* (Durham, Duke University press).

Boudreau, J.-A. (2007) 'Making new political spaces: mobilizing spatial imaginaries, instrumentalizing spatial practices, and strategically using spatial tools', *Environment and Planning A* 39:11, 2593-2611.

Bourassa, S. (1991) *The Aesthetics of Landscape* (London, Belhaven).

Bourdieu, P. (1977) *Outline of a Theory of Practice* (Cambridge, Cambridge University Press).

Bourdieu, P. (1998) *Practical Reason* (Stanford, Stanford University Press).

Bourdieu, P. (2000) *Pascalian Mediations* (London, Polity).

Bowie, M. (1987) *Freud, Proust and Lacan* (Cambridge, Cambridge University Press).

Bowie, M. (1991) *Lacan* (London, Fontana).

Boyce, R. (2003) *Risk* (Buckingham, Open Uiniversity Press).

Boyer, M. (1983) *Dreaming the Rational City* (Cambridge, MIT Press).

Bracher, M. (1993) *Lacan, Discourse, and Social Change* (Ithaca, Cornell University Press).

Bracher, M. (1994) 'On the Psychological and Social Functions of Language: Lacan's Theory of the Four Discourses', in Bracher, M., *et al.* (eds) *Lacanian Theory of Discourse* (New York, New York University Press).

Bracher, M. (1999) *The Writing Cure* (Carbondale, Southern Illinois University Press).

Bracher, M. (2000) 'How Analysis Cures According to Lacan', in Malone K., Friedlander, S. (eds) *The Subject of Lacan*, 189-208 (Albany, SUNY).

Bradley, B., Stocker, M. (2005) '"Doing and Allowing" and Doing and Allowing', *Ethics* 115, 799-808.

Bramley, G., Kirk, K. (2005) 'Does planning make a difference to urban form? Recent evidence from Central Scotland', *Environment and Planning A* 37:2, 355-378.

Brand, P. (1999) 'The Environment and postmodern Spatial Consciousness: A Sociology of Urban Environmental Agendas', *Journal of Environmental Planning and Management* 42:5, 631-648.

Brand, R., Gaffikin, F. (2007) 'Collaborative Planning in an Uncollaborative World', *Planning Theory* 6:3, 282-313.

Breger, L. (2000) *Freud* (New York, John Wiley and Sons).

Breheny, M. (1995) 'The compact city and transport energy consumption', *Transactions of the Institute of British Geographers* 20:2, 81-101.

Brenner, N. (1999) 'Globalisation as Reterritorialisation: The Re-Scaling of Urban Governance in the European Union', *Urban Studies* 36:3, 431-451.

Brent, J. (2004) 'The desire for community: Illusion, confusion and paradox', *Community Development Journal* 39:3, 213-223.

Briassoulis, H. (1999) '*Who* Plans *Whose* Sustainability? Alternative Roles for Planners', *Journal of Environmental Planning and Management* 42:6, 889-902.

Bridge, G., Watson, S. (2000) 'City interventions', in Bridge, G., Watson, S. (eds) *A Companion to the City*, 505-516 (Oxford, Blackwell).

Brito, R. (2008) 'The Critique of Ideology Revisited: A Žižekian appraisal of Habermas' Communicative Rationality', *Contemporary Political Theory* 7:1, 53-71.

Brookes, M. (1988) 'Four Critical Junctures in the History of the Urban Planning Profession: An Exercise in Hindsight', *Journal of the American Planning Association* 54, 241-248.

Bruton, M. (1974) *The Spirit and Purpose of Planning* (London, Hutchinson).

Bruton, M., Nicholson, D. (1987) *Local Planning in Practice* (London, Hutchinson).

Buchanan, A., Decamp, M. (2006) 'Responsibility for Global Health', *Theoretical Medicine and Bioethics* 27:2, 95-114.

Bulkeley, H. (2006) 'Urban sustainability: learning from best practice?' *Environment and Planning A* 38: 6, 1029-1044.

Bullard, R. (1990) *Dumping in Dixie* (Boulder, Westview Press).

Bullard, R. (1999) 'Environmental justice challenges at home and abroad', in Low N. (ed.) *Global Ethics and Environment*, 33-46 (London, Routledge).

Bullen, E., Fahey, J., Kenway, J. (2006) 'The Knowledge Economy and Innovation: Certain uncertainty and the risk economy', *Discourse: Studies in the Cultural Politics of Education* 27:1, 53-68.

Bunce, E. (2004) 'The Emergence of "Smart Growth" Intensification in Toronto: environment and economy in the new Official Plan', *Local Environment* 9:2, 177-191.

Burkitt, I. (2002) 'Technologies of the Self; Habitus and Capacities', *Journal for the Theory of Social Behaviour* 32:2, 219-237.

Burnyeat, M. (1992) 'Utopia and fantasy: the practicability of Plato's ideally just city', in Hopkins, J., Savile, A. (eds) *Psychoanalysis, Mind and Art*, 175-187 (Oxford, Blackwell).

Burton, E. (2000) 'The Compact City: Just or Just Compact? A Preliminary Analysis', *Urban Studies* 37:11, 1969-2001.

Butler, J. (1990) *Gender Trouble* (London, Routledge).

Butler, J. (1997) *The Psychic Life of Power* (Stanford, Stanford University Press).

Butler, J., Laclau, E., Žižek, S. (2000) *Contingency, Hegemony, Universality* (London, Verso).

Butler, R. (2005) *Slavoj Žižek* (London: Continuum).

Buxton, M., Scheurer, J. (2007) 'Density and Outer Urban Development in Melbourne', *Urban Policy and Research* 25:1, 91-111.

Byrne, J., Glover, L. (2002) 'A Common Future or Towards a Future Commons: Globalization and sustainable Development since UNCED', *International Review for Environmental Strategies* 3:1, 5-25.

Byrne, K., Healy, S. (2006) 'Cooperative Subjects: Towards a Post-Fantasmatic Enjoyment of the Economy', *Rethinking Marxism* 18:2, 241-258.

Campbell, H. (2006) 'Just Planning: The Art of Situated Ethical Judgement', *Journal of Planning Education and Research* 26:2, 92-106.

Campbell, H., Marshall, R. (1998) 'Acting on principle: dilemmas in planning practice', *Planning Practice and Research* 13:2, 117-128.

Campbell, H., Marshall, R. (2005) 'Professionalism and planning in Britain', *Town Planning Review* 76:2, 191-214.

Campbell, H., Marshall, R. (2006) 'Towards justice in planning: A reappraisal', *European Planning Studies* 14:2, 239-252.

Campbell, S., Currie, G. (2006) 'Against Beck: In Defence of Risk Analysis', *Philosophy of the Social Sciences* 36:2, 149-172.

Campbell, S., Fainstein, S. (2003) 'Introduction: the structure and debates of planning theory', in Campbell, S., Fainstein, S. (eds) *Readings in Planning Theory*, 1-16 (Oxford, Blackwell).

Cardew, R. (1999) 'Two Cultures, Common Purpose', *Australian Planner* 36:3, 134-141.

Carvalho, A. (2007) 'Ideological cultures and media discourses on scientific knowledge: re-reading news on climate change', *Public Understanding of Science* 16:2, 223-243.

Casakin, H. (2006) 'Assessing the use of metaphor in the design process', *Environment and Planning B: Planning and Design* 33:3, 253-268.

Catlaw, T. (2006) 'Authority, Representation, and the Contradictions of Posttraditional Governing', *The American Review of Public Administration* 36:3, 261-287.

Caudill, D. (1997) *Lacan and the Subject of Law* (New Jersey, Humanities Press).

Cavell, S. (1979) *The Claim of Reason* (Oxford, Oxford University Press).

Chan, W. (2007) 'Writing Multiculturalism? Planning for Cultural Different identities in the City of Birmingham', *Planning Theory and Practice* 8:1, 69-85.

Charles, M. (2008) 'The Masquerade, the Veil, and the Phallic Mask: Commentary', *Psychoanalysis, Culture and Society* 13:1, 24-34.

Cheshire, P. (2006) 'Resurgent Cities, Urban Myths and Policy Hubris: What We Need to Know', *Urban Studies* 43:8, 1231-1246.

Chopra, R. (2003) 'Neoliberalism as Doxa: Bourdieu's Theory of the State and the Contemporary Indian Discourse on Globalization and Liberalization', *Cultural Studies* 17:3/4, 419-444.

Christensen, K. (1985) 'Coping with Uncertainty in Planning', *Journal of the American Planning Association* 51:1, 63-73.

Christensen, K. (1999) *Cities and Complexity* (Thousand Oaks, Sage).

Cladera, J., Burns, M. (2000) 'The Liberalization of the Land Market in Spain: The 1998 Reform of Urban Planning Legislation', *European Planning Studies* 8:5, 547-564.

Cloke, P. (2002) 'Deliver us from evil? Prospects for living ethically and acting politically in human geography', *Progress in Human Geography* 26:5, 587-604.

Coaffee, J. (2006) 'From Counterterrorism to Resilience', *The European Legacy* 11:4, 389-403.

Coaffee, J., Murakami Wood, D. (2006) 'Security is coming home: rethinking scale and constructing resilience in the global urban response to terrorist risk', *International Relations* 20:4, 503-517.

Coaffee, J., Murakami Wood, D., Rogers, P., Croft, S. (2008) *The Everyday Resilience of the City* (Basingstoke, Palgrave Macmillan).

Cochrane, A. (2000) 'The Social Construction of Urban Policy', In Bridge, G., Watson, S. (eds) *A Companion to the City*, 531-542 (Oxford, Blackwell).

Colebrook, C. (2006) *Deleuze: A Guide for the Perplexed* (London, Continuum).

Concise Oxford Dictionary (1992) *Concise Oxford Dictionary* (Oxford, Clarendon Press).

Connolly, W. (1991) *Identity\Difference* (Ithaca, Cornell University Press).

Connolly, W. (1998) 'Beyond good and evil: the ethical sensibility of Michel Foucault', in Moss, J. (ed.) *The Later Foucault* (London, Sage).

Connolly, W. (2002) *Neuropolitics* (Minneapolis, University of Minnesota Press).

Connolly, W. (2005) *Pluralism* (Durham, Duke University Press).

Copjec, J. (1989) *Read My Desire* (Cambridge, MIT Press).

Copjec, J. (2002) *Imagine There's No Woman* (Cambridge, MIT Press).

Cortright, J., Mayer, H. (2004) 'Increasingly Rank: The use and Misuse of Rankings in Economic Development', *Economic Development Quarterly* 18:1, 34-39.

Cotton, D., Warren, M., Maiboroda, O., Bailey, I. (2007) 'Sustainable development, higher education and pedagogy: a study of lecturer's beliefs and attitudes', *Environmental Education Research* 13:5, 579-597.

Counsell, D., Haughton, G. (2003) 'Regional planning tensions: planning for economic growth and sustainable development in two contrasting English regions', *Environment and Planning C* 21:2, 225-239.

Cowell, R., Owens, S. (2006) 'Governing space: planning reform and the politics of sustainability', *Environment and Planning C* 24:3, 403-421.

Crang, M. (2000) 'Public Space, Urban Space and Electronic Space: Would the Real City Please Stand Up?', *Urban Studies* 37:2, 301-317.

Critchley, S. (2004) 'Encounters with other philosophers: Lévinas', in Reynolds, J., Roffe, J. (eds) *Understanding Derrida*, 127-134 (London, Continuum).

Curtis, N. (2001) *Against Autonomy* (Aldershot, Ashgate).

Cussen, K. (2000) '"Is" or "ought" in planning', *Australian Planner* 37:3, 130-132.

Cutter, S. (1993) *Living with Risk* (New York, Routledge).

Dabinett, G., Richardson, T. (1999) 'The European Spatial approach: The Role of Power and Knowledge in Strategic Planning and Policy Evaluation', *Evaluation* 5:2, 220-236.

Dagenhart, R., Sawicki, D. (1992) 'Architecture and Planning: the divergence of two fields', *Journal of Planning Education and Research* 12:1, 1-16.

Dalton, L. (2001) 'Weaving the Fabric of Planning as Education', *Journal of Planning Education and Research* 20:4, 423-436.

Daniels, T. (2001) 'Smart Growth: A New American Approach to Regional Planning', *Planning Practice and Research* 16:3/4, 271-279.

Davoudi, S. (2000) 'Sustainability: a new vision for the British planning system', *Planning Perspectives* 15:2, 123-137.

Davoudi, S. (2001) 'Planning and the Twin Discourses of Sustainability', in Layard, A., *et al.* (eds), *Planning for a Sustainable Future*, 81-99 (London, Spon).

Day, K. (2003) 'New Urbanism and the Challenges of Designing for Diversity', *Journal of Planning Education and Research* 23:1, 83-95.

Dean, J. (2001) 'Publicity's Secret', *Political Theory* 29:5, 624-650.

Dean, J. (2006) *Žižek's Politics* (London, Routledge).

Dean, M. (1999) *Governmentality* (London, Sage).

Dean, T. (1997) 'Two Kinds of Other and Their Consequences', *Critical Inquiry* 23:4, 910-920.

Dean, T. (2000) *Beyond Sexuality* (Chicago, University of Chicago Press).

Dear, M. (1986) 'Postmodernism and Planning', *Environment and Planning D* 4:3, 367-384.

Dear, M., Scott, A. (1981) *Urbanisation and Urban Planning in Capitalist Society* (London, Methuen).

Declercq, F. (2006) 'Lacan on the Capitalist Discourse: Its Consequences for Libidinal Enjoyment and Social Bonds', *Psychoanalysis, Culture and Society* 11:1, 74-83.

Deetz, S., White, W. (1999) 'Relational responsibility or dialogic ethics', in McNamee S., *et al.* (eds) *Relational Responsibility*, 111-120 (Thousand Oaks, Sage).

Department for Environment, Food and Rural Affairs [Defra] (2008) *Sustainable Development* http://www.defra.gov.uk/sustainable/government/progress/regio nal/regional_methods.htm, accessed 13 October 2008.

Deleuze, G. (1991) *Coldness and Cruelty* (New York, Zone Books).

Deleuze, G. (1994) *Difference and Repetition* (London, Athlone Press).

Deleuze, G. (1995) *Negotiations, 1972-1990* (New York, Columbia University Press).

Deleuze, G., Guattari, F. (1987) [1980] *A Thousand Plateaus* (London, Athlone Press).

Department of Sustainability and Environment (2005) <http://www.dse.vic.gov. au/melbourne2030online/content/implementation_plans/07_transport.html>, accessed 19 August 2008.

De Roo, G., Miller, D. (2000) *Compact Cities and Sustainable Urban Development* (Aldershot, Ashgate).

Derrida, J. (1978) *Writing and Difference* (London, Routledge).

Derrida, J. (1988) *Limited Inc* (Evanston, North Western University Press).

Derrida, J. (1990) 'Force of law: the "mystical foundation of authority"', *Cardozo Law Review* 11:5-6, 919-1045.

Derrida, J. (1991) 'Eating Well', in Cadava, E., *et al.* (eds) *Who Comes after the Subject?*, 96-119 (London, Routledge).

Derrida, J. (1992) *The Other Heading* (Indianapolis, Indiana University Press).

Derrida, J. (1993) 'Politics and Friendship: An Interview with Jacques Derrida', in Kaplan, A., Sprinker, M. (eds) *The Althusserian Legacy*, 183-231 (London, Verso).

Derrida, J. (1994) *Specters of Marx* (London, Routledge).

Derrida, J. (1995) *The Gift of Death* (Chicago, University of Chicago Press).

Derrida, J. (1997a) *Of Grammatology* (Baltimore, John Hopkins University Press).

Derrida, J. (1997b) *Politics of Friendship* (London, Verso).

Derrida, J. (2000a). 'Intellectual Courage: an Interview', *Culture Machine* <http://culturemachine.tees.ac.uk/Cmach/Backissues/j002/Articles/art_derr.htm>, accessed 4 October 2006.

Derrida, J. (2000b) *Of Hospitality* (Stanford, Stanford University Press).

Derrida, J. (2002) *Negotiations* (Stanford, Stanford University Press).

de Soysa, I. (2002) 'Ecoviolence: Shrinking Pie, or Honey Pot?' *Global Environmental Politics* 2:4, 1-34.

De Vries, P. (2007) 'Don't Compromise Your Desire for Development! A Lacanian/Deleuzian rethinking of the anti-politics machine', *Third World Quarterly* 28:1, 25-43.

Dews, P. 1995 *The Limits of Disenchantment* (London, Verso).

Dixon, J. (2001) 'Trends and Prospects for Planning Education in New Zealand', Paper presented at the 1st World Planning Schools Congress, 11-15 July, Shanghai, China.

Dixon, J., Dupuis, A. (2003) 'Urban Intensification in Auckland, New Zealand: A Challenge for New Urbanism', *Housing Studies* 18:3, 353-368.

Doak, J., Parker, G. (2005) 'Networked Space? The Challenge of Meaningful Participation and the New Spatial Planning in England', *Planning, Practice and Research* 20:1, 23-40.

Dolar, M. (1999) 'Where does power come from?' *New Formations* 35, 79-92.

Dolar, M. (2006) 'Hegel as the Other Side of Psychoanalysis', in Clemens, J., Grigg, R. (eds) *Jacques Lacan and the Other Side of Psychoanalysis*, 129-154 (Durham, Duke University Press).

Donnison, N. (2005) 'Bridging the gap between rhetoric and reality: making sustainability happen in Melbourne', *Creative and Sustainable Communities, Planning Institute of Australia 2005 National Congress Program and Abstracts*, 17-20 April, Melbourne, Australia.

Dor, J. (1998) *Introduction to the Reading of Lacan* (Other Press, New York).

Douglass, M. (2002) 'From global intercity competition to cooperation for livable [*sic*] cities and economic resilience in Pacific Asia', *Environment and Urbanization* 14:1, 53-68.

Downs, A. (2005) 'Smart Growth: Why We Discuss It More than We Do It', *Journal of the American Planning Association* 71:4, 367-378.

Doyle, T. (1998) 'Sustainable development and Agenda 21: the secular bible of global free markets and pluralist democracy', *Third World Quarterly* 19:4, 771-786.

Duffy, H. (1995) *Competitive Cities* (London, Taylor and Francis).

Duncan, G. (2007) 'After happiness', *Journal of Political Ideologies* 12:1, 85-108.

Dupuis, A., Thorns, D. (1998) 'Home, home ownership and the search for ontological security', *The Sociological Review* 46:1, 24-47.

Dupuis, A., Thorns, D. (2008) 'Gated Communities as Exemplars of "Forting Up" Practices in a Risk Society', *Urban Policy and Research* 26:2, 145-157.

Dyckman, J. (1964) 'Summary: planning and metropolitan systems', in Webber M., *et al.* (eds) *Explorations into Urban Structure*, 220-237 (Philadelphia, University of Pennsylvania Press).

Dyllick, T., Hockerts, K. (2002) 'Beyond the Business Case for Corporate Sustainability', *Business Strategy and the Environment* 11:2, 130-141.

Egéa-Kuehne, D. (2003) 'The Teaching of Philosophy: Renewed rights and responsibilities', *Educational Philosophy and Theory* 35:3, 271-284.

Ekberg, M. (2007) 'The Parameters of the Risk Society', *Current Sociology* 55:3, 243-366.

Elden, S. (2004) *Understanding Henri Lefebvre* (London, Continuum).

Elliot, A. (2001) *Concepts of the Self* (Cambridge, Polity).

Elliott, A. (2003) *Critical Visions* (Oxford: Rowman and Littlefield).

Ellis, G., Weekes, T. (2008) 'Making sustainability "real": using group-enquiry to promote education for sustainable development', *Environmental Education Research* 14:4, 482-500.

Esnard, A.-M. (1996) 'Professional ethics in the GIS era', paper presented at the ACSP-AESOP Joint Congress, Toronto, July.

Evanoff, R. (2005) 'Reconciling Realism and Constructivism in Environmental Ethics', *Environmental Values* 14:1, 61-81.

Evans, D. (1996) *An Introductory Dictionary of Lacanian Psychoanalysis* (London, Routledge).

Ewing, R. (1997) 'Is Los Angeles-style sprawl desirable?', *Journal of the American Planning Association* 63:1, 107-125.

Ezrahi, Y. (1990) *The Descent of Icarus* (Cambridge, Harvard University Press).

Fainstein, S. (2005) 'Cities and Diversity: Should we want it? Can we plan for it?' *Urban Affairs Review* 40:1, 3-19.

Faludi, A. (1973) *Planning Theory* (Oxford, Pergamon Press).

Featherstone, M. (2002) 'Empire and Utopia: A Psychoanalytic Critique of Totality', *Cultural Values* 6:4, 369-384.

Feinberg, J. (1980) *Rights, Justice and the Bounds of Liberty* (Princeton, Princeton University Press).

Ferraro, G. (1995) 'Planning as Creative Interpretation', in Mandelbaum S., *et al.* (eds) *Explorations in Planning Theory*, 312-327 (New Brunswick, Rutgers).

Filion, P., McSpurren, K. (2007) 'Smart Growth and Development Reality: The Difficult Co-ordination of Land Use and Transport Objectives', *Urban Studies* 44:3, 501-523.

Findlay, A., Morris, A., Rogerson, R. (1988) 'Where to live in Britain, 1988', *Cities* August, 268-276.

Finer, H. (1941) 'Administrative responsibility and democratic government', *Public Administration Review* 1:3, 335-350.

Fink, B. (1995) *The Lacanian Subject* (Princeton, Princeton University Press).

Fink, B. (1998) 'The Master Signifier and the Four Discourses', in Nobus, D. (ed.) *Key Concepts of Lacanian Psychoanalysis* (New York, Other Press).

Fink, B. (2002) 'Knowledge and Jouissance', in Barnard, S., Fink, B. (eds) *Reading Seminar XX*, 21-46 (Albany, SUNY).

Fink, B. (2004) *Lacan to the Letter* (Minneapolis, University of Minnesota Press).

Fischer, J., Ravizza, M. (1998) *Responsibility and Control* (Cambridge, Cambridge University Press).

Fishman, R. (1977) *Urban Utopias in the 20th Century* (New York, Basic Books).

Flint, J. (2003) 'Housing and ethopolitics: constructing identities of active consumption and responsibility community', *Economy and Society* 32:3, 611-629.

Florida, R. (2000) *Competing in the Age of Talent* (Pittsburgh, Mellon Foundation).

Florida, R. (2002a) 'The Economic Geography of Talent', *Annals of the Association of American Geographers* 92:4, 743-755.

Florida, R. (2002b) 'Bohemia and economic geography', *Journal of Economic Geography* 2:1, 55-71.

Florida, R. (2002c) *The Rise of the Creative Class* (New York, Basic Books).

Florida, R. (2004) *Cities and the Creative Class* (London, Routledge).

Flyvbjerg, B. (1992) 'Aristotle, Foucault and Progressive Phronesis: Outline of an Applied Ethics for Sustainable Development', *Planning Theory* 7-8, 65-83.

Flyvbjerg, B. (1998) *Rationality and Power* (Chicago, University of Chicago Press).

Flyvbjerg, B. (2001) *Making Social Science Matter* (Cambridge, Cambridge University Press).

Flyvbjerg, B., Bruzelius, N., Rothengatter, W. (2003) *Megaprojects and Risk* (Cambridge, Cambridge University Press).

Flyvbjerg, B., Richardson, T. (2002) 'Planning and Foucault: In Search of the Dark Side of Planning Theory', in Allmendinger, P., Tewdwr-Jones, M. (eds) *Planning Futures*, 44-62 (London, Routledge).

Foley, D. (1960) 'British Town Planning: One Ideology or Three?' *The British Journal of Sociology* 11:3, 211-231.

Forester, C. (2006) 'The Challenge of Change: Australian Cities and Urban Planning in the New Millennium', *Geographical Research* 44:2, 173-182.

Forester, J. (1989) *Planning in the Face of Power* (Berkeley, University of California Press).

Forester, J. (1993) *Critical Theory, Public Policy and Planning Practice* (Albany, SUNY Press).

Forester, J. (1999) *The Deliberative Practitioner* (Cambridge, MIT Press).

Forrest, D. 2000, 'Theorising empowerment thought: illuminating the relationship between ideology and politics in the contemporary era', *Sociological Research Online* 4 <http://www.socresonline.org.uk/4/4forrest.html>, accessed 23 May 2005.

Foster, J. (2001) 'Education as Sustainability', *Environmental Education Research* 7:2, 153-165.

Foucault, M. (1972) *The Archaeology of Knowledge* (London, Tavistock).

Foucault, M. (1977) *Discipline and Punish: The Birth of the Prison* (New York, Pantheon Books).

Foucault, M. (1979) *The History of Sexuality, Volume 1* (London, Allen Lane).

Foucault, M. (1980) *Power/Knowledge* (Brighton, Harvester Press).

Foucault, M. (1982) 'Afterword: The subject and power', in Dreyfus, H., Rabinow, P. (eds) *Michel Foucault*, 214-232 (Brighton, Harvester Books).

Foucault, M. (1987) 'The ethic of care for the self as a practice of freedom', *Philosophy and Social Criticism* 12:2-3, 112-131.

Foucault, M. (1988) 'Truth, power and self: an interview with Michel Foucault', in Martin, L., Gutman, H., Hutton, P. (eds) *Technologies of the Self*, 9-15 (Amherst, University of Massachusetts Press).

Foucault, M. (1991) 'Governmentality', in Burchell G., *et al.* (eds) *The Foucault Effect: Studies in Governmentality*, 87-104 (London, Harvester Wheatsheaf).

Foucault, M. (1998) 'On the Ways of Writing History', in Faubion, J. (ed.) *Aesthetics, Method, and Epistemology*, *279-295* (London, Penguin).

Foucault, M. (2001) *Fearless Speech* (Los Angeles, Semiotext(e)).

Frank, T. (1997) *The Conquest of Cool* (Chicago: University of Chicago Press).

Fraser, M. (2006) 'The ethics of reality and virtual reality: Latour, facts and values', *History of the Human Sciences* 19:2, 45-72.

Freeman, C. (2005) 'Is Sustainability an appropriate Focus for Planning Education? A Discussion Paper', *ANZAPS/GPEAN 2005 – Planning Education and Sustainability: Sustaining Planning Education Conference Proceedings*, University of South Australia, Adelaide, 30 September-2 October, 106-117.

Fressoz, J.-B. (2007) 'Beck Back in the 19th Century: Towards a Genealogy of Risk Society', *History and Technology* 23:4, 333-350.

Freud, S. (2003) *The Uncanny* (London, Penguin).

Frey, H. (1999) *Designing the City* (London, Spon).

Friedmann, J. (1987) *Planning in the Public Domain* (Princeton, Princeton University Press).

Friedmann, J. (1996) 'The Core Curriculum in Planning Revisited', *Journal of Planning Education and Research* 15:1, 89-104.

Friedmann, J. (1998) 'Planning Theory Revisited', *European Planning Studies* 6:3, 245-253.

Friedmann, J. (2000) 'The good city: in defence of utopian thinking', *International Journal of Urban and Regional Research* 24:2, 473-489.

Friedmann, J. (2002) *The Prospect of Cities* (Minneapolis, University of Minnesota Press).

Friedmann, J. (2005) 'Globalization and the emerging culture of planning', *Progress in Planning* 64:3, 183-234.

Fuery, P. (1995) *Theories of Desire* (Melbourne, Melbourne University Press).

Furedi, F. (2002) *Culture of Fear* (London, Continuum).

Gay, P. (2006) *Freud: A Life For Our Times* (London, Max Press).

Gergen, M. (1999) 'Relational responsibility: deconstructive possibilities', in McNamee, S., Gergen, K. (eds) *Relational Responsibility*, 99-109 (Thousand Oaks, Sage).

Germain, A., Gagnon, J. (2003) 'Minority Places of Worship and Zoning Dilemmas in Montréal', *Planning Theory and Practice* 4:3, 295-318.

Gibbs, D., Krueger, R. (2007) 'Containing the Contradictions of Rapid development?: New Economy Spaces and Sustainable Urban Development', in Krueger, R., Gibbs, D. (eds) *The Sustainable Development Paradox*, 66-94 (London, The Guilford Press).

Giddens, A. (1974) *Positivism and Sociology* (London, Heinemann).

Giddens, A. (1979) *Central Problems in Social Theory* (London, Macmillan).

Giddens, A. (1987) 'Structuralism, poststructuralism and the production of culture', in Giddens, A., Turner, J. (eds) *Social Theory Today* (Cambridge, Polity Press).

Giddens, A. (1991) *Modernity and Self-Identity* (Cambridge, Polity Press).

Gigante, D. (1998) 'Toward a notion of critical self-creation: Slavoj Žižek and the "Vortex of Madness"', *New Literary History* 29:1, 153-168.

Gilbert, L. (2004) 'At the Core and on the Edge: Justice Discourses in Metropolitan Toronto', *Space and Polity* 8:2, 245-260.

Gilligan, C. (1982) *In a Different Voice* (Cambridge, Harvard University Press).

Gleeson, B. (2000) 'Reflexive Modernization: The Re-enlightenment of Planning?' *International Planning Studies* 5:1, 117-135.

Gleeson, B. (2001) 'Devolution and State Planning in Australia', *International Planning Studies* 6:2, 133-152.

Gleeson, B. (2004) 'Deprogramming Planning: Collaboration and Inclusion in New Urban Development', *Urban Policy and Research* 22(3), 315-322.

Gleeson, B., Darbas, T., Lawson, S. (2004) 'Governance, Sustainability and Recent Australian Metropolitan Strategies: A Socio-theoretic Analysis' *Urban Policy and Research* 22:4, 245-366.

Gleeson, B., Low, N. (2000) *Australian Urban Planning* (Sydney, Allen and Unwin).

Glynos, J. (2002) 'Theory and evidence in the Freudian field: from observation to structure', in Glynos, J., Stavrakakis, Y. (eds) *Lacan and Science*, 13-50 (London, Karnac).

Gow, L. (2000) *Curbing the sprawl: urban growth management in the United States – lessons for New Zealand* (Wellington, Ministry for the Environment).

Gramsci, A. (1971) *Prison Notebooks* (New York, International Publishers).

Gravovic, B. (2003) 'Educating Planners of the Future', *Planning Quarterly* 151, 24-28.

Grcic, J. (1983) 'Kant and Rawls: Contrasting Concepts of Moral Theory', *Journal of Value Inquiry* 17:3, 235-240.

Greer, G. (1999) *The Whole Woman* (Anchor).

Gregory, D. (1997) 'Lacan and geography: the production of space revisited,' in Benko, G., Strohmayer, U. (eds), *Space and Social Theory*, 203-231 (Oxford, Blackwell).

Grenville, J. (2007) 'Conservation as Psychology: Ontological Security and the Built Environment', *International Journal of Heritage Studies* 13:6, 447-461.

Grey, C., Garsten, C. (2002) 'Organised and disorganised utopias: an essay on presumption', in Parker, M. (ed.) *Utopia and Organisation*, 9-23 (Oxford, Blackwell).

Griggs, S., Howarth, D. (2002) 'The work of ideas and interests in public policy', in Finlayson, A., Valentine, J. (eds) *Politics and Post-structuralism* (Edinburgh, Edinburgh University Press).

Grosz, E. (1989) *Sexual Subversions* (Sydney, Allen and Unwin).

Grosz, E. (1990) *Jacques Lacan: a feminist introduction* (London, Routledge).

Gunder, M. (1998) 'The Free Lunch Public Transport Centre: A New Zealand case study on how to acquire 2,900 new car parking spaces and $0.4b in public debt', *World Transport Policy and Practice* 4:3, 8-15.

Gunder, M. (2000a) 'Planning for joy: Bringing-forth the places of the Others' desire', in *Conference Proceedings, Habitus 2000: a Sense of Place*, Perth, Curtin University (CD-ROM).

Gunder, M. (2000b) 'Urban policy formation under efficiency: The case of the Auckland City Council's Britomart Project', in Memon, A., Perkins, H. (eds) *Environment Planning and Management In New Zealand*, 294-308 (Palmerston North, Dunmore Press).

Gunder, M. (2002a) 'Auckland's Motorway System: A New Zealand Genealogy of Imposed Automotive Progress 1946-66', *Urban Planning and Research* 20:2, 129-142.

Gunder, M. (2002b) 'Bridging Theory and Practice in Planning Education: a Story from New Zealand', *Australian Planner* 39:4, 200-204.

Gunder, M. (2003a) 'Passionate Planning for the Others' Desire: An Agonistic Response to the Dark Side of Planning', *Progress in Planning* 60:3, 236-319.

Gunder, M. (2003b) 'Planning Policy Formulation from a Lacanian Perspective', *International Planning Studies* 8:4, 279-294.

Gunder, M. (2004) 'Shaping the Planner's Ego-Ideal: A Lacanian Interpretation of Planning Education', *Journal of Planning Education and Research* 23:3, 299-311.

Gunder, M. (2005a) 'Lacan, Planning and Urban Policy Formation', *Urban Policy and Research* 23:1, 91-111.

Gunder, M. (2005b) 'The Production of Desirous Space: Mere Fantasies of the Utopian City?', *Planning Theory* 4:2, 173-199.

Gunder, M. (2005c) 'Obscuring Difference Through Shaping Debate: A Lacanian View of Planning for Diversity', *International Planning Studies* 10:2, 83-103.

Gunder, M. (2006) 'Sustainability: Planning's Saving Grace or Road to Perdition?', *Journal of Planning Education and Research* 26:2, 208-221.

Gunder, M. (2008) 'Ideologies of Certainty in a Risky Reality: Beyond the Hauntology of Planning', *Planning Theory* 7:2, 186-206.

Gunder, M. (2009) 'Imperatives of Enjoyment: Economic Development under Globalisation', in Rowe, J. (ed.) *Theories of Local Economic Development: Linking Theory to Practice*, 285-300 (Aldershot, Ashgate).

Gunder, M., Fookes, T. (1997a) 'Planning School Programs in Australia and New Zealand: A comparison of accredited programs', *Australian Planner* 34:1, 54-61.

Gunder, M., Fookes, T. (1997b) 'In Defence of Planning Praxis, Knowledge and the Profession: Planning Education and Institutions for the New Century', *Planning Practice and Research* 12:2, 133-146.

Gunder, M., Hillier, J. (2004) 'Conforming to the Expectations of the Profession: A Lacanian Perspective on Planning Practice, Norms and Values', *Planning Theory and Practice* 5:2, 217-235.

Gunder, M., Hillier, J. (2007a) 'Planning as Urban Therapeutic', *Environment and Planning: A* 39:2, 467-486.

Gunder, M., Hillier, J. (2007b) 'Problematising Responsibility in Planning Theory and Practice: On Seeing the Middle of the String', *Progress in Planning* 68:2, 57-96.

Gunder, M., Mouat, C. (2002) 'Symbolic Violence and Victimisation in Planning Processes: A Reconnoitre of the New Zealand Resource Management Act', *Planning Theory* 1:2, 125-146.

Gunder, M., Searle, G. (2007) 'Not the Only Game in Town: A Lacanian Analysis of Metropolitan Planning in Sydney since 1995', *Conference of The Australian and New Zealand Association of Planning Schools*, 14-16 September, University of Otago, Dunedin.

Habermas, J. (1972) *Knowledge and Human Interests* (London, Heinemann).

Habermas, J. (1979) *Communication and the Evolution of Society* (Boston, Beacon Press).

Habermas, J. (1984) *The Theory of Communicative Action, Volume 1* (Boston, Beacon Press).

Habermas, J. (1987) *The Theory of Communicative Action, Volume 2* (Cambridge, Polity Press).

Habermas, J. (2001) *On the Pragmatics of Social Interaction* (Cambridge, MIT Press).

Hacking, I. (1981) *Scientific Revolutions* (Oxford, Oxford University Press).

Hajer, M. (1995) *The Politics of Environmental Discourse* (Oxford, Oxford University Press).

Haji, I., Cuypers, S. (2005) 'Moral responsibility, love, and authenticity', *Journal of Social Philosophy* 36:1, 106-126.

Hall, P. (2001) 'Sustainable cities or town cramming?', in Layard, A., *et al.* (eds) *Planning for a Sustainable Future*, 101-114 (London, Spon).

Hardy, D. (2000) *Utopian England* (London, Spon).

Hardy, J. (2002) 'Lévinas and Environmental Education', *Educational Philosophy and Theory* 34:4, 459-476.

Hardy, J. (2008) 'Stratification of environmental education and education for sustainable development in Australia: an analysis of positions vacant advertisements', *Environmental Education Research* 14:2, 165-174.

Hardy, N. (2007) 'On Lacan and the "Becoming-ness" of Organizations/Selves' *Organization Studies* 28:11, 1761-1773.

Harper, T., Stein, S. (1983) 'The environmental professions: moral and professional responsibilities', *Journal of Environmental Education* 14:3, 27-32.

Harper, T., Stein, S. (1995) 'Contemporary procedural ethical theory and planning theory', in Hendler, S. (ed.) *Planning Ethics*, 49-65 (New Brunswick, Centre for Urban Policy Research Press).

Harper, T., Stein, S. (2006) *Dialogical Planning in a Fragmented Society* (New Brunswick, Centre for Urban Policy Research Press).

Harvey, D. (1995) 'The Environment of Justice', in Merrifield, A., Swyngedouw, E. (eds) *The Urbanization of Injustice*, 65-99 (London, Lawrence and Wishart).

Harvey, D. (1999) 'Consideration on the environment of justice', in Low, N. (ed.) *Global Ethics and Environment*, 109-130 (London, Routledge).

Harvey, D. (2000) *Spaces of Hope* (Edinburgh, Edinburgh University Press).

Harvey, D. (2005) *A Brief History of Neo-Liberalism* (Oxford, Oxford University Press).

Haslam, S. (2001) *Psychology in Organizations* (London, Sage).

Hasson, E. (2005) 'Risk, modernity and history', *International Journal of Law in Context* 1:4, 315-334.

Haughton, G. (1999) 'Environmental Justice and the Sustainable City', *Journal of Planning Education and Research* 18:3, 233-243.

Haughton, G., Counsell, D. (2004) 'Regions and sustainable development: regional planning matters', *The Geographical Journal* 170:2, 135-145.

Healey, P. (1997) *Collaborative Planning* (London, Macmillan).

Healey, P. (1999) 'Institutionalist analysis, communicative planning and shaping places', *Journal of Planning Education and Research* 19:2, 111-122.

Healey, P. (2002) 'On creating the "city" as a collective resource', *Urban Studies* 39:10, 1777-1793.

Healey, P. (2003) 'Creativity and urban governance: an institutionalist perspective' presented at ECPR Workshop 21, Edinburgh. Copy available from author.

Healey, P. (2005) *Collaborative Planning,* second edition (London, Palgrave Macmillan).

Healey, P. (2007) *Urban Complexity and Spatial Strategies: Towards a relational planning for our times* (New York, Routledge).

Healey, P., de Magalhaes, C., Madanipour, A., Pendlebury, J. (2002) *Shaping City Centre Futures: conservation, regeneration and institutional capacity* (CREUE, University of Newcastle, Newcastle-upon-Tyne).

Healey, P., Shaw, T. (1994) 'Changing meanings of 'environment' in the British planning system', *Transactions of the Institute of the British Geographers* 19:4, 425-438.

Healy, S. (2004) 'A "post-foundational" interpretation of risk: risk as "performance"', *Journal of Risk Research* 7:3, 277-296.

Healy, S. (2005) 'Towards a Vocabulary for Speaking of the Engagement of Things in Discourse', *Journal of Environmental Policy and Planning* 7:3, 239-256.

Hendler, S. (1996) 'On the use of models in planning ethics', in Mandelbaum, S., *et al.* (eds) *Explorations in Planning Theory*, 400-413 (New Brunswick, Centre for Urban Policy Research Press).

Hendler, S. (2005) 'Towards a Feminist Code of Planning Ethics', *Planning Theory and Practice* 6:1, 53-69.

Hendrix, H. (1967) 'The Ontological Character of Anxiety', *Journal of Religion and Health* 6:1, 46-65.

Hillier, J. (2002) *Shadows of Power* (London: Routledge).

Hillier, J. (2003a) 'Agon'ising Over Consensus – Why Habermasian Ideals Cannot be "Real"', *Planning Theory* 2:1, 37-59.

Hillier, J. (2003b) 'Puppets of Populism', *International Planning Studies* 8:2, 157-166.

Hillier, J. (2004) '"But tight jeans are better!": moral improvisation and ethical judgement in local planning decision-making', in Lee, R., Smith, D.M. (eds) *Geographies and Moralities*, 211-227 (Oxford, Blackwell).

Hillier, J. (2005) 'Straddling the post-structuralist abyss: between transcendence and immanence?', *Planning Theory* 4:3, 271-299.

Hillier, J. (2006) 'Multiethnicity and the Negotiation of Place', in Neill, W., Schwedler, H.-U. (eds) *Cultural Inclusion in the European City*, 74-87 (London, Palgrave Macmillan).

Hillier, J. (2007) *Stretching Beyond the Horizon: A Multiplanar Theory of Spatial Planning and Governance* (Aldershot, Ashgate).

Hillier, J. (2008a) 'Plan(e) speaking: a multiplanar theory of spatial planning', *Planning Theory* 7:1, 24-50.

Hillier, J. (2008b) 'Interplanary practice: towards a Deleuzean-inspired methodology for creative experimentation in strategic spatial planning', in van den Broeck J., *et al.* (eds) *Empowering the Planning Fields*, 23-41 (Leuven, Acco).

Hillier, J. (2009) 'Assemblages of Justice: the 'ghost ships' of Graythorp', *International Journal of Urban and Regional Research*, forthcoming.

Hillier, J., Gunder, M. (2003) 'Planning Fantasies? An Exploration of a Potential Lacanian Framework for Understanding Development Assessment Planning', *Planning Theory* 2:3, 225-248.

Hillier, J., Gunder, M. (2005) 'Not Over Your Dead Bodies! A Lacanian Interpretation of Planning Discourse and Practice', *Environment and Planning: A* 37:6, 1049-1066.

Hock, C. (2007) 'Making Plans: Representation and Intention', *Planning Theory* 6:1, 16-35.

Hoffman, S., Krumholz, N., O'Brien, K. (2000) 'How Capital Budgeting Helped a Sick City: Thirty Years of Capital Improvement Planning in Cleveland', *Public Budgeting and Finance* 20:1, 24-37.

Holloway, L. (2002) 'Virtual Vegetables and Adopted Sheep, Ethical Relation, Authenticity and Internet-Mediated Food Production Technologies', *Area* 34:1, 70-81.

Hoogenboom, M., Ossewaarde, R. (2005) 'From Iron Cage to Pigeon House: The Birth of Reflexive Authority', *Organizational Studies* 26:4, 601-619.

Hook, D. (2008) 'Absolute Other: Lacan's 'Big Other' as Adjunct to Critical Social Psychological Analysis?', *Social and Personality Psychology Compass* 2:1, 51-73.

Hopkins, L. (2001) 'Planning As Science: Engaging Disagreement', *Journal of Planning Education and Research* 20:4, 309-406.

Howe, E. (1992) 'Professional roles and the public interest in planning', *Journal of Planning Literature* 6:3, 230-248.

Howe, E. (1994) *Acting on Ethics in City Planning* (New Jersey, Rutgers University Press).

Howe, E., Kaufman, J. (1979) 'The ethics of contemporary American planners', *Journal of the American Planning Association* 45:3, 243-255.

Howe, E., Kaufman, J. (1981) 'The values of contemporary American planners', *Journal of the American Planning Association* 47:3, 266-278.

Howe, J., Langdon, C. (2002) 'Towards a Reflexive Planning Theory', *Planning Theory* 1:3, 209-225.

Howell-Moroney, M. (2008) 'A description and exploration of recent state-led smart-growth efforts', *Environment and Planning: C* 26:4, 778-695.

Howes, H. (2004) 'An Environment for Prosperity and Quality Living Accommodating Growth in the Thames Valley', *Corporate Social Responsibility and Environmental Management* 11:1, 35-47.

Hudson, B. (1979) 'Comparison of Current Planning Theories: Counterparts and Contradictions', *Journal of the American Planning Association* 45:4, 387-398.

Huggins, R. (2003) 'Creating a UK Competitive Index: Regional and Local Benchmarking', *Regional Studies* 37:1, 89-96.

Hunt, T. (2004) *Building Jerusalem* (London, Weidenfeld and Nicholson).

Hutchens, B. (2004) *Lévinas* (London, Continuum).

Innes, J. (1995) 'Planning theory's emerging paradigm: communicative action and interactive practice', *Journal of Planning Education and Research* 14:3, 183-189.

Innes, J. (1996) 'Planning through consensus building', *Journal of the American Planning Association* 62:4, 460-172.

Innes, J., Booher, D. (1999) 'Consensus Building and Complex Adaptive Systems', *Journal of the American Planning Association* 65:4, 412-423.

Innes, J., Booher, D. (2002) 'Network power in collaborative planning', *Journal of Planning Education and Research* 21:4, 221-236.

Irigaray, L. (1985) *Speculum of the Other* (Ithaca, Cornell University Press).

Irvine, C. (2005) 'The other side of silence: Lévinas, medicine and literature', *Literature and Medicine* 24:1, 8-18.

Irwin, A. (2001) *Sociology and the Environment* (Oxford, Polity Press).

Jacobs, C., Heracleous, L. (2006) 'Constructing Shared Understanding: The Role of Embodied Metaphors in Organizational Development', *The Journal of Applied Behavioural Science* 42:2, 207-226.

Jacobs J., Gelder, K. (1998) *Uncanny Australia* (Melbourne, Melbourne University Press).

Jacobs, M. (1991) *The Green Economy* (Concord, Pluto).

Jacobsen, M., Tester, K. (2007) 'Sociology, Nostalgia, Utopia and Mortality: A Conversation with Zygmunt Bauman', *European Journal of Social Theory* 10:2, 305-325.

jagodzinski, j. [*sic*] (2002) 'A Strange Introduction: My Apple Thing', in j. jagodzinski (ed.) *Pedagogical Desire*, xiii-lx (London, Bergin and Garvey).

Jameson, F. (2003) 'Imaginary and Symbolic in Lacan: Marxism, psychoanalytic criticism, and the problem of the subject', in Žižek, S. (ed.) *Jacques Lacan, Volume III*, 3-43 (London, Routledge).

Jameson, F. (2005) *Archaeologies of the Future* (London, Verso).

Jarvis, D. (2007) 'Risk, Globalisation and the State: A Critical appraisal of Ulrich Beck and the World Risk Society Thesis', *Global Society* 27:1, 23-46.

Jasanoff, S. (1999) 'The Songlines of Risk', *Environmental Values* 8:2, 135-152.

Jentsch, B. (2006) 'Land use Planning and The Consequences of "Smart Growth"', *Sociation Today* 4:2,<http://www.ncsociology.org/sociationtoday/v42/jentsch. htm>, accessed 25 July 2008.

Jepson, J. (2001) 'Sustainability and Planning: Diverse Concepts and Close Associations', *Journal of Planning Literature* 15:4, 499-510.

Jessop, B. (1999) *Reflections on globalisation and its (il)logic(s),* Department of Sociology, Lancaster University, <http://www.lancs.ac.uk/fass/sociology/ research/resalph.htm#ik>, accessed 22 August 2007.

Jessop, B. (2000) 'The Crisis of the National Spatio-Temporal Fox and the Tendential Ecological Dominance of Globalising Capital', *International Journal of Urban and Regional Research* 24:2, 323-360.

Johnston, A. (2005) *Time Driven* (Evanston, Northwestern University Press).

Johnston, A. (2008) *Žižek's Ontology* (Evanston, Northwestern University Press).

Jonas, A., While, A. (2007) 'Greening the Entrepreneurial City? Looking for Spaces of Sustainability Politics in the Competitive City', in Krueger, R., Gibbs, D. (eds) *The Sustainable Development Paradox*, 123-159 (London, Guilford Press).

Jonas, H. (1984) *The Imperative of Responsibility* (Chicago, University of Chicago Press).

Jones, C., Spicer, A. (2005) 'The Sublime Object of Entrepreneurship', *Organization* 12:2, 223-246.

Jordan, A. (2008) 'The governance of sustainable development: taking stock and looking forwards', *Environment and Planning C* 26:1, 17-33.

Junge, M. (2001) 'Zygmunt Bauman's poisoned gift of morality', *British Journal of Sociology* 52:1, 105-119.

Kant, I. (1934) *Critique of Pure Reason* (London, Dent).

Kant, I. (1959) *Foundations of the Metaphysics of Morals* (Indianapolis, Bobbs-Merrill Company).

Kant, I. (1990) *Foundations of the Metaphysics of Morals and What is Enlightenment* (London, Collier Macmillan).

Kapstein, E. (2006) *Economic Justice in an Unfair World* (Princeton, Princeton University Press).

Katz, P. (1994) *The New Urbanism* (San Francisco, McGraw Hill).

Kaufman, J. (1980) 'Land planning in an ethical perspective', *Journal of Soil and Water Conservation*, November-December, 255-258.

Kay, S. (2003) *Slavok Žižek* (Cambridge, Polity).

Keil, R., Boudreau, J.-A. (2005) 'Is there regionalism after municipal amalgamation in Toronto?', *City* 9:1, 9-22.

Keynes, J. (1921) *A Treatise on Probability* (London, Macmillan).

Kierkegaard, S. (2006) *Fear and Trembling* (Cambridge, Cambridge University Press).

Kipfer, S., Keil, R. (2002) 'Toronto Inc? Planning the Competitive City in the New Toronto', *Antipode* 34:2, 227-264.

Kitching G. (2003) *Wittgenstein and Society* (Aldershot, Ashgate).

Knight, F. (1921) *Risk, Uncertainty and Profit* (New York, Houghton Mifflin).

Kochis, B. (2005) 'On Lenses and Filters: The Role of Metaphor in Policy theory', *Administrative Theory and Praxis* 27:1, 24-50.

Kohn, J. (2003) 'Introduction', in Kohn, J. (ed.) *Responsibility and Judgement*, vii-xxxvii (New York, Schocken Books).

Kovacevic, F. (2003) 'Lacanians and the Fate of Critical Theory', *Angelaki: Journal of the Theoretical Humanities* 8:3, 109-131.

Kristeva, J. (1970) *Le Texte du Roman* (The Hague, Mouton de Gruyter).

Kristeva, J. (1982) *Powers of Horror* (New York, Columbia University Press).

Krips, H. (2003) 'Extract from Fetish. An Erotics of Culture', in Žižek S. *Jacques Lacan, Volume III*, 143-184 (London, Routledge).

Krips, H. (2008) The Hijab, the Veil, and Sexuation', *Psychoanalysis, Culture and Society* 13:1, 35-47.

Krogstrup, J., Svendsen, G. (2004) 'Can the EU Persuade the US to Rejoin the Kyoto Agreement', *Energy and Environment* 15:3, 427-435.

Krueger, R., Agyeman, J. (2005) 'Sustainability schizophrenia or "actual existing sustainabilities?" toward a broader understanding of the politics and promise of local sustainability in the US', *Geoforum* 36:4, 410-417.

Krueger, R., Savage, L. (2007) 'City-Regions and social reproduction: a "Place" for Sustainable Development?' *International Journal of Urban and Regional Research* 31:1, 215-223.

Lacan, J. (1977) *Ecrits: A Selection* (London, Norton).

Lacan, J. (1988a) *The Seminar, Book I, 1953-1954* (Cambridge, Cambridge University Press).

Lacan, J. (1988b) *The Seminar, Book II, 1954-1955* (Cambridge, Cambridge University Press).

Lacan, J. (1992) *The Ethics of Psychoanalysis 1959-1960* (London, Routledge).

Lacan, J. (1993) *The Psychoses* (London, Routledge).

Lacan, J. (1994) *The Four Fundamental Concepts of Psycho-Analysis* (London, Penguin).

Lacan, J. (1998) *The Seminar, Book XX, 1972-1973* (London, Norton).

Lacan, J. (2006) *Ecrits* (London, Norton).

Lacan, J. (2007) *The Seminar of Jacques Lacan: Book XVII* (London, Norton).

Laclau, E. (1989) 'Preference', in S. Žižek *The Sublime Object of Ideology*, ix-xv (London, Verso).

Laclau, E. (1996) *Emancipation(s)* (Verso, London).

Laclau, E. (2000) 'Identity and Hegemony' in Butler J., *et al.* (eds) *Contingency, Hegemony, Universality*, 44-89 (Verso, London).

Laclau, E. (2002) 'Democracy and the question of power', in Hillier, J., Rooksby, E. (eds) *Habitus: a sense of place*, 37-50 (Aldershot, Ashgate).

Laclau, E. (2003) 'Why do empty signifiers matter to politicians?' in Žižek S. (ed.) *Jacques Lacan, Volume III*, 305-313 (London, Routledge).

Laclau, E. (2005) *On Populist Reason* (London, Verso).

Laclau, E., Mouffe, C. (1985) *Hegemony and Socialist Strategy* (London, Verso).

Lacy, M. (2002) 'Deconstructing Risk Society', *Environmental Politics* 11:4, 42-62.

Laitin, D. (2006) 'The Perestroikan Challenge to Social Science', in Schram, S., Caterino, B. (eds) *Making Political Science Matter*, 33-55 (New York, New York University Press).

Landry, C. (2006) *The Art of City Making* (London, Earthscan).

Lang, H. (2003) 'Language and Finitude', in Žižek S. (ed.) *Jacques Lacan, Volume III*, 221-265 (London, Routledge).

Lankao, P. (2007) 'Are we missing the point? Particularities of urbanization, sustainability and carbon emissions in Latin American cities', *Environment and Urbanization* 19:1, 159-175.

Lash, S. (2007) 'Power after Hegemony: Cultural Studies in Mutation', *Theory, Culture and Society* 24:3, 55-78.

Latour, B. (1993) *We Have Never Been Modern* (Hemel Hempstead, Harvester Wheatsheaf).

Latour, B. (2000) 'When things strike back: a possible contribution of "science studies" to the social sciences', *British Journal of Sociology* 51:1, 107-123.

Latour, B. (2003) 'Is *Re*-modernization Occurring – And If So, How to Prove It?', *Theory, Culture and Society* 20:2, 35-48.

Lavin C. (2006) 'Fear, Radical Democracy, and Ontological Methadone', *Polity* 38:2, 254-275.

Law, J. (2003) 'Networks, relations, cyborgs: on the social study of technology', Centre for Science Studies, Lancaster University. <http://www.comp.lancs. ac.uk/sociology/soc042jl.html>, accessed 26 June 2004.

Law-Yone, H. (2007) 'Another Planning Theory? Rewriting the Meta-Narrative', *Planning Theory* 6:3, 315-326.

Leccardi, C. (2008) 'New biographies in the "risk society"? About future and planning', *21st Century Society* 3:2, 119-129.

Lefebvre, H. (1991) *The Production of Space* (Oxford, Blackwell).

Lefebvre, H. (1996) *Writings on Cities* (Oxford, Blackwell).

Lefebvre, H. (2003) *The Urban Revolution* (Minneapolis, University of Minnesota Press).

Leo, C., Anderson, K. (2006) 'Being Realistic About Urban Growth', *Journal of Urban Affairs* 28:2, 169-189.

LeRoy, S., Singell, L. (1989) 'Knight on Risk and Uncertainty', *Journal of Political Economy* 95:2, 394-406.

Leuenberger, D., Watkin, M. (2007) 'Sustainable Development in Public Administrative Planning: An Exploration of Social Justice, Equity, and Citizen Inclusion', *Administrative Theory and Praxis* 29:3, 394-411.

Leupin, A. (2004) *Lacan Today* (New York, Other Press).

Lever, W., Turok, I. (1999) 'Competitive Cities: Introduction to the Review', *Urban Studies* 36:5/6, 791-793.

Lévinas, E. (1969) *Totality and Infinity* (Pittsburgh, Duquesne University Press).

Lévinas, E. (1985) *Ethics and Infinity* (Pittsburgh, Duquesne University Press).

Lévinas, E. (1989) *The Lévinas Reader* (Oxford, Basil Blackwell).

Lévinas, E. (1993) *Outside the Subject* (Stanford, Stanford University Press).

Lévinas, E., Kearney, R. (1986) 'Dialogue with Emmanuel Lévinas', in Cohen, R. (ed.) *Face to Face with Lévinas*, 12-33 (Albany, SUNY).

Levitas, R. (1990) *The Concept of Utopia* (Herts., Phillip Allen).

Levitas R, (2003) 'Introduction: the elusive idea of utopia', *History of the Human Sciences* 16:1, 1-10.

Levitas, R. (2007) 'Looking for the blue: The necessity of utopia', *Journal of Political Ideologies* 12:3, 289-306.

Levy, J. (1992) 'What has happened to planning?' *Journal of the American Planning Association* 58:1, 81-84.

Lidskog, R., Soneryd, L., Uggla, Y. (2006) 'Knowledge, Power and Control – Studying Environmental Regulation in Late Modernity', *Journal of Environmental Policy and Planning* 7:2, 89-106.

Lindahl, E. (2002) 'Face to Face', *Pietisten* 17:1, <http://www.pietisten.org/ summer02/facetoface.html>, accessed 26 January 2006.

Lleywelyn, J. (1991) *The Middle Voice of Ecological Conscience* (New York, St Martin's Press).

Loose, R. (2002) 'A Lacanian approach to clinical diagnosis and addiction', in Glynos, J., Stavrakakis, Y. (eds) *Lacan and Science*, 263-289 (London, Karnac).

Lovell, T. (2003) 'Resisting with Authority: Historical Specificity, Agency and the Performative Self', *Theory, Culture and Society* 20:1, 1-17.

Lucas, K., Fuller, S. (2005) 'Putting the "E" into LSPs: Representing the environment within Local Strategic Partnerships (LSPs) in the UK', *Local Economy* 10:5 461-475.

Lucy, N. (2004) *A Derrida Dictionary* (Oxford, Blackwell).

Luke, T. (2008) 'The politics of true convenience or inconvenient truth: struggles over how to sust in capitalism, democracy, and ecology in the 21st century', *Environment and Planning A* 40:8, 1811-1824.

Lupton, D., Tulloch, J. (2002) 'Life Would be Pretty Dull without Risk: Voluntary Risk-Taking and its Pleasures', *Health, Risk and Society* 4, 113-124.

Lynch, K. (1981) *A Theory of Good City Form* (Cambridge, MIT Press).

MacDonald, K. (2005) 'What is planning?', *Planning,* 13 May, 25.

Malecki, E. (2007) 'Cities and regions competing in the global economy: knowledge and local development policies', *Environment and Planning C* 25:5, 638-654.

Mandelbaum, S. (1996) 'Making and Breaking Planning Tools', *Computers, Environments and Urban Systems* 20:2, 71-84.

Mandelbaum, S. (2000) *Open Moral Communities* (Cambridge, MIT Press).

Mannberg, M., Wihlborg, E. (2008) 'Communicative Planning – Friend or Foe? Obstacles and Opportunities for Implementing Sustainable Development Locally', *Sustainable Development* 16:1, 35-43.

Mannheim, K. (1960 [1936]) *Ideology and Utopia* (London, Routledge).

Marcuse, P. (1995) 'Not Chaos, but Walls: Postmodernism and the Partitioned City', in Watson, S., Gibson, K. (eds) *Postmodern Cities and Spaces,* 243-253 (London, Blackwell).

Marcuse, P. (1998) 'Sustainability is not enough', *Environment and Urbanization* 10:2, 103-111.

Marcuse, P. (2000) 'Cities in Quarters', In Bridge G., Watson, S. (eds) *A Companion to the City*, 270-281 (Oxford, Blackwell).

Marini, M. (1992) *Jacques Lacan* (New Brunswick, Rutgers).

Markusen, A. (2003) 'Fuzzy Concepts, Scanty Evidence, Policy Distance: The Case for Rigour and Policy Relevance in Critical Regional Studies', *Regional Studies* 37:6/7, 701-717.

Marshall, G. (2007) 'Commanded to Enjoy. The Waning of Traditional Authority and its Implications for Public Administration', *Administrative Theory and Praxis* 29:1, 102-114.

Martell, L. (2008) 'Beck's cosmopolitan politics', *Contemporary Politics* 14:2, 129-143.

Martin, E., Beatley, T. (1993) 'Our Relationship with the Earth: Environmental Ethics in Planning Education', *Journal of Planning Education and Research* 12:2, 117-126.

Masselos, J. (1995) 'Postmodern Bombay: Fractured Discourses', in Watson, S., Gibson, K. (eds) *Postmodern Cities and Spaces,* 199-215 (London: Blackwell).

Massey, D. (2004) 'Geographies of responsibility', *Geografiska Annaler* 86B:1, 5-18.

Massey, D. (2005) *For Space* (London, Sage).

May, T. (2005) *Gilles Deleuze* (Cambridge, Cambridge University Press).

McCann, E. (2004) '"Best Places": interurban competition, quality of life and popular media discourse', *Urban Studies* 41:10, 1909-1929.

McCann, E. (2007) 'Inequality and Politics in the Creative City-Region: Questions of Liveability and State Strategy', *International Journal of Urban and Regional Research* 31:1, 188-196.

McDonald, G. (1996) 'Planning as Sustainable Development', *Journal of Planning Education and Research* 15:3, 225-236.

McFee, W. (1916) *Casuals of the Sea: the Voyage of a Soul* (New York, Doubleday).

McGowan, T. (2004) *The End of Dissatisfaction?* (Albany, SUNY).

McGowan, T. (2008) 'The Case of the Missing Signifier', *Psychoanalysis, Culture and Society* 13:1, 48-66.

McGuirk, P. (2004) 'State, strategy, and scale in the competitive city: a neo-Gramscian analysis of the governance of "global Sydney"', *Environment and Planning: A* 36:6, 1019-1043.

McGuirk, P. (2005) 'Neoliberalist Planning? Re-thinking and Re-casting Sydney's Metropolitan Planning', *Geographical Research* 43:1, 59-70.

McGuirk, P. (2007) 'The Political Construction of the City-region: Note from Sydney', *International Journal of Urban and Regional Research* 31:1, 179-187.

McGuirk, P., O'Neill, P. (2002) 'Planning a Prosperous Sydney: the challenges of planning urban development in the new urban context', *Australian Geographer* 33:3, 301-316.

McLoughlin, B. (1992) *Shaping Melbourne's Future?* (Cambridge, Cambridge University Press).

McManus, P., Haughton, G. (2006) 'Planning with Ecological Footprints: a sympathetic critique of theory and practice', *Environment and Urbanization* 18:1, 113-127.

McMichael, A., Butler, C., Folke, C. (2003) 'New Visions for Addressing Sustainability', *Science* 302, 12 December, 1919-1920.

Meadows, D.H., Meadows, D.L., Randers, J., Behrens, W. (1972) *The Limits to Growth* (New York, Universe).

Medd, W. (2002) 'Complexity in the wild: action in local welfare', in Finlayson A., Valentine J. (eds) *Politics and Post-structuralism,* 130-144 (Edinburgh, Edinburgh University Press).

Mees, P. (2003) 'Paterson's Curse: the Attempt to revise Metropolitan Planning in Melbourne', *Urban Policy and Research* 21:3, 287-299.

Merrifield, A. (2000) 'Henri Lefebvre: a socialist in space', in Crang, M., Thrift, N. (eds) *Thinking Space,* 167-182 (Routledge, London).

Metselaar, S. (2005) 'When neighbours become numbers: Lévinas and the inhospitality of Dutch asylum policy', *parallax* 11:1, 61-69.

Middlemiss, L. (2008) 'Influencing individual sustainability: a review of evidence on the role of community-based organisations', *International Journal of Environment and Sustainable Development* 7:1, 78-93.

Miller, J., Hoel, L. (2002) 'The "smart growth" debate: best practices for urban transportation planning', *Socio-Economic Planning Sciences* 36:1, 1-24.

Ministry for the Environment [MfE] (2005) *New Zealand Urban Design Protocol* (Wellington, Ministry of Environment).

Ministry for the Environment [MfE] (2008) *Urban Design Case Studies: Local Government* (Wellington, Ministry for the Environment).

Mitchell, J. (1974) *Psychoanalysis and Feminism* (London, Allen Lane).

More, T. (1965 [1516]) *Utopia* (Harmondsworth, Penguin).

Morel, G. (2000) 'Science and Psychoanalysis', *Umbra(a): A journal of the unconscious – Science and Truth,* 65-79 (Buffalo, SUNY).

Mouffe, C. (2000) *The Democratic Paradox* (London, Verso).

Moulaert, F., Cabaret, K. (2006) 'Planning, Networks and Power Relations: Is Democratic Planning Under Capitalism Possible?' *Planning Theory,* 5:1, 51-70.

Mulgan, R. (2000) '"Accountability": an ever-expanding concept?' *Public Administration* 78:3, 555-573.

Murakami Wood D., Coaffee J. (2007) 'Lockdown! Resilience, resurgence and the stage-set city', in Atkinson, R., Helms, G. (eds) *Securing an Urban Renaissance* (Bristol, Policy Press).

Murdoch, J. (2004) 'Putting planning in its place: planning, sustainability and the urban capacity study', *Area* 36:1, 50-58.

Murdoch, J., Abram, S. (2002) *Rationalities of Planning* (Aldershot, Ashgate).

Myers, T. (2003) *Slavoj Žižek* (London, Routledge).

Mythen, G. (2007) 'Reappraising the Risk Society Thesis: Telescopic Sight or Myopic Vision?', *Current Sociology* 55:6, 793-813.

Næss, P. (2001) 'Urban Planning and Sustainable Development', *European Planning Studies* 9:4, 503-524.

Needham, B. (2006) *Planning, Law and Economics* (London, Routledge).

Neighborhood Park Council (2007) *Open Space San Francisco: 2100*, <http://www.sfnpc.org/open_space_2100>, accessed 8 October 2008.

Neuman, M. (2005a) 'Notes on the Uses and Scope of City Planning Theory', *Planning Theory* 4:2, 123-145.

Neuman, M. (2005b) 'The Compact City Fallacy', *Journal of Planning Education and Research* 25:1, 11-26.

Newman, P., Kenworthy, J. (1989) *Cities and Automobile Dependency* (Aldershot: Gower Technical).

Newman, S. (2001) *From Bakunin to Lacan* (Oxford, Lexington Books).

Newman, S. (2004) 'New reflections on the theory of power: a Lacanian perspective', *Contemporary Political Theory,* 3:1, 148-167.

Nixon, H., Lejano, R., Funderburg, R. (2006) 'Planning Methodology for Predicting Spatial Patterns of Risk Potential fro, Industrial Land Use', *Journal of Environmental Planning and Management* 49:6, 829-847.

Nobus, D. (2004) 'The Punning of Reason', *Angelaki* 9:1, 189-201.

November, V. (2008) 'Spatiality of Risk', *Environment and Planning: A* 40:7, 1523-1527.

Nussbaum, M. (2001a) *Upheavals of Thought,* Cambridge, (Cambridge University Press).

Nussbaum, M. (2001b) 'The Enduring Significance of John Rawls', *The Chronicle,* July 20, 2001, <http://www.sc.ehu.es/sfwpbiog/acdr/Archivo/nussbaum-rawls. PDF>, accessed 2 October 2006.

O'Byrne, A. (2005) 'Pedagogy without a Project: Arendt and Derrida on Teaching, Responsibility and Revolution', *Studies in Philosophy and Education* 24: 389-409.

O'Connor, K. (2003) 'Melbourne 2030: A Response', *Urban Policy and Research* 21:2, 211-215.

Office of the Deputy Prime Minister [ODPM] (2005a) *Best Value Performance Indicators,* <http://www.bvpi.gov.uk> (home page), accessed 29 November 2005.

Office of the Deputy Prime Minister [ODPM] (2005b) *Local Development Framework Monitoring* (London, ODPM).

O'Malley, L., Patterson, M., Kelly-Holmes, H. (2008) 'Death of a metaphor: reviewing the "marketing as relationships" frame', *marketing theory* [*sic*] 8:2, 167-187.

O'Neill, J. (2005) 'Environmental values through Thick and Thin', *Conservation and Society* 3:2, 479-500.

O'Neill, O. (1985) *Faces of Hunger* (London, Allen and Unwin).

O'Neill, O. (1996) *Toward Justice and Virtue* (Cambridge, Cambridge University Press).

O'Riordan, T. (1988) *The Politics of Sustainability* (London, Belhaven Press).

Orr, D. (1992) *Earth in Mind* (Washington, Island Press).

Orr, D., Ehrenfeld, D. (1995) 'None So Blind: The Problem of Ecological Denial', *Conservation Biology* 9:5, 985-987.

Osborne, T., Rose, N. (1999) 'Governing cities: notes on the spatialisation of virtue', *Environment and Planning D* 17, 737-760.

Pacione, M. (2007) 'Sustainable Urban Development in the UK: Rhetoric or reality?' *Geography* 92:3, 248-65.

Pallagst, K. (2007) *Growth Management in the US* (Aldershot, Ashgate).

Parker, I. (2004) *Slavok Žižek* (London, Pluto).

Parker, M. (2002) 'Utopia and the organisational imagination', in Parker M. (ed.) *Utopia and Organisation,* 1-8 (Oxford, Blackwell).

Parnell, S., Robinson, J. (2006) 'Development and Urban Policy: Johannesburg's City Development Strategy', *Urban Studies* 43:2, 337-355.

Patton, P. (2003) 'Concept and Politics in Derrida and Deleuze', *Critical Horizons* 4:2, 157-175.

Patton, P. (2004) 'Politics', in Reynolds, J., Roffe, J. (eds) *Understanding Derrida*, 26-36 (New York, Continuum).

Pearce, D. (1993) *Blueprint 3* (London, Earthscan).

Pease, B. (2002) 'Rethinking empowerment: a postmodern appraisal for emancipatory practice', *British Journal of Social Work* 32, 135-147.

Peck, J., Tickell, A. (2002) 'Neoliberalizing Space', *Antipodes* 34:3, 380-404.

Pellizzoni, L. (2004) 'Responsibility and Environmental Governance', *Environmental Politics* 13:3, 541-565).

Peratti-Watel, P. (2003) 'Neutralization theory and the denial of risk: some evidence from cannabis use among French adolescents', *British Journal of Sociology* 54:1, 21-42.

Perloff, H. (1957) *Education for Planning* (Baltimore, John Hopkins University Press).

Pestieau, K., Wallace, M. (2003) 'Challenges and Opportunities for Planning in the Ethno-culturally Diverse City: A Collection of Papers – Introduction', *Planning Theory and Practice* 4:3, 253-258.

Pile, S. (1993) 'Human agency and human geography revisited: a critique of "new models" of the self', *Transactions of the Institute of British Geographers* 18, 122-139.

Pile, S. (1996) *The Body and the City* (London, Routledge).

Pile, S. (1998) 'Freud, dreams and imaginative geographies,' in Elliott A. (ed.) *Freud 2000,* 204-234 (Cambridge, Polity).

Pile, S. (2000) 'Sleepwalking in the modern city: Walter Benjamin and Sigmund Freud in the world of dreams', in Bridge, G., Watson, S. (eds) *A Companion to the City*, 75-86 (Oxford, Blackwell).

Pile, S. (2005) *Real Cities* (London, Sage).

Pinder, D. (2002) 'In defence of utopian urbanism: imagining cities after the "end of utopia"', *Geografiska Annale,* 84B:3-4, 229-241.

Plato (1992) *The Republic* (Indianapolis, Hackett).

Pløger, J. (2001a) 'Millennium Urbanism – Discursive planning', *European Urban and Regional Studies* 8:1, 63-72.

Pløger, J. (2001b) 'Public participation and the art of governance', *Environment and Planning: B* 28:2, 219-241.

Pløger, J. (2004) 'Strife: urban planning and agonism', *Planning Theory* 3:1, 71-92.

Pløger, J. (2006) 'In Search of Urban Vitalis', *Space and Culture*, 9:4, 382-399.

Popke, J. (2003) 'Poststructuralist ethics: subjectivity, responsibility and the space of community', *Progress in Human Geography* 27:3, 298-316.

Popke, J. (2004) 'The face of the other: Zapatismo, responsibility and the ethics of deconstruction', *Social and Cultural Geography* 5:2, 301-317.

Popke, J. (2006) 'Geography and ethics: everyday mediations through case and consumption', *Progress in Human Geography* 30:4, 504-512.

Porter, M. (1995) 'The Competitive Advantage of the Inner City', *Harvard Business Review* 73:3, 55-71.

Porter, M. (2000) 'Location, Competition, and Economic Development: Local Clusters in a Global Economy', *Economic Development Quarterly* 14:1, 15-34.

Porter, M. (2003) 'The Economic Performance of Regions', *Regional Studies* 37:6/7, 545-578.

Pupavac, V. (2004-5) 'International therapeutic governance', *The CSD Bulletin* 11:2/12:1, 36-37.

Quinn, B. (2006) 'Transit-Oriented Development: Lessons from California', *Built Environment* 32:2, 311-322.

Raco, M. (2005a) 'A Step Change or a Step Back? The Thames Gateway and the Re-birth of the Urban Development Corporations', *Local Economy* 20:2, 141-153.

Raco, M. (2005b) 'Sustainable Development, Rolled-out Neoliberalism and Sustainable Communities', *Antipode* 37:2, 324-347.

Raco, M. (2006) 'Sustainable Urban Planning and the Brownfield Development Process in the United Kingdom: Lessons from the Thames Gateway', *Local Environment* 11:5, 499-513.

Raco, M. (2008) 'Key Worker Housing, Welfare Reform and the New Spatial Policy in England', *Regional Studies*, 42:5, 737-751.

Ragland, E. (1996) 'The Discourse of the Master', In Apollon, W., Feldstein, R. (eds) *Lacan, Politics, Aesthetics* (Albany, SUNY).

Ragland, E. (2004) *The Logic of Sexuation* (Albany, SUNY).

Ragland, E. (2008) 'The Masquerade, the Veil, and the Phallic Mask', *Psychoanalysis, Culture and Society* 13:1, 8-23.

Ragland-Sullivan, E. (1986) *Jacques Lacan and the Philosophy of Psychoanalysis* (Urbana, University of Illinois Press).

Rankin, K. (2003) 'Anthropologies and geographies of globalization', *Progress in Human Geography* 27:6, 708-734.

Ratner, B. (2004) '"Sustainability" as a Dialogue of values: Challenges to the Sociology of Development', *Sociological Inquiry* 74:1, 50-69.

Rawls, J. (1971) *A Theory of Justice* (Cambridge, Harvard University Press).

Rawls, J. (1993a) 'The Law of Peoples', *Critical Inquiry* 20:1, 36-38.

Rawls, J. (1993b) *Political Liberalism* (Chicago, Chicago University Press).

Rawls, J. (2001) *Justice as Fairness* (Cambridge, Harvard University Press).

Reade, E. (1987) *British Town and Country Planning* (Milton Keynes, Open University Press).

Rees, W. (1992) 'Ecological footprints and appropriated carrying capacity: what urban economics leaves out', *Environment and Urbanization* 4:2, 121-130.

Rees, W. (1995) 'Achieving sustainability: reform or transformation?', *Journal of Planning Literature* 9:4, 343-361.

Rees, W. (2002) 'Globalization and sustainability: Conflict or Convergence?', *Bulletin of Science, Technology and Society* 22:4, 249-268.

Rees, W. (2003) 'Economic Development and Environmental Protection: An Ecological Economics Perspective', *Environmental Monitoring and Assessment* 86:1, 29-45.

Reynolds, J. (2004) 'Decision', in Reynolds, J., Roffe, J. (eds) *Understanding Derrida*, 46-53 (New York, Continuum).

Richardson, T. (2002) 'Freedom and Control in Planning: Using Discourse in the Pursuit of Reflexive Practice', *Planning Theory and Practice* 3(3), 353-361.

Ricoeur, P. (1992) *Oneself as Another* (Chicago, Chicago University Press).

Robinson, J. (2008) 'Developing ordinary cities: city visioning processes in Durban and Johannesburg', *Environment and Planning A* 40:1, 74-87.

Roffe, J. (2004) 'Ethics', in Reynolds, J. and Roffe, J. (eds) *Understanding Derrida*, 37-45 (New York, Continuum).

Rohe, W., Stegman, M. (1994) 'The Effects of Homeownership on the Self-Esteem, Perceived Control and Life Satisfaction of Low-Income people', *Journal Of the American Planning Association* 60:2, 173-184.

Rose, N. (1994) 'Medicine, history and the present', in Jones, C., Porter, R. (eds), *Reassessing Foucault*, 48-72 (London, Routledge).

Rose, N. (1996) *Inventing Our Selves* (Cambridge, Cambridge University Press).

Rose, N. (1999) *Powers of Freedom* (Cambridge, Cambridge University Press).

Rose, N. (2001) 'Community, citizenship and the Third Way', in Merydyth, D., Minson, J. (eds), *Citizenship and Cultural Policy*, 1-17 (London, Sage).

Roudinesco, E. (1997) *Jacque Lacan* (New York, Columbia University Press).

Rowe, J. (2005) 'Economic Development: From a New Zealand perspective', in Rowe, J. (ed.) *Economic Development in New Zealand*, 1-14 (Aldershot, Ashgate).

Rowe, J. (2009) 'Moving the Discipline Beyond Metaphors', in Rowe J. (ed.) *Theories of Local Economic Development: Linking Theory to Practice*, 301-328 (Aldershot, Ashgate).

Royal Town Planning Institute [RTPI] (2001) *New Vision for Planning* (London, RTPI).

RTPI (2003) *Education Commission Report* (London, RTPI).

Runde, J., Mizuhara, S. (eds) (2003) *The Philosophy of Keynes' Economics* (London, Routledge).

Ruti, M. (2008) 'The Fall of Fantasies: A Lacanian Reading of Lack', *Journal of the American Psychoanalytic Association* 56:2, 483-508.

Sack, R. (2003) *A Geographical Guide to the Real and the Good* (New York, Routledge).

Safouan, M. (2004) *Four Lessons of Psychoanalysis* (New York, Other Press).

Sager, T. (1994) *Communicative Planning Theory* (Aldershot, Ashgate).

Saito, A., Thornley, A. (2003) 'Shifts in Tokyo's World City Status and the Urban Planning response', *Urban Studies* 40: 4, 665-685.

Salecl, R. (1994) 'Deference to the Great Other: Discourse of Education', in Bracher, M., *et al.* (eds) *Lacanian Theory of Discourse* (New York, New York University Press).

Sandercock, L. (1990) *Property, Politics, and Urban Planning: A History of Australian City* (New Brunswick, Transaction Publishers).

Sandercock, L. (1997) 'The Planner Tamed: Preparing planners for the twenty-first century', *Australian Planner* 34:2, 90-95.

Sandercock, L. (1998) *Towards Cosmopolis* (Chichester: Wiley).

Sandercock, L. (2003a) 'Out of the Closet: The Importance of Stories and Storytelling in Planning Practice', *Planning Theory and Practice* 4:1, 11-28.

Sandercock, L. (2003b) 'Planning in the Ethno-cultural Diverse City: A Comment', *Planning Theory and Practice* 4:3, 319-323.

Sandercock, L. (2003c) *Mongrel Cities* (London, Continuum).

Sandercock, L. (2004) 'Towards a Planning Imagination for the 21st Century', *Journal of the American Planning Association* 70:2, 133-141.

Santilli, P. (2007) 'Culture, Evil and Horror', *American Journal of Economics and Sociology* 66:1, 173-193.

Sanyal, B. (2005) 'Strategizing to Overcome Institutional Resistance to Planning in Developing Countries', *Planning Theory* 4:3, 225-246.

Sarkissian, W. (1996) 'With a Whole Heart: Nurturing an Ethic of Caring for Nature in the Education of Australian Planners', PhD Thesis (Perth, Murdoch University) <http://wwwlib.murdoch.edu.au/adt/browse/view/adt-MU20051109.104544>, accessed 22 September 2008.

Sarup, M. (1993) *Poststructuralism and Postmodernism* (Harlow, Longman).

Saussure, F. (2006) *Writings in General Linguistics* (Oxford, Oxford University Press).

Savić, O. (2005) 'Introduction – duty of unconditioned hospitality', *parallax* 11:1, 1-5.

Schaer, R., Claeys, G., Sargent, L. (2000) *Utopia* (Oxford, Oxford University Press).

Scheffler S. (2004) 'Doing and Allowing', *Ethics*, 114, 215-239.

Schön, D., Rein, M. (1994) *Frame Reflection* (New York, BasicBooks).

Schroeder, J. (1998) 'The End of the Market: A Psychoanalysis of Law and Economics', *Harvard Law Review* 112:2, 483-558.

Schroeder, J. (2000) 'Rationality in Law and Economic Scholarship', *Oregon Law Review* 79:1, 147-252.

Schwickert, E-M. (2005) 'Gender, morality, and ethics of responsibility: complementing teleological and deontological ethics' (trans. Miller S.C.), *Hypatia*, 20:2, 164-187.

Scott, A. (2003) 'Assessing public perception of landscape: from practice to policy', *Journal of Environmental Policy and Planning* 5:2, 123-144.

Scott, A. (2008) 'Inside the City: On Urbanisation, Public policy and Planning', *Urban Studies* 45:4, 755-772.

Scott, J. (2007) 'Smart Growth as Urban Reform: A Pragmatic "Recoding" of the New Regionalism', *Urban Studies* 44:1, 15-35.

Searle, G., Byrne, J. (2002) 'Selective Memories, Sanitised Futures: Constructing Visions of Future Place in Sydney', *Urban Policy and Research* 20:1, 7-25.

Shankar, A., Whittaker, J., Fitchet, J. (2006) 'Heaven knows I'm miserable now', *Marketing Theory* 6:4, 485-505.

Sharpe, M. (2001) 'Che Vuoi?'/'What Do You Want?' *Arena* 16, 101-120.

Sharpe, M. (2006) 'The Aesthetics of Ideology, or "The Critique of Ideological Judgement" in Eagleton and Žižek', *Political Theory* 34:1, 95-120.

Shen, Q., Zhang, F. (2007) 'Land-use changes in a pro-smart-growth state: Maryland, USA', *Environment and Planning A* 39:6, 1457-1477.

Shildrick, M. (2003) 'Relative Responsibilities', *Women: a cultural review* 14:2, 182-194.

Shmueli, D., Kaufman, S., Ozawa, C. (2008) 'Mining Negotiation Theory for Planning Insights', *Journal of Planning Education and Research* 27:3, 359-364.

Silvia, E. (2002) 'Indecision Factors when Planning for Land Use Change', *European Planning Studies* 10:3, 335-358.

Simmel, G. (2000) 'The Metropolis and Mental Life', in Farganis J. (ed.) *Readings in Social Theory,* 147-157 (New York, McGraw Hill).

Skriabine, P. (2004) 'Clinic and Topology: The Flaw in the Universe', in Ragland, E, Milovanovic, D. *Lacan: Topologically Speaking* (New York, Other Press).

Smart, B. (1995) 'The subject of responsibility', *Philosophy and Social Criticism* 21:4, 93-109.

Smart, B. (1998) 'Foucault, Lévinas and the subject of responsibility', in Moss, J. (ed.) *The Later Foucault*, 78-92 (London, Sage).

Smith D.W. (2003) 'Deleuze and Derrida, immanence and transcendence: two directions in recent French thought', in Patton, P., Protevi, J. (eds) *Between Deleuze and Derrida*, 46-66 (London, Continuum).

Snary, C. (2004) 'Understanding Risk: The Planning Officers' Perspective', *Urban Studies* 41:1, 33-55.

Snow, M. (2004) 'Towards an urban design agenda for Queensland', *Australian Planner* 41:2, 22-24.

Soja, E. (1996) *Thirdspace* (Oxford, Blackwell).

Soja, E. (2000) *Postmetropolis* (Oxford, Blackwell).

Soroos, M. (2001) 'Global Climate Change and the Futility of the Kyoto Process', *Global Environmental Politics* 1:2, 1-9.

Sparti D. (2000) 'Responsiveness as responsibility', *Philosophy and Social Criticism* 26:5, 81-107.

Spence, K. (2005) 'World Risk Society and War Against Terror', *Political Studies* 53:2, 284-302.

Spender, D. (1980) *Man Made Language* (London, Routledge, Kegan, Paul).

Stacey, R. (1996) *Complexity and Creativity in Organisations* (San Francisco, Berrett-Koehler).

Stavrakakis, Y. (1999) *Lacan and the Political* (London, Routledge).

Stavrakakis, Y. (2003) 'Re-Activating the Democratic Revolution: The Politics of Transformation Beyond Reoccupation and Conformism', *parallax* 9:2, 56-71.

Stavrakakis, Y. (2007) *The Lacanian Left* (Albany, SUNY).

Stegall, N. (2006) 'Designing for Sustainability: A Philosophy for Ecological Intentional Design', *Design Issues* 22:2, 56-63.

Stein, S., Harper, T. (2003) 'Power, Trust, and Planning', *Journal of Planning Education and Research* 23:1, 125-139.

Steinmetz, G. (2006) 'Bourdieu's Disavowal of Lacan: Psychoanalytic Theory and the Concepts of "Habitus" and "Symbolic Capital"', *Constellations* 13:4, 445-464.

Sternberg, E. (2000) 'A Integrative Theory of Urban Design', *Journal of the American Planning Association* 66:3, 265-278.

Storper, M., Manville, M. (2006) 'Behaviour, Preferences and Cities: Urban Theory and Urban Resurgence', *Urban Studies* 43:8, 1247-1274.

Sturrock, J. 2003. *Structuralism* (Oxford, Blackwell).

Swearingen White, S., Mayo, J. (2004) 'Learning Expectations in Environmental Planning: Predictions and Interpretations', *Journal of Planning Education and Research* 24:1, 78-88.

Swyngedouw, E. (2007) 'Impossible "Sustainability" and the Postpolitical Condition', in Krueger, R., Gibbs, D. (eds) *The Sustainable Development Paradox*, 13-40 (London, The Guilford Press).

Tajbakhsh, K. (2001) *The Promise of the City* (Berkeley, University of California Press).

Talen, E. (2002) 'The Social Goals of New Urbanism', *Housing Policy Debate* 13:1, 165-188.

Talen, E., Ellis, C. (2004) 'Cities as Art: Exploring the Possibility of an Aesthetic Dimension in Planning', *Planning Theory and Practice* 5:1, 11-32.

Taylor, N. (1992) 'Professional ethics in town planning: what is a code of professional conduct for?' *Town Planning Review* 63:3, 227-241.

Tewdr-Jones, M. (1999) 'Discretion, Flexibility, and Certainty in British Planning: Emerging Ideological Conflicts and Inherent Political Tensions', *Journal of Planning Education and Research* 18:3, 244-256.

Tewdwr-Jones, M. (2002) 'Personal Dynamics, Distinctive Frames and Communicative Planning', in Allmendinger, P. (ed.) *Planning Futures,* 65-92 (London, Routledge).

Thomas, I., Nicita, J. (2002) 'Sustainability Education and Australian Universities', *Environmental Education Research* 8:4, 475-292.

Thompson A. (2006) 'Environmentalism, moral responsibility and the doctrine of doing and allowing', *Ethics, Place and Environment* 9:3, 269-278.

Thompson, S. (2003) 'Planning and Multiculturalism: A Reflection on Australian Local Practice', *Planning Theory and Practice* 4:3, 275-293.

Thrift, N. (1993) 'The arts of living, the beauty of the dead: anxieties of being in the work of Anthony Giddens', *Progress in Human Geography* 17:1, 111-121.

Thrift N. (2000a) 'With child to see any strange thing: everyday life in the city', in Bridge, G., Watson, S. (eds) *A Companion to the City*, 398-409 (Oxford, Blackwell).

Thrift N. (2000b) 'Entanglements of power: shadows?', in Sharp, J., Routledge, P., Philo, C., Paddison, R. (eds) *Entanglements of Power,* 269-278 (London, Routledge).

Thrift, N. (2004) 'Intensities of feeling: Towards a Spatial Politics of Affect', *Geografiska Annaler* 86B: 1, 57-78.

Thrift, N. (2008) *Non-Representational Theory* (Abington, Routledge).

Throgmorton, J. (1993) 'Planning as a Rhetorical Activity: Survey Research as a Trope in Arguments About Electric Power Planning in Chicago', *Journal of the American Planning Association* 59:3, 334-346.

Throgmorton, J. (1996) *Planning as Persuasive Storytelling* (Chicago, University of Chicago Press).

Throgmorton, J. (2008) 'The Bridge to Gretna: Three Faces of a Case', *Planning Theory and Practice* 9:2, 187-208.

Tierney, K. (1999) 'Towards a Critical Sociology of Risk', *Sociological Forum* 14:2, 215-242.

Tong, R. (1987) 'Ethics and the policy analyst: the problem of responsibility', in Fischer, F., Forester, J. (eds) *Confronting Values in Policy Analysis,* 192-211 (Thousand Oaks, Sage).

Torfing, J. (1999) *New Theories of Discourse* (Oxford, Blackwell).

Tregoning, H., Agyeman, J., Shenot, C. (2002) 'Sprawl, Smart Growth, and Sustainability', *Local Environment* 7:4, 341-347.

Trifonas, P. (2003) 'Derrida, Lyotard and the orientations of a new academic responsibility', *Democracy and Nature* 9:1, 107-123.

Troy, P. (1996) *The Perils of Urban Consolidation* (Sydney, Federation Press).

Troy, P. (2000) 'Urban Planning in the Late Twentieth Century', in Bridge G., Watson, S. (eds) *A Companion to the City,* 543-554 (Oxford, Blackwell).

Turok, I. (2004) 'Cities, Regions and Competitiveness', *Regional Studies* 38:9, 1069-1083.

Ungar, S. (2001) 'Moral panic versus the risk society: the implications of the changing sites of social anxiety', *British Journal of Sociology* 52:2, 271-291.

Upton, R. (2002) 'Planning praxis: ethics, values and theory', *Town Planning Review* 73:3, 253-269.

Urry, J., Dingwall, R., Gough, I. (Editors), Ormerod, P., Massey, D., Scott, J., Thrift, N. 'What is 'social' about social science?' *21st Century Society* 2:1, 95-119.

Van den Berg, A., Hartig, T., Staats, H. (2007) 'Preferences for Nature in Urban Societies: Stress, restoration, and the Pursuit of Sustainability', *Journal of Social Issues* 63:1, 79-96.

Van Eeten, M., Roe, E. (2000) 'When Fiction Conveys Truth and Authority', *Journal of the American Planning Association* 66:1, 58-67.

Van Haute P. (2002) *Against Adaptation* (New York, Other Press).

Van Houtum, H. (2002) 'Borders of Comfort: Spatial Economic Bordering Processes in the European Union', *Regional and Federal Studies* 12:4, 37-58.

Verhaeghe, P. (1997) *Does the Woman Exist?* (New York, Other Press).

Verhaeghe, P. (2001) *Beyond Gender* (New York, Other Press).

Verhaeghe, P. (2002) 'Causality in science and psychoanalysis', in Glynos, J., Stavrakakis, Y. (eds) *Lacan and Science*, 119-145 (London, Karnac).

Vighi, F., Feldner, H. (2007) 'Ideology Critique or Discourse Analysis? Žižek against Foucault', *European Journal of Political Theory* 6:2, 141-159.

Wacquant, L. (2004) 'Critical Thought as Solvent of *Doxa*', *Constellations* 11:1, 97-101.

Waddell, B., Pollock, G. (1999) 'Auckland's Internal Growing Pains', *Planning Quarterly*, 135, 9-11.

Waldron, J. (1991) 'Homelessness and the issue of freedom', *UCLA Law Review* 39, 295-324.

Wamsler, C. (2006) 'Mainstreaming risk reduction in urban planning and housing: a challenge for international aid organisations', *Disasters* 30:2, 151-177.

Ward, K., Jonas, A. (2004) 'Competitive city-regionalism as a politics of space: a critical reinterpretation of the new regionalism', *Environment and Planning: A* 36:12, 2119-2139.

Washington, R., Strong, D. (1997) 'A Model for Teaching Environmental Justice In a Planning Curriculum', *Journal of Planning Education and Research* 16:3, 280-290.

Watson, D. (2004) *Watson's Dictionary of Weasel Words, Contemporary Cliches, Cant and Management Jargon* (Sydney, Vintage).

Watson, V. (2003) 'Conflicting Rationalities: Implications for Planning Theory and Ethics', *Planning Theory and Practice* 4(4), 395-407.

Watson, V. (2006) 'Deep Difference: Diversity, Planning and Ethics', *Planning Theory* 5:1, 31-50.

Watts D. (1999) *Small Worlds* (Princeton, NJ, Princeton University Press).

Watts D. (2003) *Six Degrees* (London, Heinemann).

Weber, M. (2002) *The Protestant Ethic and the Spirit of Capitalism* (Los Angeles, Roxbury).

Weber, M. (2004) 'Politics as a Vocation', in Owen, D., Strong, T. (eds) *The Vocational Lectures*, 32-94 (Cambridge, Hackett Publishing).

Weiss, M. (2002) *The Rise of the Community Builders* (Knoxville, Beard Books).

Western Australian Planning Commission [WAPC] (2005) *Statement of Planning Policy 3: Urban Growth and Settlement. Draft* (Perth, WAPC).

Wheeler, S. (2000) 'Planning for Metropolitan Sustainability', *Journal of Planning Education and Research* 20:2, 133-145.

Wheeler, S. (2008) 'Regions, Megaregions, and Sustainability', *Regional Studies* DOI: 10.1080/0034300701861344, accessed 15 August 2008.

Whitehead, A. (1985) *Process and Reality* (New York: Free Press).

Wildavsky, A. (1973) 'If Planning is Everything, Maybe it's Nothing', *Policy Sciences* 4:2, 127-153.

Williams G. (2006) 'Infrastructures of responsibility': the moral tasks of institutions', *Journal of Applied Philosophy* 23:2, 207-221.

Wolf-Powers, L. (2005) 'Up-Zoning New York City's Mixed-Use Neighborhoods: Property-Led Economic Development and the Anatomy of a Planning Dilemma', *Journal of Planning Education and Research* 2005; 24:4, 379-393.

Wollin, R. (2006) *The Frankfurt School Revisited* (New York, Routledge) World Commission on Environment and Development [WCED] (1987) *Our Common Future* (Oxford, Oxford University Press)

World Commission on Environment and Development [WCED] (1987) *Our Common Future* (Oxford, Oxford University Press).

Ye, L., Mandpe, S., Meyer, P. (2005) 'What *Is* "Smart Growth" – Really?', *Journal of Planning Literature* 19:3, 301-315.

Yiftachel, O. (1994) 'The Dark Side of Modernism: Planning as Control of Control of an Ethnic Minority', in Watson, S., Gibson, K. (eds) *Postmodern Cities and Spaces* (Oxford, Blackwell).

Yiftachel O. (1995) 'Planning as Control: Policy and Resistance in a Deeply Divided Society', *Progress in Planning* 44:2, 115-184.

Yiftachel, O. (1998) 'Planning and Social Control: Exploring the Dark Side', *Journal of Planning Literature* 12(4), 395-406.

Yiftachel, O. (2000) 'Social Control, Urban Planning and the Ethno-Class Relations: Mizahi Jews in Israel's "Development Towns"', *International Journal of Urban and Regional Research* 20:2, 418-438.

Yiftachel, O. (2006) 'Re-Engaging Planning Theory? Towards "South-Eastern" Perspectives', *Planning Theory* 5:3, 211-222.

Yigitcanlar, T., O'Connor, K., Westerman, C. (2008) 'The making of knowledge cities: Melbourne's knowledge-based urban development experience', *Cities* 25:1, 63-72.

Young, I.M. (2003) *Political Responsibility and Structural Injustice*, The Lindley Lecture, Department of Philosophy, The University of Kansas, Kansas.

Young, I.M. (2004) 'Responsibility and Global Labor Justice', *The Journal of Political Philosophy* 12:4, 365-388.

Young, I.M. (2006) 'Responsibility and Global Justice: A Social Connective Model', *Social Philosophy and Policy Foundation* 23:1, 102-130.

Žižek, S. (1989) *The Sublime Object of Ideology* (London, Verso).

Žižek, S. (1991) *Looking Awry* (Cambridge, MIT Press).

Žižek, S. (1993) *Tarrying with the Negative* (Durham, Duke University Press).

Žižek, S. (1994a) *The Metastases of Enjoyment* (London, Verso).

Žižek, S. (1994b) 'A Hair of the Dog That Bit You', in Bracher M., *et al.* (eds) *Lacanian Theory of Discourse*, 46-73 (New York: New York University Press).

Žižek, S. (1994c) 'Introduction: the spectre of ideology', in Žižek S. (ed.) *Mapping Ideology,* 1-33 (London, Verso).

Žižek, S. (1996) *The Indivisible Remainder: On Schelling and Related Matters* (London, Verso).

Žižek, S. (1997a) *The Plague of Fantasies* (London, Verso).

Žižek, S. (1997b) *The Abyss of Freedom* (Ann Arbour, University of Michigan Press).

Žižek, S. (1997c) 'Multiculturalism, or, the Cultural Logic of multinational Capitalism', *New Left Review* 225 (September/October), 28-51.

Žižek, S. (1998a) 'Four Discourses, Four Subjects', in Žižek S. (ed.) *cognito and the unconscious*, 74-113 (London, Duke University Press).

Žižek, S. (1998b) 'The seven veils of fantasy', Nobus, D. (ed.) *Key Concepts of Lacanian Psychoanalysis*, 190-218 (London, Rebus press).

Žižek, S. (1998c) 'The Interpassive Subject', *Traverses*, <http://homepage. newschool.edu/~quigleyt/vcs/interpassive.pdf>, accessed 5 November, 2008.

Žižek, S. (1999a) 'The Spectre of Ideology', in Wright, E., Wright, E. (eds) *The Žižek Reader*, 55-86 (Oxford, Blackwell).

Žižek, S. (1999b) 'Fantasy as a Political Category: A Lacanian Approach', in Wright, E., Wright, E. (eds) *The Žižek Reader*, 89-101 (Oxford, Blackwell).

Žižek S. (1999c) *The Ticklish Subject: The Absent Centre of Political Ontology* (London, Verso).

Žižek S. (1999d) 'The undergrowth of enjoyment: how popular culture can serve as an introduction to Lacan', in Wright, E., Wright, E. (eds) *The Žižek Reader,* 11-36 (Oxford, Blackwell).

Žižek, S. (1999e) *The Žižek Reader* (Oxford, Blackwell).

Žižek, S. (2001a) *Did Somebody Say Totalitarianism?* (London, Verso).

Žižek, S. (2001b) *Welcome to the Desert of the Real* (London, Verso).

Žižek, S. (2002a) *For they know not what they do* (London, Verso).

Žižek, S. (2002b) *Revolution at the Gates* (London, Verso).

Žižek, S. (2002c) 'The Real of Sexual Difference', in Barnard S., Fink B. (eds) *Reading Seminar XX*, 57-75 (Albany, SUNY).

Žižek, S. (2002d) *Welcome to the Desert of the Real* (London, Verso).

Žižek, S. (2003) *The Puppet and the Dwarf* (Cambridge, MIT Press).

Žižek, S. (2004a) *Organs without Bodies* (London, Routledge).

Žižek, S. (2004b) *'Iraq: The Borrowed Kettle'* (London, Verso).

Žižek, S. (2005a) *Interrogating the Real* (London, Continuum).

Žižek, S. (2005b) 'The politics of jouissance', *Lacanian Ink* 24/25, 126-155.

Žižek, S. (2005c) 'Neighbors and Other Monsters: A Plea for Ethical Violence', in Žižek, S., *et al.* (eds) *The Neighbor: Three Inquiries in Political Theology*, 134-190 (Chicago, University of Chicago Press).

Žižek, S. (2006a) *The Parallax View* (Cambridge, MIT Press).

Žižek, S. (2006b) *How to Read Lacan* (London, Norton).

Žižek, S. (2006c) 'Notes towards a politics of Bartleby: The ignorance of chicken', *Comparative American Studies* 4:4, 375-394.

Žižek, S. (2007) 'Introduction: Robespierre, Or, The "Divine Violence" of Terror', in Robespierre, M., *Virtue and Terror* (London, Verso).

Žižek, S. (2008a) *In Defence of Lost Causes* (London, Verso).

Žižek, S. (2008b) 'The Prospects of Radical Politics Today', *International Journal of Baudrillard Studies* 5:1, <http://www.ubishops.ca/BaudrillardStudies/vol5_1/pf/v5-1-article3-Žižek_pf.html >, accessed 24 July 2008.

Žižek, S. (2008c) 'Tolerance as an Ideological Category', *Critical Enquiry* 34:4, 660-682.

Žižek, S. (2008d) *Violence* (New York, Picador).

Žižek, S., Daly, G. (2004) *Conversations with Žižek* (Cambridge, Polity).

Zöllner, E. (2004) 'The economic value of urban design', *Australian Planner* 41:2, 40.

Zupančič, A. (1998) 'The Subject of the Law,' in Žižek, S. (ed.) *cognito and the unconscious*, 41-73 (Durham, Duke University Press).

Zupančič, A. (2000) *Ethics of the Real* (London, Verso).

Zupančič, A. (2003) *The Shortest Shadow* (Cambridge, MIT Press).

Zupančič, A. (2006) 'When Surplus Enjoyment Meets Surplus Value', in Clemens, J., Griggs, R. (eds) *Jacque Lacan and the Other Side of Psychoanalysis*, 155-178 (Durham, Duke University Press).

# Index